HOT TOPICS

A STUDENT COMPANION

Susan Freeman

A.R.E. Publishing, Inc.
Denver, Colorado

Pages 10, 11, 167: Selections from *Love and Sex: A Modern Jewish Perspective* by Robert Gordis reprinted with permission.

Pages 166, 171, 173, 185-186: Reprinted from *This Is My Beloved, This Is My Friend* (pp. 27-28, p. 13, pp. 30-36), by Elliot N. Dorff, © 1996, The Rabbinical Assembly.

Pages 20, 23, 179, 185, 191, 193, 200, 201: Reprinted from *Matters of Life and Death*, Elliot N. Dorff, 1998 © The Jewish Publication Society with permission of the publisher, The Jewish Publication Society.

Pages 163, 172, 179, 186, 201-202: Reprinted from *Does God Belong in the Bedroom?* Michael Gold, 1992 © The Jewish Publication Society with permission of the publisher, The Jewish Publication Society.

Published by:
A.R.E. Publishing, Inc.
Denver, Colorado
www.arepublish.com

Library of Congress Control Number: 2004109008
ISBN 0-86705-088-8

Printed in the United States of America
10   9   8   7   6   5   4   3   2   1

Dedication

This book is dedicated to my sons,
Benjamin Freeman Graubart and Ilan Freeman Graubart.

Acknowledgements

Special thanks to Steve Arons, Steve Brodsky, Dr. Hal Blumenfeld, Dr. Michelle Brody, Pamela Cosman, Dr. Robert Dorit, Efraim Eisen, Rosalie Eisen, Joel Feldman, Rabbi Nancy Flam, Carol Freeman, Dr. Joyce Freeman, Samuel Freeman, Shayna Friedman,Rabbi Philip Graubart, Claudia Levin, Laura Michaels, Rana Morissey, Dr. Susan Mosler, Dorothy Nemetz, Jody Rosenbloom, Pamela Schwartz, and Abbie Steiner.

Contents

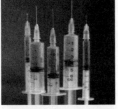

INTRODUCTION

What Are Hot Topics?

Abortion. The ethics of business. Euthanasia. Animal experimentation. The death penalty. The ethics of war. Sex outside of marriage. These "hot topics" are some of the most controversial issues of our day. We see and hear stories of them daily on the front page of our newspapers, and nightly on our television newscasts. These complex issues, with so many angles to consider and viewpoints to integrate, are of special interest to you as you learn to live in a world that is often filled with contradictions. The world changes quickly, yet we can look to Jewish teachings to help us understand these sensitive subjects and form worthy responses to them.

The topics mentioned above are just a few of the controversial subjects this book examines. You will have opportunities to read, study, reflect, and respond to these and many other issues. This book won't attempt to tell you the "right" answer to any dilemma, but will instead describe a range of possible responses and guide you through the process of identifying competing priorities and values. Looking at an issue from many perspectives — including through a "Jewish lens" — will help you learn how to weigh decisions carefully, clarify your own beliefs and values, and make informed choices.

What's In This Book?

With a few variations, each chapter of *Hot Topics: A Student Companion* includes several sections that will allow you to explore an issue in depth, think about real-world scenarios, and study ancient and modern texts that will shed light on the topic at hand. Along the way, you'll have opportunities to think, discuss, write, debate, and explore further.

Overview

The Overview provides an introduction to the topic — the essential dilemma, moral challenges, and ethical questions that are raised by the sub-

ject. Then, background information, major considerations and controversies are presented, usually from both general and Jewish perspectives.

General Perspectives

In this section, you will find factual information, relevant secular laws, modern attitudes, sociological factors, and ideas and theories about each topic, drawn from thinkers in the Jewish and non-Jewish worlds. These resources will help you begin to grasp the complexity of the issues as we face them today.

Jewish Perspectives

This book assumes that our goal is to respond to contemporary dilemmas from an authentic Jewish place. This requires us to engage with our tradition, our heritage, our sacred books and brightest thinkers. As Jews, we do not base our actions solely on an article we've read in the *New York Times* or in a prestigious medical journal; at the same time, we don't limit our decision making to personal whims, agendas, impressions, or gut feelings. In this section we'll look at Jewish sacred texts and other historical documents, as well as contemporary Jewish views: theories, *halachic* (Jewish legal) opinions, and ongoing debates. These sources will help us to analyze the layers of insights in our tradition, and to respond to critical issues with Jewish wisdom and moral integrity.

Summary of the Overview

The Overview wraps up with a few short statements that summarize the critical points of each issue. Your teacher or leader may have you "preview" an issue by reading this section first, and then go back to the beginning of the chapter for the detailed view.

Scenarios

Each chapter includes two or more scenarios, "real-life" situations that raise thought-provoking questions. In most chapters, the objective of the scenarios is to illustrate how attitudes toward the topic have changed over time. As you read them, imagine yourself in a different time or place, and try to personalize the abstract ideas to make them meaningful and relevant to you.

Journaling: An Opportunity for Discussion, Research, and Personal Reflection

Following the scenarios is a section called, "For Thought and Discussion" that asks you to consider the issues and responses presented in the scenarios. This is the first opportunity you will have to express your own views on the topic, based on everything you have learned so far. While we've provided a few "starter" journal pages at the back of this book, we strongly suggest that you create your own "Hot Topics Journal," a place where you can answer the questions that appear in this book and jot down thoughts or questions of your own. Your journal will also make an excellent "scrapbook," a place to collect relevant articles and stories from newspapers, magazines, or the Internet that shed light on the topic at hand. Your Hot Topics Journal can be a three-ring binder or a spiral-bound notebook, but it should have plenty of room to write as well as a place to collect interesting articles that you find. It will serve as a logbook of your discovery of each Hot Topic.

Text Study

The "heart" of our study of each topics is the Text Study section, comprised of texts drawn from a wide range of Jewish and general sources. By studying these, you will begin to grasp the nuances and complexities of often opposing considerations. You'll notice that in most cases the texts are presented in an "On The One Hand" and "On The Other Hand" format, providing you with two valid, defensible Jewish viewpoints. Again, there is no "right" answer, but two opposing points of view to help you identify competing priorities and values, clarify your own beliefs and values, and make informed choices.

The *What Do You Think?* section that follows each pair of texts is another opportunity for writing in your Hot Topics Journal, or for collecting interesting stories and articles you may find as you clarify your own position on each topic.

Related Middot and Mitzvot

Rounding out each topic is a list of related *middot* (Jewish virtues) and mitzvot (commandments) that relate directly to the topic. These virtues, values, qualities, and actions support and enhance ethical decision-making, and can help us extend the process of making moral choices beyond simply "going through the motions." They help understand *how* we do things — the underlying values we bring to our decisions — as opposed to just *why* we do them.

Where Do I Go From Here?

The thing that makes any topic a "Hot Topic" is that there are no easy answers — you will likely struggle with some of these issues throughout your life. Hopefully, you'll be interested in exploring the topics further, and this section provides you with numerous resources in the forms of books and articles, Web sites, and films, for further exploration.

Your teacher or leader will also present you with a variety of interesting activities and challenges related to each hot topic, activities that delve deeper into the key issues and ideas, explore the related *middot* and mitzvot, and hands-on activities that will get you out and involved in your community or the world.

Do The Right Thing!

Underlying this *Student Companion* is the notion that studying hot topics allows us to become more informed about the issues. But just as significant, if not more so, is the value of becoming more aware and tolerant of many different points of view. You will be encouraged to foster empathy — recognizing and appreciating the challenging and often painful struggles people go through enhances our humanity. Ethics calls upon us to "do the right thing." But to be *a compassionate person doing the right thing* is what "a good Jew" aspires to. That is the ultimate goal!

Enjoy your journey as you explore these Hot Topics!

PART

I

Body, Health, Medicine

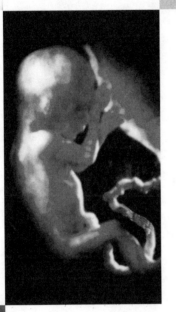

Abortion

Cloning and other
Genetic Technologies

Euthanasia

Harmful Behaviors:
Smoking, Drinking, and
Over/Undereating

CHAPTER 1
ABORTION

Overview

When does life begin? For what reasons might abortion be acceptable? For any reason? Under limited circumstances? Never? Who decides? Is the decision completely up to the pregnant woman herself? Do others, such as the woman's partner, family members, her religious community, the government, have a legitimate stake in a woman's decision to continue or to terminate a pregnancy? Such questions stir up controversy and impassioned feelings. Responses to these questions form the crux of the debate concerning abortion. In this chapter we will examine opinions on what defines a person, what circumstances may and may not justify abortion, and what role society should play in regulating the personal decisions of the individual.

The Jewish Perspective

There is no one clear-cut position on abortion. To grasp Jewish opinion on this subject, it is helpful to highlight areas of agreement, and then examine areas in which there is more dissent.

Defining a Person

From a Jewish legal point of view, a fetus in the womb is not a person until it is born (Sanhedrin 72b). The consensus notion is this: full human life deserves more consideration that "potential life," yet potential life is valued.

Over the years, Jewish sources have attempted to specify various stages of fetal development. For example, until the fortieth day, a pregnancy is said to consist of "mere fluid" (*Yebamot* 69b). Thus, until that day, abortion opinions tend to be more lenient. Other sources consider the fetus to be an organic part of the mother's body (*Chullin* 58a, *Arachin* 7a, Text #1a and 1b below). Wrestling with these and other notions of personhood is integral to the Jewish ethical process of assessing whether termination of a pregnancy is justified.

When Is Abortion Acceptable?

Jewish discussion over the ages has devoted serious consideration to a broad range of potentially legitimate reasons for abortion. These include: saving a mother from great pain, severe emotional anguish, or public shame; in cases of rape; and/or when there is medical evidence indicating a deformed or diseased fetus. However, other possible reasons, such as using abortion as a means of selecting the gender of a baby or as a form of birth control, would be unacceptable to most Jewish religious leaders.

While there are perspectives, even in traditional Jewish circles, that reflect a liberal attitude toward abortion, we are not to take such decisions lightly. We also value potential life, and the abundant discussion about abortion reflects our impulse to protect it. The challenge is how to do so appropriately and wisely.

Who Decides?

The widely accepted Jewish view is that abortion decisions do not belong in the domain of government. Abortion decisions are private, and should belong with the pregnant woman in consultation with supportive and compassionate individuals who have her essential needs and beliefs at heart. These individuals might include family members, a rabbi, and medical or psychological professionals.

To make a "Jewish" decision also involves study of Jewish sources. We have seen that many Jewish legal sources recognize a woman's emotional pain, anguish, and/or shame as providing sufficient grounds for permitting abortion. Pressing emotional needs can undercut other considerations. A woman's feelings about her pregnancy could influence an abortion decision to such an extent that, in effect, the decision could be seen as originating from her, as being chosen by her. This allowance for a woman's psychological needs — clearly a Jewish perspective — most closely supports the principle of reproductive choice.

The Jewish Council for Public Affairs advocates for women's right to choose. However, the Union of Orthodox Jewish Congregations has expressed concerns that the Council's policy usurps a rabbi's role in deciding each case based on Jewish law.

General Perspectives

Defining a Person

Just as people have different beliefs concerning afterlife, we have different beliefs about the essence of life before birth. The Jewish position is that life begins at birth — that a fetus is a full person only once the greater part of its body (or head) has entered the world. In contrast, other religious groups believe that life begins at conception, and consider an embryo a person who has a soul. They may assert that deliberately ending fetal life is a violent crime. Some anti-abortionists equate abortion with murder. Such impassioned beliefs make the abortion issue extremely controversial and fraught with emotion. Perhaps the only thing we can say for sure is that there is a range of views. The questions of what a soul is, how it exists, and when it enters the body are matters of individual religious belief.

When Is Abortion Acceptable?

Generally, various political, medical, ethical, and/or religious groups will look at two key considerations: 1) for what reasons might an abortion be justified, and 2) up until what, if any, stage (i.e., trimester) in the pregnancy may an abortion be performed.

In 1959, the American law Institute proposed new guidelines that addressed the reasons that an abortion might be justified. The Institute's "Model Penal Code"[1] permitted physicians to terminate a pregnancy:

- If they believed it threatened the life of the pregnant woman or would critically impair her physical or mental condition.
- If the child would be born with a grave physical or mental defect.
- If the pregnancy resulted from rape or incest.
- If the need for abortion was approved by two physicians.

Despite these guidelines, attaining a legal abortion in America nonetheless remained very difficult.

A turning point in abortion rights in America was the 1973 Supreme Court decision in the case of Roe v. Wade. It allowed unrestricted abortion in the first trimester, reasonably regulated abortion in relation to the woman's health in the second trimester, and permitted states to prohibit abortion, except when necessary to preserve the woman's life or health, in the third trimester. Those who oppose abortion have made efforts to impose increasing restrictions on and limit access to the procedure. The issue continues to be a volatile one.

Who Decides?

Public officials face the challenge of creating laws that reflect their nation's essential values and principles. The United States is a democratic country that officially upholds such values as separation of church and state, civil liberties (including the right to privacy), equality of opportunity (e.g., access to health services), and equality of protection for citizens. Abortion laws remain liberal when these values are emphasized, but abortion laws become more restrictive when officials assert that protecting citizens includes fetuses. Underlying restrictive abortion laws is the belief that fetal life is no different in worth from full human life.

Summary of the Overview

The paragraphs below summarize key Jewish considerations regarding abortion:

1. An embryo is potential life. Jewish tradition regards potential life respectfully even though we may not equate it in value to full human life.

2. Reasons to abort must be evaluated thoughtfully as a decision to abort is a serious matter. Abortion is a legitimate option when a woman's life is in imminent danger due to her pregnancy. Rabbis and scholars weigh in differently regarding abortion for other reasons, such as: the fetus is deformed or diseased, the pregnancy is causing the woman great emotional anguish, or the pregnancy is a result of an illicit union. On balance, Judaism is on the more liberal side of the spectrum in accepting abortion for reasons other than a life threatening situation.

3. Weighing the possibility of abortion usually begins with the pregnant woman. Her physical condition, her personal situation, and the community in which she lives all may be factored into a decision. A woman may decide on her own or choose to consult with others. She may relinquish the decision to religious authorities. If she lives in a place where abortion laws are restrictive, she may have no choice at all. That is, the law will dictate the course her pregnancy must take given her particular circumstances.

Scenarios: Jews Living in Different Communities

Below are two imaginary scenarios followed by questions intended to stimulate thought and spark discussion. Read each scenario and reflect, either individually or in a group discussion, on the questions in the "For Thought and Discussion" section that follows. Then continue on to the "Text Study" section to see what Jewish and other sources have to say on the subject. Finally, you may wish to come back and discuss the questions a second time, to see if your views have changed.

Scenario I: A Jewish Community in Jerusalem in 1900

Devorah, a 16-year-old, was raped by her uncle. From this violent act, she is pregnant. She feels anguish, shame, and anger regarding her circumstances. Her uncle has been punished for his crime. Meanwhile, Devorah faces an unwanted pregnancy. Chances are reasonable that she would give birth to a healthy infant. However, she cannot bear to go through with the pregnancy and either raise the child or give it up for adoption. She wants an abortion.

While not all rabbis would feel abortion is appropriate in Devorah's situation, her own rabbi supports her in her wish to terminate the pregnancy. She is referred to a respected midwife who prescribes herbs for her that induce abortion.

Scenario II: In America in 1900

Debra, a 16-year-old, was raped by her uncle. From this violent act, she is pregnant. She feels anguish, shame, and anger regarding her circumstances. Her uncle has been punished for his crime. Meanwhile, Debra faces an unwanted pregnancy. Chances are reasonable that she would give birth to a healthy infant. However, she cannot bear to go through with the pregnancy and either raise the child or give it up for adoption. She wants an abortion.

However, abortion is illegal. Her rabbi supports her in her wish to terminate the pregnancy, yet he feels he must caution her against following through with the procedure since it is illegal. Furthermore, because abortion is unregulated, it is potentially dangerous.

Despite the caution, Debra proceeds to arrange for an illegal abortion. From a neighbor she obtains the name of a person who performs abortions. Debra does not realize that the person is unqualified and goes through with the procedure. There are complications that the abortion provider is ill-equipped to handle. Debra barely makes it through. Her reproductive organs are permanently scarred. She will never be able to give birth to children in the future.

For Thought and Discussion:

How do the facts change from Devorah's situation to Debra's?

Which situation offered the rabbi more flexibility in guiding the young woman?

In your opinion, is that flexibility ultimately a good or bad thing for society? Defend your answer.

Text Study

The questions of defining a person, when abortion should be acceptable, and who should make that decision are difficult and controversial. Jewish textual sources provide many answers, but these answers often highlight the tension between seemingly opposing considerations. The chart on the next page poses the questions and offers two opposing points of view. Text sources supporting each of these points of view follow.

1. Should abortion be permitted?

On the One Hand:

Abortion deliberately ends life in its earliest stages. Permitting abortion forces us to wrestle with our sacred obligation to protect life.

A. I hereby declare today, with heaven and earth as my witnesses, that I have put before you life and death, blessing and curse. Choose life, that you and your descendants may live (Deuteronomy 30:19).

On the Other Hand:

A fetus is not equivalent to a full human being; it is potential life.

a. The fetus is as the thigh of its mother (*Chullin* 58a).

b. . . . for [the fetus] is her body (Arachin 7a).

c. If a woman is pregnant, the semen, until the fortieth day is only a mere fluid (*Yevamot* 69b).

d. [Capital punishment is not imposed on one who, during a scuffle, causes a pregnant woman to miscarry because there is] no form [yet to the fetus] . . . (*Septuagint* translation of Exodus 21:22).

What Do You Think?

Outline the tension that exists between the two views presented in the texts above.

Do you agree that we have a sacred obligation to protect life? If so, where does this obligation come from? Consider these questions:

Does the fetus have a soul?

Is the fetus part of the mother's body?

Does the status of the fetus change over the course of the pregnancy (e.g., in the first trimester or the first 40 days versus in the last trimester)?

What do you believe about life in the womb and from where do you derive your beliefs?

2. What is our duty to protect an unborn fetus?

On the One Hand:

Even potential life is to be valued.

A. When two men scuffle and one deals a blow to a pregnant woman, so that her children abort forth, but (other) harm does not occur, he is to be fined, yes, fined, as the woman's spouse imposes for him, and the matter placed before the judges . . . (Exodus 21:22).

B. He who indulges in marital intercourse on the ninetieth day [of pregnancy, when it was thought to injure the embryo], it is as though he had shed blood (*Niddah* 31a).

C. As the Mishnah states regarding a one day old infant, that capital punishment is prescribed for murdering it, for a one day old infant, but not for a fetus . . . nevertheless with regard to keeping the laws (i.e., of Shabbat) we set them aside for it (i.e., we may break the laws of Shabbat in order to save a fetus) . . . since the Torah declared "set aside one Sabbath that someone might keep many Sabbaths" (*Halachot Gedolot*).

On the Other Hand:

Our duty to protect potential life differs from our duty to protect living human beings.

a. But if harm should occur [to the pregnant woman herself], then shall you give life for life (Exodus 21:23).

b. It was necessary for the Torah to write "he that smites a man [*ish*] so that he dies shall surely be put to death" [Exodus 21:12]. For had the Torah written only "whoso kills any person [*nefesh*] the murderer shall be slain" [Numbers 35:30], one would have concluded that capital punishment is applied to one who destroys a fetus (*Sanhedrin* 84b).

Making an Ethical Decision about Abortion: Questions to Consider

The Question	On the One Hand	On the Other Hand
1. Should abortion be permitted? (see page 6)	Abortion deliberately ends life in its earliest stages. Permitting abortion forces us to wrestle with our sacred obligation to protect life.	A fetus is not equivalent to a full human being; it is *potential* life.
2. What is our duty to protect an unborn fetus? (see page 6)	Even *potential* life is to be valued.	Our duty to protect *potential* life differs from our duty to protect living human beings.
3. What status does a fetus have as part of the mother? (see page 8)	A fetus is an organic part of the mother's body. Aborting it is like wounding oneself, and wounding oneself is prohibited.	When the fetus is not yet fully developed (but "merely fluid"), aborting is not "wounding." There is no established organ to wound.
4. Who has the right to decide life or death? (see page 8)	God alone pronounces life and death.	When your life is threatened, you are permitted to protect yourself from the danger that "pursues" you.
5. Under what circumstances relating to the health of the mother would abortion be justified? (see page 9)	One area of leniency for justifying abortion is when the mother's life is in danger.	There are legitimate needs for terminating a pregnancy, other than imminent danger to a mother's physical health, that justify abortion.
6. Under what circumstances relating to the health of the fetus would abortion be justified? (see page 9)	Justifying abortion to prevent the birth of a defective, retarded, or deformed infant is unacceptable.	Aborting when sufficient medical evidence indicates the infant will be born deformed is permissible.
7. Who should determine the course of an individual human being's life? (see page 10)	The course of our existence is not solely in our hands.	It is up to individual human beings to steer the course of their lives as best they can determine, including what happens to their bodies.
8. Who should be responsible for setting standards regarding abortion? (see page 11)	Society has a stake in the life of the fetus.	No objective standard exists for permitting or prohibiting abortion. Abortion is a private issue.

Which of these texts offers the most compelling argument about fetal status? Defend your answer.

The Bible states that a fine is to be imposed on a man who, in the midst of a scuffle with another man, causes a pregnant woman standing by to miscarry. Do you think a fine is the appropriate punishment?

In Talmudic days, it was thought that engaging in sexual intercourse during certain stages of pregnancy could damage the fetus. Nowadays, in healthy pregnancies, we know this is not a concern. The underlying message, however is relevant — that is, that potential life has value. How might this message be applied in discussions on the ethics of abortion? How do our obligations to protect potential life differ from our obligations to protect full human life?

3. **What status does a fetus have as part of the mother?**

On the One Hand:

A fetus is an organic part of the mother's body. Aborting it is like wounding oneself, and wounding oneself is prohibited.

A. It is prohibited for people to injure themselves or their peers (Maimonides, *Laws of Injury and Damage* 5:1).

On the Other Hand:

When the fetus is not yet fully developed (but "merely fluid"), aborting is not "wounding." There is no established organ to wound.

a. Once abortion is viewed as the wounding of a limb (in this case of the mother), then prior to the formation of the fetus, which takes place at 40 days, there cannot be any organ to be wounded (Basil F. Herring, contemporary scholar, explaining Rabbi Weinberg's opinion in *Responsa Seridei Ish*, Jerusalem, 1966, vol. 3, no. 127).

Which of these texts presents a more compelling argument? Why?

Do you think a reasonable argument against abortion is that it is equivalent to deliberately wounding yourself? Why or why not?

4. **Who has the right to decide life or death?**

On the One Hand:

God alone pronounces life and death.

A. "I [God] will kill and I will make to live" (Deuteronomy 32:39).

On the Other Hand:

When your life is threatened, you are permitted to protect yourself from the danger that "pursues" you.

a. If a woman in labor has a [life threatening] difficulty, one dismembers the embryo within her, removing it limb by limb, for her life takes precedence over its life. But once its greater part [*Tosefta Yevamot* 9: "head"] has emerged, it may not be harmed, for we do not set aside one life for another (*Ohalot* 7:6).

b. " . . . removing it limb by limb." This is because as long as it has not emerged into the world it is not a human being [*lav nefesh hu*], and therefore it can be killed in order to save its mother (Rashi, *Sanhedrin* 72b).

c. [We are commanded] not to have compassion on the life of the pursuer. The sages ruled that when a woman has difficulty in labor, one may dismember the embryo within her, either with drugs or surgery, because [the fetus] is like a pursuer seeking to kill her. But once the head has emerged, [the fetus] is not to be harmed, for we do not set aside one life for another. This is the natural course of the world (Maimonides, *Mishneh Torah, Hilchot Rotzayach* 1:9).

Jewish Sages agree that when a woman's life is in danger due to her pregnancy, abortion is an acceptable option. Do you agree with the reasoning presented in these texts?

Imagine someone saying that we should "let nature take its course," and not interfere with God's plans. How would you respond to such an opinion with regard to abortion?

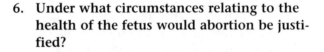

5. **Under what circumstances relating to the health of the mother would abortion be justified?**

On the One Hand:

One area of leniency for justifying abortion is when the mother's life is in danger.

A. See #4a and #4c above.

On the Other Hand:

There are legitimate needs for terminating a pregnancy, other than imminent danger to a mother's physical health, that justify abortion (see also #6a, b, and c below).

a. [Abortion is permitted, provided] there is great need, and as labor has not yet begun, even if it is not to save the mother's life but only to save her from evil caused by great pain (*Responsa She'elat Ya'abetz*, Altona, 1739, no. 43).

b. It is clear that abortion is not permitted without reason . . . but for a reason, even if a weak reason, such as to prevent [a woman from] public shame, we have precedent and authority [i.e., *Arachin* 7a] to permit it (*Responsa Mishpetei Uziel*, *Choshen Mishpat* 3:46, Tel Aviv, 1935).

c. We would therefore permit abortion in the case of Thalidomide babies [whose exposure to that drug likely will result in deformity], cases of rape and the like, not because such a fetus has no right to life but because it constitutes a threat to the health of the mother. This is an area of controversy. Many authorities would dis-

agree and limit abortion to cases in which the threat to the life of the mother is direct. We would not permit abortions that are prompted merely by the desire of the mother not to have another child (Rabbi Isaac Klein, "Abortion and Jewish Tradition," in Conservative Judaism, 1970).

What Do You Think?

A pregnancy that is causing imminent danger to a woman's life is one reason to induce abortion. What other motivations do these texts mention for seeking abortion? Do you believe some of these motivations are more acceptable than others? Explain.

On what do you base your beliefs concerning acceptable versus unacceptable reasons for abortion — that is, would you say your beliefs express your own personal feelings, that they represent Jewish values, or that they reflect universal truths?

6. **Under what circumstances relating to the health of the fetus would abortion be justified?**

On the One Hand:

Justifying abortion to prevent the birth of a defective, retarded, or deformed infant is unacceptable.

A. No matter how deformed a baby might be, the fact that it is born of a human mother gives it human status, and therefore absolute equality with other humans in its claim to life (Rabbi Eliezer Fleckeles, *Teshuvah me-Ahavah*, 19th c., as explained by Basil F. Herring, *Jewish Ethics and Halachah for Our Time*, p. 42).

B. Abortion . . . is considered actual murder, whether the fetus is pure or illegitimate, [for] regular fetuses or those which are suffering from Tay-Sachs [abortion] is strictly prohibited . . . (Rabbi Moshe Feinstein, *Iggrot Moshe, Choshen Mishpat*, 2, 49).

On the Other Hand:

Aborting when sufficient medical evidence indicates the infant will be born deformed is permissible.

a. [Where there is a possibility of a deformed fetus, abortion may be granted on account that] the possibility is causing severe anguish to the mother (Rabbi David Feldman, *Birth Control in Jewish Law*, New York: 1968, p. 292).

b. If there is good reason to suspect that the baby will be born deformed and experience pain, one can incline to permit an abortion prior to 40 days of pregnancy, and even to permit this as long as three months of pregnancy have not yet passed and there is no fetal movement (Rabbi Eliezer Waldenberg, *Responsa Tzitz Eliezer*, 9:237).

c. With regard to an abortion because of the Tay Sachs disease . . . in which the consequences are so grave if the pregnancy and childbirth are allowed to continue, it is permissible to terminate the pregnancy until seven months have elapsed . . . [Moreover, according to some scholarly opinion, abortion is permitted] for a Jewish woman whenever that matter was necessary for her health even when her life was not at stake . . . And therefore, ask yourself is there a greater need [that would justify terminating the pregnancy]. Pain and suffering greater than the woman in our case [can bear] . . . will be inflicted upon her if she gives birth to such a creature whose very being is one of pain and suffering. And [the infant's] death is certain within a few years . . . Add to that the pain and suffering of the infant . . . This would seem to be the classic case in which abortion may be permitted, and it doesn't matter what type of pain and suffering is endured, physical or emotional, as emotional pain and suffering is to a large extent much greater than physical pain and suffering (Rabbi Eliezer Waldenberg, *Responsa Tzitz Eliezer*, 13:102; adapted).

What Do You Think?

Aborting because the infant may be deformed is a particularly charged subject. After reviewing these texts, why do you think this is so?

Do you believe one rationale is more valid than the other? Explain.

7. Who should determine the course of an individual human being's life?

On the One Hand:

The course of our existence is not solely in our hands.

A. The alleged right of abortion on demand is generally supported by the argument that a woman has rights over her own body. This is a contention which Judaism, and indeed all high religion, must reject on both theological and ethical grounds as being essentially a pagan doctrine. It is basic Jewish teaching that human beings are not masters of their own bodies, because they did not create themselves; male and female alike have been fashioned by God in God's image (Robert Gordis, *Love & Sex: A Modern Jewish Perspective*, 1977, p. 145; adapted).

On the Other Hand:

It is up to individual human beings to steer the course of their lives as best they can determine, including what happens to their bodies.

a. According to Reform principles . . . every person owns his/her own body, with the ultimate right, consequently, to determine what that body shall do and experience. This being the case, it is a Reform presumption that whatever exists within the confines of a person's body and is physically connected to it is part of that body, and therefore entirely under the authority of the person whose body it is . . . No entity — state, religious institution, or individual — has taken even beginning steps to demonstrate objectively that a fetus is a person or that the entity possesses a moral right to override a woman's authority over her own body (Alvin Reines, "Reform Judaism, Bioethics and Abortion" in *Journal of Reform Judaism*, 1990).

What Do You Think?

How does Reform Judaism depart from the traditional Jewish attitude about ownership of the body? Are you comfortable with this departure? Why or why not?

Which of the above two texts do you feel makes a more worthy point, and why?

Is it possible to accept the ideas in both passages, or does one text necessarily cancel out the other?

⟫◈⟪

8. **Who should be responsible for setting standards regarding abortion?**

On the One Hand:

Society has a stake in the life of the fetus.

A. The law on abortion is and should be liberal, to meet genuine cases of hardship and misery that are not soluble in any other way. But society has an obligation to educate its members to ethical standards that rise above the level of abortion on demand. In other words, abortion should be legally available but ethically restricted, to be practiced only for very good reasons. Men and women must be persuaded that though the abortion of a fetus is not equivalent to taking an actual life, it does represent the destruction of potential life and must not be undertaken lightly or flippantly (Robert Gordis, *Love & Sex: A Modern Jewish Perspective*, 1977, p. 147).

B. Under Israeli law, abortion is permitted if carried out in a recognized medical institution, with the woman's approval, and according to one or more of the following criteria: if the birth would endanger the woman's life or injure her physical or emotional health; if it can be determined that the child would be born either physically or mentally handicapped; if the pregnancy was the result of rape, incestuous relations, or intercourse outside of marriage; if the

woman is under the age of 16 or over 40 (Robert Gordis, *Love & Sex: A Modern Jewish Perspective*, 1977, p. 147-148; adapted).

On the Other Hand:

No objective standard exists for permitting or prohibiting abortion. Abortion is a private issue.

a. From the testimony of the religious, philosophic, and scientific communities of the world viewed as a whole, it is evident that there is no generally accepted objective standard for determining whether a fetus is a human being or part of the mother in which it exists (Alvin Reines, "Reform Judaism, Bioethics and Abortion" in *Journal of Reform Judaism*, 1990).

b. Abortion is an intensely complex and personal decision, one which raises profound moral and religious questions that the government cannot and should not attempt to answer for every individual (Raymond A. Zwerin and Richard J. Shapiro, *Judaism and Abortion*, Washington, D.C.: Religious Coalition for Abortion Rights).

c. The diversity of religious views in this country, on the sensitive issue of abortion, requires that abortion decisions must remain with the individual, to be made on the basis of conscience and personal religious principles and free from government interference (*Words of Choice*, Washington, D.C., Coalition for Abortion Rights, 1991).

What Do You Think?

Does one rationale strike you as being more religiously driven than the other? Explain.

What are some of the possible ways a society could influence and/or dictate abortion decisions (e.g., through laws, education, grassroots organizing, and so on)? How should society be involved in abortion decisions, if at all? That is, does society have obligations in terms of regulating, educating about, or guaranteeing equal access to the procedure?

Does society have responsibilities for protecting fetal life?

Related Middot and Mitzvot

Practicing these virtues and commandments supports the process of addressing abortion issues in an ethical manner.

Anavah (Humility): In making abortion decisions, humility is in order. No one but the pregnant woman herself experiences the full impact and possibly agony of an abortion decision. We must be conscious of respecting each other's beliefs and refraining from assumptions about the universal rightness of our own personal values.

Eino Samayach BeHora'ah (Not delighting in Rendering Decisions): We are not to take abortion decisions lightly, but rather recognize that terminating a pregnancy is a significant act.

Lo Levayesh (Not Embarrassing Others): Certain pregnancies are the result of circumstances a woman feels a need to keep private. She should not be made to endure public scrutiny and judgment over what may be a painful and sensitive situation.

Lo Ta'amod al Dam Rayecha (Do Not Stand Idly by the Blood of Your Neighbor): When abortions were illegal, women still sought them, sometimes at the cost of their lives (from botched procedures). We must take care not to create a situation that restricts abortion to such an extent that women will endanger their lives in order to terminate a pregnancy.

Pikuach Nefesh (Saving a Life): When a pregnancy endangers a woman's life, the priority is to save her, even though the fetus may have to be aborted.

Rachamim (Compassion): Treating a woman facing an unwanted pregnancy with compassion paves the way for a wise decision concerning her situation.

Yirah (Awe and Reverence): The process of conception, gestation, and birth is mysterious and wondrous. Reverence for God requires us to weigh abortion decisions carefully and responsibly.

Where Do I Go From Here?

As you have gleaned from the many perspectives presented here, it's difficult to ever be finished thinking about an issue like abortion. Your teacher will present you with activities designed to help you continue to interact with these perspectives, decide which ones feel right to you, which ones do not, and why. This is all meant to help you develop your own take on abortion, and it's a process that should stay with you long after you leave the classroom.

We've barely scratched the surface of this complex and challenging issue, and you may wish to explore further on your own. Following is a list of suggested resources that you may find helpful.

Books and Articles

Abraham, Abraham S. *The Comprehensive Guide To Medical Halachah.* Jerusalem and New York: Feldheim Publishers, 1996.

Cytron, Barry D., and Earl Schwartz. *When Life Is in the Balance.* New York: United Synagogue of America, 1986.

Freeman, Susan. *Teaching Jewish Virtues: Sacred Sources and Arts Activities.* Denver, CO: A.R.E. Publishing, Inc., 1999.

Gordis, Robert. *Love & Sex: A Modern Jewish Perspective.* New York: Farrar Straus Giroux, 1978.

Kadden, Barbara Binder, and Bruce Kadden. *Teaching Mitzvot: Concepts, Values, and Activities.* Rev. ed. Denver, CO: A.R.E. Publishing, Inc., 2003.

Mackler, Aaron L., ed. *Life & Death Responsibilities in Jewish Biomedical Ethics.* New York: The Jewish Theological Seminary of America, 2000.

Rein, Mei Ling. *Abortion: An Eternal Social and Moral Issue.* Wylie, TX: Information Plus Reference Series, 2000.

Religious Coalition for Abortion Rights, "Personhood and the Bible in the Abortion Debate," 1991.

Reiss, Glynis Conyer. "Abortion." In *Where We Stand: Jewish Consciousness on Campus,* edited by Allan L. Smith. New York: UAHC Press, 1997.

Rosner, Fred. *Modern Medicine and Jewish Ethics*. Hoboken, NJ: KTAV Publishing House, Inc. and New York: Yeshiva University Press, 1991.

Wahrman, Miriam Z. *Brave New Judaism: When Science and Scripture Collide*. Waltham, MA: Brandeis University, 2002.

Zwerin, Raymond A., and Richard J. Shapiro. *Judaism and Abortion*. Washington, DC: Religious Coalition for Abortion Rights, n.d.

Web Sites

A Heart Breaking Choice: www.aheartbreaking-choice.com
> *A site for parents who have interrupted a wanted pregnancy because of a poor medical diagnosis.*

Center for Reproductive Law and Policy: www.crlp.org
> *A nonprofit legal advocacy organization dedicated to promoting and defending women's reproductive rights worldwide.*

Focus on the Family: www.family.org
> *The web site of Focus on the Family, a conservative Christian organization whose mission is to preserve traditional values and the institution of the family.*

NARAL Pro-Choice America (formerly The National Abortion and Reproductive Rights Action League): www.naral.org
> *NARAL is the political arm of the pro-choice movement and a strong advocate of reproductive freedom and choice.*

National Council of Jewish Women: www.ncjw.org
> *Works to improve the quality of life for women, children and families and strives to ensure individual rights and freedoms for all.*

Planned Parenthood: www.plannedparenthood.org
> *Advocates for reproductive self-determination.*

Religious Coalition for Reproductive Choice: www.rcrc.org
> *Works to ensure reproductive choice through the moral power of religious communities.*

Teenwire from Planned Parenthood Federation of America: www.teenwire.com
> *The Planned Parenthood Federation of America Web site for young people needing information about all aspects of sexual health.*

Films

The following commercial films deal with the issue of abortion in a frank and mature manner, and some of them may not be appropriate for younger students. Check with parents or teachers before viewing.

The Cider House Rules (1999, 126 minutes, rated PG-13)
> A young boy, raised in an orphanage, is trained to be a physician by a compassionate doctor who performs illegal abortions. Available from video stores.

If These Walls Could Talk (1996, 95 minutes, rated R)
> A trilogy of stories set in the same house, but with different occupants and spanning over 40 years, deals with various women and moral crisis over unexpected pregnancies and their choice of abortion. Available from video stores, or online from the HBO Store at http://store.hbo.com.

A Private Matter (1992, 89 minutes, rated PG-13)
> The true story of Romper Room host "Miss Sherri" Finkbine (played by Sissy Spacek), who, after the devastating effects of Thalidomide were discovered in the early 1960s, sparked a firestorm of controversy with her determination to obtain an abortion. Available from video stores, or online from the HBO Store at http://store.hbo.com.

CHAPTER 2
CLONING AND OTHER GENETIC TECHNOLOGIES

Overview

Note: Understanding of a number of biotechnological terms is important for this chapter. See the "Glossary" on page 29 for definitions of these important terms.

Introduction

Why the interest in cloning and other genetic technologies? Two major reasons are their therapeutic promise and their potential to address infertility. Current scientific developments are encouraging regarding these two goals. Who can argue with such good intentions — healing people and helping people to have children? As it happens, there is plenty to argue about.

One critical ethical dilemma rests on this classical question: Do the ends justify the means? In other words, gene therapies may allow a person to overcome an illness or even avoid getting a disease in the first place. That would be the goal or the "ends". But achieving that goal — the "means" — might involve an ethically murky process.

A related concern is this: With genetic technologies, we may end up creating more, possibly worse problems than we solve. Thus, another critical ethical dilemma is this: Do the ends justify (all) the ends?

Related dilemmas may arise. Possibly only elite (wealthy) members of society will have the means to access the technology. Another concern is that society may neglect important responsibilities as it channels substantial resources to genetic-related health procedures. For example, funds committed to genetics may divert needed money away from schools, environmental protection, or aid to individuals in need.

These and other ethical questions present daunting obstacles as research goes ahead. Some recommend putting a stop to this line of scientific inquiry. Others suggest vigilant regulation of genetic technologies. Still others favor only limited regulation, believing scientists and potential beneficiaries should be free to make their own decisions regarding experiments and treatments.

Jewish Perspectives

Finding traditional Jewish sources that apply neatly to modern genetic science is not easy. Primarily, we must look toward overarching Jewish principles to help us respond to the ethical challenges.

Reasons to Pursue Genetic Technologies

Pikuach Nefesh (Saving a Life): To save one life is equivalent to saving a whole world (*Sanhedrin* 4:5). Genetic technologies may help save lives.

Rofeh Cholim (Healing the Sick): This mandate teaches that it is our obligation to heal. Genetic technologies hold great promise in treating and curing disease.

Mechabayd Zeh et Zeh (To Honor One Another): This *middah* requires us to respect the dignity of each individual. We honor others when we respond to their suffering. New therapies may allow for suffering individuals to cope with their illness with an improved sense of dignity.

"Choose life" (Deuteronomy 30:19): This passage suggests that though there may be risks involved in genetic procedures, we should pursue the most life-affirming options.

Pru u'Revu (Be Fruitful and Multiply, Genesis 1:28): The first commandment in the Torah imparts an important Jewish value, reinforced by Jewish social traditions. Cloning may allow individuals to have biologically related children when other fertility treatments fail.

Reasons for Caution

Anavah (Humility): This principle would caution us not to overreach in our efforts to be *k'Elohim*, like God.

HaNeshama be'kirbee (The Soul That is Within Me), a phrase found in our morning liturgy, teaches we are integrated, whole beings and not simply mechanical objects. We must be wary of technologies that diminish the sacredness of human life.

"One may not sacrifice one life to preserve another." (*Mishneh Torah, Hilchot Yesodei Hatorah* 5:7): We must question the morality of creating a person essentially for the purpose of serving the needs of another person (for example, parents having a child to supply an older sibling with compatible, healthy cells or tissue).

God intends each human being to be unique: The rabbis of the Talmud extol God's ability to make each person an original: "Each individual was created alone . . . to proclaim the greatness of the Holy One. For if a person strikes many coins from one die, they all resemble one another; in fact, they are exactly alike. But though the Sovereign of Sovereigns, the Holy One Who is Blessed, fashioned every person from the die of the first man, not a single one of them is like his/her fellow" (*Sanhedrin* 38a). Judaism appreciates individual uniqueness. A practice that deliberately stifles uniqueness calls for caution.

Self-idolization: Self-idolization can be a threat when people replicate themselves through cloning, essentially a self-involved act. Although we do not actually attain immortality through a clone, genetic self-perpetuation can cause undue focus on the self.

"Teach us to number our days so that we may attain a heart of wisdom" (Psalms 90:12): God's wisdom is countered when we try to endlessly prolong life.

Bal Tashchit (Do not destroy): This important Jewish principal is liable to be violated in researching and applying genetic therapies, which require the use of genetic material, including embryos, female eggs, and/or other tissue.

Additional Considerations

B'tzelem Elohim, in God's image did God create humankind (Genesis 1:27): Some might say that God is the Creator, and that when we engage in cloning we presume a role that is not legitimately ours. Yet, the mysteries of the universe do not disappear just because researchers gain ground in cloning. Mysteries will always remain despite the scientific discoveries that humans make.

Use of embryonic material: Genetic technologies may require the use of an embryo — or hundreds of embryos — that will be destroyed in the process. While Judaism does not equate an embryo with full life, it is potential life and should be valued and treated with respect. Some Jews may be troubled by the possible disregard for the sanctity of human life, even in its most elemental form. They worry that a factory-type attitude toward embryos may develop.

Use of community resources: Long ago communities understood the need to allocate resources carefully. The Talmud lists ten things a worthy community must provide (see Text Study #5a below). Genetic technologies are expensive, yet the potential benefits to humankind are priceless. There must be open debate on the ethics of spending priorities.

Access to treatments: As already mentioned, genetic therapies are very expensive. Should only those who can afford them benefit? A Jewish perspective would urge us to avoid medical practices that allow access only by the wealthy.

Who are the parents? This question involves complicated scientific details and *halachic* (Jewish legal) rules. An egg may come from one woman, the genetic material, might come from the same woman, a different woman, or a man. The man may be the husband of the egg donor, the gene donor, or the womb provider, or he may not be related to them at all. Despite such complex matters, reputable halachic scholars believe we can effectively resolve questions of paternity and maternity.

General Perspectives

The following two sections are adapted from the ideas of Dr. Avraham Steinberg, Director of the Center for Medical Ethics at Hebrew University and author of a paper entitled "Human Cloning — Scientific, Moral and Jewish Perspectives."

Potential Medical Benefits:

- Renewing the activity of damaged cells may improve the prognosis for debilitating illnesses. For example, renewing or replacing damaged brain cells might benefit sufferers of Parkinson's or Alzheimer's Disease. Renewing or replacing these cells would require cloning technology, but not the full cloning of human beings.

- Curbing the proliferation of cancerous cells could lead to cures for certain malignant diseases. This would also require only cloning technology, not the full cloning of human beings.

- Humans created with similar immunities could serve as organ donors for one another. However, scientists are focused on the cloning of organs rather than the cloning of human beings as organ donors.

- Cloning technologies could enable animals to become potential sources of transplant organs for humans.

- Cloning could help infertile couples for whom other modern reproductive techniques haven't worked.[1]

Potential Disadvantages and Concerns:

- Cloning adds another dimension to the questionable morality of eugenics (manipulating embryonic genes to attain preferred characteristics), a potentially unsettling situation that deserves ethical examination.

- Creating large groups of people with similar appearance and personality would compromise the individuality of every member. This scenario would challenge our value of respecting people precisely because they are unique individuals.

- The loss of genetic variation among clones could cause genetic inbreeding, and may lead to problematic consequences.

- "Black markets" for "designer" fetuses with desirable traits could arise.

- New technologies could lead to confusion about the definition and determination of parenthood.

- There is potential for worrisome effects on societal order — our ideals of homes and families.[2]

A Jewish Approach

With compelling reasons to pursue genetic technology, and chilling reasons to avoid such efforts, where should Judaism stand? A moderate and reasonable conclusion would be to proceed, but with

great caution. Dr. Abraham Steinberg (who was quoted in the "General Perspectives" section above) offers these practical suggestions:[3]

> The Parliaments of the Western world should establish a multi-disciplinary, international committee that will examine the positive and negative aspects of the topic before us . . . Furthermore, this international committee should be given credence to judge all the positive and negative aspects of the genetics of the future. The purpose of this committee will include the following tasks:
>
> - Recommendations for the methods of research and development of these technologies
>
> - Recommendations for the application of these technologies.
>
> - International supervision on the application and implementation of the use of these technologies, modeled after the supervision over unconventional weapons.
>
> - Supervision over the allotments for research and application of these technologies.

Summary of the Overview

The paragraphs below summarize the key Jewish considerations concerning cloning and genetic engineering:

1. Cloning and other genetic technologies have potential benefits in the realms of healing and fertility. They also have potentially worrisome consequences.

2. A ban on genetic research and development is not realistic, and may be unwise, as well.

3. Judaism shares many of the general moral concerns expressed concerning genetic technologies. In addition, Judaism has concerns that specifically reflect our values and beliefs.

4. Because of the ethical issues associated with cloning and other genetic technologies, rigorous regulation and supervision are an absolute necessity. The goal is to nurture scientific advances which enhance humanity, minimize dangerous risks, and avoid destructive mistakes.

Scenarios: A Few Possible Directions in Genetic Technologies

Below are three imaginary scenarios followed by questions intended to stimulate thought and spark discussion. Read each scenario and reflect, either individually or in a group discussion, on the questions in the "For Thought and Discussion" section that follows. Then continue on to the "Text Study" section to see what Jewish and other sources have to say on the subject. Finally, you may wish to come back and discuss the questions a second time, to see if your views have changed.

Scenario I

Dave is 70 years old. He is in great physical health, but his mental faculties are declining. A medical exam and some tests confirm what the family fears: Dave is showing the beginning signs of Alzheimer's Disease. Fortunately, he is an excellent candidate to participate in experimental genetic-based treatments.

Medical scientists develop a therapy compatible with Dave's genetic make-up. So far, Dave is responding well. Doctors feel hopeful that Dave will improve. Though these treatments are very expensive, researchers expect they will be able to bring down the costs as they perfect the procedure.

Scenario II

David is 70 years old. He has begun to suffer from a degenerative muscle condition. Genetic researchers believe that if they were able to replace some of David's degenerating tissue with healthy tissue, his health could improve greatly. David would like to have himself cloned, with the clone serving as a source for healthy muscle tissue. David's son and daughter-in-law say they are willing to raise the cloned child since David doesn't feel prepared to take that on. David is a wealthy man and cost is no obstacle. He is willing to spend whatever it takes for the chance to overcome his debilitating health problems.

Scenario III

Same scenario as II above, except "Davey" is a cat with a degenerative muscle disease. The interest in, decisions about, and funding for cloning Davey come from the cat's owners.

For Thought and Discussion

Should an expensive treatment that is still in its experimental stages be made available to candidates who might benefit from it? If that candidate can't afford the treatment, should it still be offered to him? If so, at who's expense?

Should a human being be allowed to clone himself in order to obtain tissue and organs? Why or why not?

Should the cloning of animals as a source of tissue and organs for other animals be allowed? Why or why not?

Text Study

Though cloning and genetic engineering are very new technologies, they raise ethical questions with which Judaism has dealt for thousands of years. Jewish sources, both our ancient texts and contemporary writings, provide many answers, but these answers often highlight the tension between seemingly opposing considerations. The chart on the next page poses the questions and offers two opposing points of view. Text sources supporting each of these points of view follow.

1. **Should genetic research be unrestricted, strictly regulated, or banned entirely?**

   On the One Hand:

   Banning the development of new scientific ideas (technologies) is unrealistic and possibly unwise. Genetic research will continue to evolve over the next decades.

   A. Is it, then, any wonder that [humans] should try to do in [their] own small way what God did in the beginning? (Gershom Scholem, quoted in *The Great Jewish Cities of Central and Eastern Europe* by Eli Valley, Northvale, NJ: Jason Aronson, Inc., 1999, p. 44.)

   B. There is no stopping human inquisitiveness, and once we begin to ask questions, it's only a matter of time before we begin to take steps to answer them and then to

Ethical Responses to Cloning and Genetic Engineering: Questions to Consider

The Question	On the One Hand	On the Other Hand
1. Should genetic research be unrestricted, strictly regulated, or banned entirely? (see page 18)	Banning the development of new scientific ideas is unrealistic and possibly unwise. Genetic research will continue to evolve over the next decades.	We must direct genetic science by regulating who does the research, who supervises the efforts, and who benefits from or receives applications of the research.
2. Should the use of embryonic cells and/or tissue be allowed for medical research? (see page 20)	Promising genetic research and techniques involve use of embryos which essentially are clusters of pre-life cells.	Embryos may not be full human beings with souls, but they embody early-stage life. We must question the ethics of meddling in an embryo's natural development.
3. To what extent should healing and preserving life supercede other values? (see page 22)	If we have the ability to improve the physical quality of human life, we should do so.	Human beings are more than just bodies.
4. Should the cloning of human beings for the purpose of helping infertile couples to have children be allowed? (see page 22)	Cloning will help infertile couples bring children into the world who carry the genetic imprint of one of them.	There are values that transcend passing along our genes.
5. Should the cloning of human beings for the purpose of curing illness and genetic disorders be allowed? (see page 23)	Cloning and related gene manipulation techniques will help us find cures to devastating illnesses and genetic disorders.	The hurdles for using cloning to find cures are daunting: including, expense, individually tailoring therapies, access (by the wealthy and privileged only?), safety, environmental issues, and unforeseen detrimental genetic consequences affecting future generations.
6. Should the cloning of human beings for the purpose of providing healthy tissue and/or organs be allowed? (see page 24)	A cloned individual can provide healthy tissue/organs to its ill counterpart without the problems of immune incompatibility. Creating a new organ (without the full body) is another possibility.	Manufacturing some people to serve others is coercive and an abuse of power. In creating an organ, we take risks that it will evolve in abnormal and frightening ways.

(continued on next page)

7. Should cloning or the manipulation of genes for the purpose of producing desirable characteristics in human beings be allowed? (see p. 26)	Cloning will help us as a society to improve the quality of our species by cloning special individuals or isolating favorable genetic qualities to pass on to the next generation.	The practice of eugenics is hubris. That is, manipulating genes for the purpose of producing "desirable" characteristics is sacrilegious arrogance. It turns humans into objects and creates a breeding ground for racism.

act on the answers. (Alan Meisel, "The Jerusalem Report," April 16, 1998)

C. The Jewish demand that we do our best to provide healing makes it important that we take advantage of the promise of cloning to aid us in finding cures for a variety of diseases and in overcoming infertility . . . To pretend that human cloning will not take place if it is banned in experiments funded with government money is simply unrealistic; it will happen with private funds in the United States and/or abroad. (Rabbi Elliot N. Dorff, *Matters of Life and Death*, p. 322-323)

On the Other Hand:

We must direct genetic science by regulating: who does the research, who supervises the efforts, and who benefits from or receives applications of the research.

a. The dangers of cloning . . . require that it be supervised and restricted. Specifically, cloning should be allowed only for medical research or therapy; clones must be recognized as having full and equal status with other fetuses or human beings, with the equivalent protections; and careful policies must be devised to determine how cloning mistakes will be identified and handled . . . (Rabbi Elliot N. Dorff, *Matters of Life and Death*, p. 322-323)

b. It is indefensible to initiate uncontrolled experiments with incalculable effects on the balance of nature and the preservation of [humankind's] incomparable spirituality without the most careful evaluation of the likely consequences beforehand . . . (Rabbi Immanuel Jakobovits, *Jewish Medical Ethics*, pp. 261)

c. There are certain inevitabilities in life, and I'm afraid [cloning] is one of them. Passing laws to prohibit the practice won't work. We need to face up to the challenge and try to assure that science and technology work for us rather than sabotaging us. That should be the aim first of public debate and then of law. (Alan Meisel, "The Jerusalem Report," April 16, 1998)

What Do You Think?

Of the six texts above, whose words do you find most compelling and why?

What might be the consequences of banning research related to cloning?

What might be the consequences of encouraging research?

——✦——

2. **Should the use of embryonic cells and/or tissue be allowed for medical research?**

On the One Hand:

Promising genetic research and techniques involve use of embryos which essentially are clusters of pre-life cells.

Note: For more detailed Jewish views on the status and nature of the embryo, see the chapter on abortion beginning on page 3.

Texts A, B, and C are from traditional Jewish sources, and texts D and E reflect modern science.

A. If a woman is pregnant, the semen, until the fortieth day, is only a mere fluid. (*Yevamot* 69b)

B. [Capital punishment is not imposed on one who, during a scuffle, causes a pregnant woman to miscarry because there is] no form [yet to the fetus]. . . (*Septuagint* translation of Exodus 21:22).

C. If a woman in labor has a [life-threatening] difficulty, one dismembers the embryo within her, removing it limb by limb, for her life takes precedence over its life. But once its greater part has emerged, it may not be harmed, for we do not set aside one life for another (*Ohalot* 7:6) . . . [The embryo can be removed "limb by limb"] because, as long as it has not emerged into the world, it is not a human being [*lav nefesh hu*], and therefore it can be killed in order to save its mother (Rashi, *Sanhedrin* 72b).

D. A four to five day old embryo is called a blastocyst. Between six and nine days old, an embryo implants itself on the uterine wall.

> Blastocyst: A hollow sphere of some 250 cells that develop four to five days after an egg is fertilized. Inside is a clump of about 30 cells, the inner cell mass, from which the embryo develops. When removed and grown in the lab, cells from the inner cell mass are called embryonic stem cells ("Glossary," *New York Times* "Science Times," p. D10).

E. Embryonic stem cells . . . have two attributes that make them attractive for regenerative medicine.[4] They are versatile, in that they can be turned into any other type of tissue or cell in the body, at least in theory. And they can be easily multiplied in culture, providing an ample supply of cells (Andrew Pollack, "Scientists Seek Ways to Rebuild the Body, Bypassing the Embryo," *New York Times* "Science Times," p. D6).

On the Other Hand:

Embryos may not be full human beings with souls, but they embody early-stage life. We must question the ethics of meddling in an embryo's natural development.

a. He who indulges in marital intercourse on the ninetieth day [of pregnancy, when it was thought to injure the embryo], it is as though he had shed blood (*Niddah* 31a).

b. From the perspective of an Orthodox Christian reverend and scholar:

> Sometime during the development of a human person, from the moment of conception until birth, that person becomes "ensouled." We will never know when or how that occurs. Once a human zygote forms and begins to develop, it is committed to becoming a human person. Because we do not know when or how that person obtains a soul, we must not interfere with that development in any deleterious way at any time. We must treat the developing embryo with dignity and respect because we do not know when it becomes a person (Rev. Dr. Demetri Demopulos, "Cloning: Sanctity or Utility," from *Reflections, Newsletter of the Program for Ethics, Science, and the Environment,* Department for Philosophy, Oregon State University, Special Edition, May 1997).

What Do You Think?

After reading the above texts, do you see a conflict between Judaism and science? Explain.

Suppose a scientist wants to conduct his/her research in ways consistent with Judaism. Can the scientist use embryos (under forty days old) as freely in experiments as he/she might use any other cells (for example, from a carrot or a mouse)?

To what extent, if at all, do you believe Jews should heed Rev. Demopulos' words?

3. **To what extent should healing and preserving life supercede other values?**

On the One Hand:

If we have the ability to improve the physical quality of human life, we should do so.

A. I hereby declare today, with heaven and earth as my witnesses, that I have put before you life and death, blessing and curse. Choose life, that you and your descendants may live. (Deuteronomy 30:19)

B. If one destroys a single person, Scripture considers it as if he/she had destroyed the whole population of the world. And if one saves the life of a single person, Scripture considers it as though he/she saves the whole world (*Sanhedrin* 4:5). See also Text #1C above.

On the Other Hand:

Human beings are more than just bodies.

a. Teach us to number our days so that we may attain a heart of wisdom. (Psalms 90:12)

b. Judaism upholds the values of perpetuating life and healing. Still, we may find these thoughts of a Hindu scholar and spiritual leader challenging. He eloquently questions the degree of value we should attach to our physical bodies.

"Those who think the Self is the body will lose their way in life . . . It is true that the body is perishable, but within it dwells the imperishable Self . . . " (*Chandogya Upanishad*). The supreme purpose of life is to reveal the divine spark that is latent within every one of us. When we hear about important scientific discoveries like the splitting of the atom or the cloning of a sheep, we can always ask ourselves: "Will this help me in my search for realizing God, who is enshrined in the depths of my consciousness?" (Sri Eknath Easwaran, "Brave New World," from *Reflections, Newsletter of the Program for Ethics, Science, and the Environment,* Department for Philosophy, Oregon State University, Special Edition, May 1997)

What Do You Think?

Which of these passages about body and soul resonates most with you? Why?

Do Sri Eknath Easwaran's words contradict the Jewish texts #3A and B? Explain.

Judaism suggests that each of us has a spark of the Divine within us. That is, we, who are created in the Divine image, come to life because God "breathes the soul-breath" into each one of us. Does cloning put undue emphasis on our physical beings?

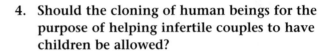

4. **Should the cloning of human beings for the purpose of helping infertile couples to have children be allowed?**

On the One Hand:

Cloning techniques will help infertile couples bring children into the world who carry the genetic imprint of one of them.

A. Be fruitful and multiply. (Genesis 1:28)

B. Show me a young man who is sterile, whose family was obliterated by the Holocaust and who is the last in a genetic line. I would advise cloning him to create a descendant. (Rabbi Moshe Tendler, "The Right Situation," [op-ed] *New York Times,* December 12, 1997, A22)

On the Other Hand:

There are values that transcend passing along our genes.

a. If God's goal is to populate the earth with men and women who are exact genetic copies, the commandment ["be fruitful and multiply"] could mean, "Replicate yourselves," and cloning would fit the bill. But look around you — we are clearly not genetic replicas of each other. The diversity of our species suggests that what God has in mind is not replication, but reproduction. Children are not genetic replicas of either parent. They are a product of their union; genetic heirs of both parents, they are genetically unique (Harvey L. Gordon, M.D., "Human Cloning and the Jewish Tradition," in *Bioethics, Program Guide X: Cloning*, UAHC Department of Jewish Family Concerns).

b. Sexual reproduction carries the promise that each individual represents something new, something unique that may enhance the species (Morton D. Prager, Ph.D., "Cloning," in *Bioethics, Program Guide X: Cloning*, UAHC Department of Jewish Family Concerns).

c. In the circumstance where a procedure with unsure consequences and uncertain implications is the only way to produce progeny, liberal Judaism offers several ways to continue to pass one's endowment to future generations — through charitable acts and donations, creations such as books and music that we leave behind, and the memories with which we grace others (Dr. Stephen M. Modell, "Four Cloning Scenarios from the Perspective of Science and the Jewish Tradition," in *Bioethics, Program Guide X: Cloning*, UAHC Department of Jewish Family Concerns).

d. Cloning is less a treatment for infertility than a treatment for vanity. It is a way to produce an exact genetic replica of yourself that will walk the earth years after you're gone (Charles Krauthammer, "Of Headless Mice . . . And Men," *Time Magazine*, January 19, 1998).

What Do You Think?

Contrast the argument presented by the first grouping of texts to that of the second.

Which "On the One Hand" or "On the Other Hand" position and grouping of texts is stronger (#4A and B or #4a-d)? Explain your response.

5. **Should the cloning of human beings for the purpose of curing illness and genetic disorders be allowed?**

On the One Hand:

Cloning and related gene manipulation techniques will help us find cures to devastating illnesses and genetic disorders.

A. Since the function of medicine, as construed in Jewish sources, is to aid God in the process of healing, research into further ways to accomplish that end finds enthusiastic endorsement within Jewish ideology and law (Rabbi Elliot N. Dorff, *Matters of Life and Death*, p. 310).

On the Other Hand:

The hurdles for using cloning to find cures are daunting: including, expense, individually tailoring therapies, access (by the wealthy and privileged only?), safety, environmental issues, and unforeseen detrimental genetic consequences affecting future generations.

a. A community should not spend so much on medical needs that other needs are compromised. The services of a surgeon is just one of ten things that a worthy community must provide:

> A scholar should not reside in a city where [any] of the following ten things is missing: (1) A court of justice . . . ; (2) a charity fund . . . ; (3) a synagogue; (4) public baths; (5) toilet facilities; (6) a circumciser (*mohel*); (7) a surgeon; (8) a notary; (9) a slaughterer (*shochet*); and (10) a schoolmaster. Rabbi Akiba [included] several kinds of fruit because they are beneficial for eyesight (*Sanhedrin* 17b).

b. The Talmud sets forth the ideal that everyone in need of healing will have access to it, regardless of their means to pay.

> Abba the blood-letter [an ancient type of medical healer] placed a box outside his office where his fees were to be deposited. Whoever had money put it in, but those who had none could

come in without feeling embarrassed. When he saw a person who was in no position to pay, he would offer him some money, saying to him, "Go, strengthen yourself [after the bleeding procedure]" (*Ta'anit* 21b).

c. To what extent should we go to take health and safety risks for the possibility of gaining something useful?

> We are commanded to remove all obstacles and sources of danger from all places in which we live (Maimonides, *The Commandments*, vol. 1, p. 197).

d. For sufficient tissue to use in genetic therapies, Scientists must create more tissue than they will use as they develop genetic therapies. The tissue might include embryonic tissue, adult cells, partially developed organs, etc. Surplus and abnormally developed tissue/clones must be destroyed (or preserved in their quasi-living state). The laws of Bal Tashchit, instructing us not to be destructive or wasteful, originate in the Torah:

> The Eternal God took the man and placed him in the garden of Eden, to till it and tend it (Genesis 2:15).

e. Germ-line gene therapy (GLGT) manipulates cells involved in reproduction.

> Whatever changes are introduced into the germ line will perpetuate themselves in subsequent generations . . . An error introduced by the procedure will (in an almost biblical sense) visit itself unto the fourth generation (Exodus 34:7) and beyond (Dr. Stephen M. Modell, "Four Cloning Scenarios from the Perspective of Science and the Jewish Tradition," in *Bioethics, Program Guide X: Cloning*, UAHC Department of Jewish Family Concerns).

f. There is a difference between purely reproductive technologies, such as in vitro fertilization (IVF), and genetic technologies, which try to change the shape of future organisms ("The Politics of Genes:

America's Next Ethical War" in *The Economist*, April 14, 2001, p. 21).

g. "Many of the animal clones that have been produced show serious developmental abnormalities . . . " (Stephen G. Post, quoting a British expert on fertility in "The Judeo-Christian Case against Human Cloning," *Biotechnology*, p. 103)

What Do You Think?

According to Jewish sources, at what point do the obstacles to genetic therapies become too high to sourmount?

For the following, give examples of when you think the hurdle would become so prohibitively high that you could no longer justify potential therapeutic benefits:

Expense: The expense would be too high if . . .

Individually tailoring therapies: The effort of tailoring a therapy to an individual's particular needs would become overly burdensome if . . .

Access: If therapeutic treatments were only available to wealthy and other privileged people . . .

Safety: If we couldn't be sure a genetic therapy was safe . . .

Environmental issues: We must limit the numbers of animals and human embryos that we develop and discard because . . .

Unforeseen detrimental genetic consequences affecting future generations: The amount of risk we should be willing to take is . . .

6. **Should the cloning of human beings for the purpose of providing healthy tissue and/or organs be allowed?**

On the One Hand:

A cloned individual can provide healthy tissue/organs to its ill counterpart without the problems of immune incompatibility. Creating a new organ (without the full body) is another possibility.

A. Show me a child whose survival depends on transplantation of bone marrow. I would advise cloning to save the child's life. A child produced for this purpose would then be doubly loved (Rabbi Moshe Tendler, "The Right Situation" [op-ed] *New York Times,* December 12, 1997, A22).

B. Embryonic cells seem less antagonistic to the immune system than are ordinary cells . . . Adult stem cells, if they could be extracted from each patient as need arose, could be used without any risk of immune rejection (Nicholas Wade, "In Tiny Cells, Glimpses of Body's Master Plan," *New York Times,* December 18, 2001, D8).

C. The promise of embryonic stem cells for medicine rests on more than their powers to morph [transform] into any body tissue. In the lab, they exhibit another amazing property — the ability to assemble spontaneously into structures seen in living tissues [e.g., blood vessels, glands, heart muscle] . . . The cells are just engineered to self-assemble, given the right cues and conditions (Nicholas Wade, "In Tiny Cells, Glimpses of Body's Master Plan," *New York Times,* December 18, 2001, D8).

D. It would almost certainly be possible to produce human bodies without a forebrain . . . These human bodies without any semblance of consciousness would not be considered persons, and thus it would be perfectly legal to keep them "alive" as a future source of organs (Lee Silver, Princeton biologist quoted by Charles Krauthammer in "Of Headless Mice . . . And Men," *Time Magazine,* January 19, 1998).

On the Other Hand:

Manufacturing some people to serve others is coercive and an abuse of power. In creating an organ, we take risks that it will evolve in abnormal and frightening ways.

a. It is a cardinal principle of Judaism that one may not sacrifice one life to preserve another . . . (see *Mishneh Torah, Hilchot Yesodei Hatorah* 5:7). One might argue this principle does not apply to the current situation since the donor clone will continue to live after contributing bone marrow. Let us suppose, however, that the cloned person is to be considered a constant source of bone marrow for the original [sibling], which might occur, say, in a case of chronic leukemia . . . This condition is not unlike the relationship between Isaac and his brother Ishmael. There were natural rivalries between Sarah and Hagar (Ishmael's mother) and between Isaac and Ishmael, so that eventually Abraham banished Hagar and Ishmael and ceded patriarchy to Isaac. Who is to say that a child born to service another will not be taken for granted or gain a lesser status in parental eyes if their contribution to a brother or sister is a recurrent necessity? There is also the question of the emotional impact on the cloned, developing child . . . (Dr. Stephen M. Modell, "Four Cloning Scenarios from the Perspective of Science and the Jewish Tradition," in *Bioethics, Program Guide X: Cloning,* UAHC Department of Jewish Family Concerns).

b. When prominent scientists are prepared to acquiesce in — or indeed encourage — the deliberate creation of deformed and dying quasi-human life [for example, as part of one's "own personal, precisely tissue-matched organ farm"], you know we are facing a bioethical abyss. There is no grosser corruption of biotechnology than creating a human mutant and disemboweling it at our pleasure for spare parts (Charles Krauthammer, "Of Headless Mice . . . And Men," *Time Magazine,* January 19, 1998).

c. Injected into mice, the unchanged [embryonic stem] cells form not an embryo but a grisly tumor full of hair and teeth and known as a "monster cancer" or teratoma (Nicholas Wade, "In Tiny Cells, Glimpses of Body's Master Plan," *New York Times,* December 18, 2001, D8).

What Do You Think?

Do Jewish sources voice valid concerns for the cloning of another human being for the use of tissue and organs? Why or why not?

When might you justify the use of a clone and/or a "manufactured" organ for therapeutic use?

When might you say doing such things is prohibited?

Where should Judaism stand on the matter of "manufacturing" organs for therapeutic use? Explain.

——◆——

7. **Should cloning or the manipulation of genes for the purpose of producing desirable characteristics in human beings be allowed?**

On the One Hand:

Cloning will help us as a society to improve the quality of our species by cloning special individuals or isolating favorable genetic qualities to pass on to the next generation.

A. Many people now argue that science is allowing a healthier, non-coercive version of eugenics, practiced by caring parents as opposed to a racist state . . . ("The Politics of Genes: America's Next Ethical War" in *The Economist,* April 14, 2001, p. 22).

B. An example of pre-birth genetic screening:

> A Jewish committee in New York that is concerned to prevent genetic disease organizes tests to discourage Ashkenzi Jews who carry the Tay-Sachs mutation from marrying each other. But it went further . . . with the specific selection of "Baby Adam", from among 15 healthy embryos, because he had the right bone marrow to help his sister, who had a rare disease. ("The Politics of Genes: America's Next Ethical War" in *The Economist,* April 14, 2001, p. 22).

On the Other Hand:

The practice of eugenics is hubris. That is, manipulating genes for the purpose of producing "desirable" characteristics is sacrilegious arrogance. It turns humans into objects and creates a breeding ground for racism.

a. The argument (that "cloning will help us as a society to improve the quality of our species . . . ") is often used, but it relies on a flawed understanding of the genetics of populations. If we were to prevent the reproduction of all individuals exhibiting a genetic disease, we would have very little effect on the frequency of the defective gene in the human population. We are not really "improving the species" by pursuing cloning. On the other hand . . . if we can avoid individual suffering by prescreening embryos, are we not obliged to do so? (Robert Dorit, Professor of Biology, Smith College, February 2002).

b. Cloning is another blow to the necessary sense of humility we should have in dealing with the mysteries of life (Rabbi David Wolpe, quoted by Barbara Trainin Blank in "The Ethics of Cloning," *Hadassah Magazine,* June/July 1997).

c. For many people, the difficulties come when biotechnology leaps from stopping disease to adding advantages — enhancing the genes that make you more intelligent, more musical, or less homosexual (as it may yet do: it can't at present) ("The Politics of Genes: America's Next Ethical War" in *The Economist,* April 14, 2001, p. 22).

d. The sex of children is already up for sale. At first, [one] institute helped couples with hereditary diseases that tend to occur in boys. Now it offers "family balancing" to couples who want to choose their next child from "the under-represented gender" ("The Politics of Genes: America's Next Ethical War" in *The Economist,* April 14, 2001, p. 22).

What Do You Think?

Why would Judaism (and other religion-based ethics) prohibit this practice?

When might a person argue in favor of eugenics?

When might a person oppose eugenics?

Related Middot and Mitzvot

Practicing these virtues supports ethical decision-making regarding cloning and other genetic technologies.

Anavah: Humility. Just because we can do something, doesn't mean we should. Focusing on healing and cooperating with international regulations will help us maintain humility as we pursue genetic technologies.

Mechabayd Zeh et Zeh: Honoring the Dignity of Each Individual. Before going ahead with a genetic procedure, we must carefully evaluate how it will affect the dignity of any and all persons involved.

Rofeh Cholim: Healing the Sick. We have a duty to heal suffering in our midst. Genetic technologies may prove to be an important tool in working toward that aim.

Samayach B'Chelko: Contentment with One's Lot. Perhaps this includes contentment with there being one version of our genes in the world (or two if we're an identical twin). Cloning ourselves is reaching beyond what we reasonably should expect to be our life's "portion."

Sho-eyl U'Maysheev: Asking and Answering Questions. Genetic technologies raise many important and difficult questions. We must encourage vibrant discussion and debate about these questions. Hopefully, in doing so, our society's decisions will be well-reasoned and will prove as wise as possible.

Yirah: Awe and Reverence. Despite human "advances" in the sciences, we must not lose sight of God's role as the ultimate Source of Mystery in the universe.

Where Do I Go From Here?

As you can see, cloning and genetic engineering are highly charged, emotional issues with many religious, social, and cultural implications. You should develop your opinions about such issues only after in-depth consideration. As a Jew, that consideration includes delving into the Jewish sources that relate to the matter. As you continue to explore these issues, your teacher will present you with activities designed to help you consider the various perspectives, decide which ones feel right to you, which ones do not, and why. This is all meant to help you develop your own take on cloning and genetic engineering, and it's a process that should stay with you long after you leave the classroom.

We've barely scratched the surface of this complex and challenging issue, and you may wish to explore further on your own. Following is a list of suggested resources that you may find helpful.

Books and Articles

Angier, Natalie. "Defining the Undefinable: Being Alive." In *The New York Times, Science Times,* December 18, 2001.

Blank, Barbara Trainin. "The Ethics of Cloning." In *Hadassah Magazine,* June/July 1997.

Dorff, Elliot N. *Matters of Life and Death: A Jewish Approach To Modern Medical Ethics.* Philadelphia, PA: The Jewish Publication Society, 1998.

Duenes, Steve, and Kris Goodfellow. "The Embryonic Journey and Its Milestones." In *The New York Times, Science Times,* December 18, 2001.

Freeman, Susan. *Teaching Jewish Virtues: Sacred Sources and Arts Activities.* Denver, CO: A.R.E. Publishing, Inc., 1999.

"From Cloning To Cures." *The New York Times,* editorial. August 4, 2001.

Kass, Leon R., and Daniel Callahan. "Ban Stand: Cloning's Big Test." *The New Republic,* August 6, 2001.

Kolata, Gina. *Cloning: The Road To Dolly and the Path Ahead.* New York: William Morrow and Company, Inc., 1998.

Krauthammer, Charles. "Of Headless Mice . . . And Men." *Time Magazine*, January 19, 1998.

Messina, Lynn, ed. *Biotechnology,* from the series *The Reference Shelf* , Vol. 72, No. 4. New York: The H.W. Wilson Company, 2000.

Pollack, Andrew. "Scientists Seek Ways to Rebuild the Body, Bypassing the Embryos" and "Use of Cloning to Tailor Treatment Has Big Hurdles, Including Cost." *The New York Times, Science Times*, December 18, 2001.

Post, Stephen G. "The Judeo-Christian Case against Human Cloning." *America*, June 21-28, 1997. Included in *Biotechnology*, from the series *The Reference Shelf* , Vol. 72, No. 4, edited by Lynn Messina. New York: The H.W. Wilson Company, 2000.

Reisner, Avram I. "Curiouser and Curiouser: Genetic Engineering of Nonhuman Life." In *Life and Death Responsibilities in Jewish Biomedical Ethics,* edited by Aaron L. Mackler. New York: The Louis Finkelstein Institute of The Jewish Theological Seminary, 2000.

Rosner, Fred. *Modern Medicine and Jewish Ethics.* Hoboken, NJ: KTAV Publishing House, Inc. and New York: Yeshiva University Press, 1991.

Steinberg, Avraham. "Human Cloning — Scientific, Moral and Jewish Perspectives." Paper delivered to The Institute for Jewish Medical Ethics of the Hebrew Academy of San Francisco, www.ijme.org/Content/Transcripts/Steinberg/scloning.htm., 1998.

Tendler, Moshe. "The Right Situation" (Op-ed) *New York Times*, December 12, 1997, A22.

UAHC Committee of the UAHC Department of Jewish Family Concerns. *Bioethics, Program Guide X: Cloning.* New York: Union of American Hebrew Congregations, Summer, 1998.

Vorspan, Albert, and David Saperstein. *Tough Choices.* New York: UAHC Press, 1992.

Wade, Nicholas. "Apostle of Regenerative Medicine Foresees Longer Health and Life," and "In Tiny Cells, Glimpses of Body's Master Plan." *The New York Times, Science Times*, December 18, 2001.

Web Sites

Advanced Cell Technology, Inc.: www.advanced-cell.com
"Involved in the research and development of technologies of Nuclear Transfer for human therapeutics and animal cloning."

Genetic Savings and Clone: www.savingsand-clone.com
A commercial enterprise with a special interest in cloning pets.

Jewish Law: www.jlaw.com
Articles and commentary examining halachah, Jewish issues, and secular law.

National Academy of Sciences: www.nationalacademies.org
Search the database for "cloning" or "genetic engineering."

National Institute of Health: www.nih.gov
Governmental organization of the United States Department of Health and Human Services. Search the database for "cloning" or "genetic engineering."

Why Biotech?: www.whybiotech.com
Focused on supporting, explaining, and defending genetic research primarily for agricultural purposes.

Films

The following commercial films, though fictitious and/or humorous, may be valuable for illustrating certain aspects of the topic of cloning. They may not be appropriate for younger students — check with parents or teachers before viewing.

The 6th Day (1999, 123 minutes, rated PG-13)
A futuristic Arnold Shwarzenegger action film about a man who meets a clone of himself and stumbles into a grand conspiracy about clones taking over the world. Available from video stores.

Multiplicity (1996, 117 minutes, rated PG-13)
A comedy about an overworked and over-scheduled man who clones himself to make more time for his wife and family. Available from video stores.

Glossary

Adult DNA Cloning
Cell nuclear replacement, in which an existing animal is duplicated. Sheep and other mammals have been cloned using this technique. The scientist removes the nucleus containing the DNA from an embryonic cell and replaces it with the nucleus from an adult animal cell. Next, the embryonic cell undergoes several rounds of cell division. It is then implanted in a surrogate's womb to develop into a new animal. This technique possesses the potential for cloning human beings, that is, producing a twin of an existing person.

Blastocyst
Four to five days after an egg is fertilized, a hollow sphere of about 250 cells develops. This is the blastocyst. Within is a clump of approximately 30 cells, the inner cell mass. The embryo develops from this inner cell mass. "Embryonic stem cells" is the term used for cells attained from the inner cell mass and grown in a laboratory.

Cloning
With this technique, a scientist may replicate a single gene, DNA segments, a cell, or an entire organism.

DNA
DNA, or deoxyribonucleic acid, is a long, double-stranded molecule coiled inside a cell. Nucleotides are subunits of a DNA molecule. They designate specific genetic information.

Embryo Cloning
This technique produces monozygotic (identical) twins or triplets. It duplicates nature's process of producing twins or triplets. A medical technician removes one or more cells from a fertilized embryo and prompts the cell(s) to develop into one or more duplicate embryos. The result is genetically identical twins or triplets. Scientists have used the technique for many years on various species of animals. Comparable experimentation on humans has been very limited.

Embryonic Stem Cells
See "Blastocyst" above. These cells seem to be pluripotent. That is, they seem to have the poten-tial to grow into any of the body's 260 or so cell types, though they cannot create a new individual on their own. In contrast, the egg cell is considered totipotent, meaning it can develop into a complete embryo.

Eugenics
Manipulating embryonic genes to attain preferred characteristics; for example, eye color, sex of the baby, correction of a genetic disease indicator, etc.

Gene
An ordered string of DNA nucleotides that transmit hereditary characteristics.

Gene Therapy
New DNA or an entire gene is transferred into an individual. Typically, the goal in replacing a damaged or missing gene is to assist in restoring the gene's intended function. See also the related term, "Therapeutic Cloning."

Parthenogenesis
An egg develops into an embryo without fertilization. This kind of reproduction does not occur naturally in mammals. Rather, scientists simulate fertilization, using chemicals or electricity to prompt certain animals' eggs to divide. Experiments with human eggs are the next step.

Stem Cells
Master cells from which the specialized cells of tissues and organs form. Stem cells have the capacity to reproduce indefinitely.

Therapeutic Cloning
The goal of therapeutic cloning is to produce a healthy copy of a sick person's tissue or organ for transplant. From perhaps a patient's skin cell, a medical technician removes the nucleus. The nucleus is inserted into a donated human egg cell without its own nucleus. The egg cell reprograms the patient's cell nucleus back to its totipotent state. That is, the reformatted patient's cell has regained its potential to form a complete embryo (i.e., any of a number of cells). Embryonic stem cells are cultured from the egg once it becomes a 5-day-old embryo. These new, "flexible" embry-

onic stem cells are changed into healthy (therapeutic) cells for injection into the patient. Perhaps the new cells will be changed into healthy liver tissue for a patient who has a diseased liver. In the therapeutic cloning process, the embryo dies. This technique has the potential to decrease reliance on other people for organ transplants, to eliminate the need for "waiting lists." Since the transplant would use the sick person's original DNA, taking immunosuppressant drugs would not be necessary. There would be less likelihood that the patient's body would "reject" the new tissue or organ.

CHAPTER 3
EUTHANASIA AND ASSISTED SUICIDE

Overview

Euthanasia literally means "a good death." Sometimes called "mercy killing," euthanasia is an act of inducing death painlessly. This chapter explores the challenges that come with wanting to honor the sacredness of life, yet feeling conflicted when it seems the best way to end the relentless suffering of those we love is by helping them to die. Over the last 50 years, medical understanding and technological advances have raised questions and concerns never imagined by our ancestors. We will look at the impact of some of these changes. As we delve into this complex subject, the reader will note that not every type of euthanasia is treated in the same way (see the Glossary on page 43 for definitions of types).

The Jewish Perspective

The Value of Compassion

Judaism clearly professes that life is sacred and that we must do whatever we can to protect and preserve it. We believe that murder is forbidden, as is "standing idly by" when another is in danger. Injuring another person (Exodus 21) or oneself (*Baba Kama* 8:6-7) is condemned.

However, our tradition also stresses the value of compassion for those who are suffering. How might we alleviate pain, how might we comfort those who are ailing? To be a righteous Jew is to keep concerns of loving-kindness at the forefront of our minds, and then to act accordingly.

Beyond these general principles, the discussion gets more complicated. Sure, Jews can agree that murder is wrong and that compassion is good. But when talking about euthanasia, making decisions based on these notions is far more complex. For instance, one physician might consider it "compassionate" to administer an increasingly lethal dose of medication to a patient who is suffering greatly from a terminal illness (which may alleviate pain but hasten death, as in "double effect," see Glossary, page 43). Another physician might refuse to prescribe any treatment that could hasten death. This second physician would argue that administering lethal quantities of medication is equivalent to murder and can hardly be called "compassionate."

Defining Life and Death

To remove life support machines from a person who is dead surely is not "murder." Brain activity, the ability to breathe on one's own, and the presence of a heartbeat are measures authorities may use to define life and death. If it is determined that a patient has no brain activity (is "brain dead"), disconnecting him/her from a respirator or a heart-lung machine is not especially controversial from a Jewish perspective, as there is a valid argument that the person is dead. However, Jewish sources are not always in agreement on how to define death in more complex situations (for example, if some minimal brain activity is discerned, yet the patient's breathing and/or heartbeat cannot be sustained on the patient's own).

Caring for the Dying Patient

There is more agreement about "routine" treatment. For example, providing food is part of routine treatment, and thus, withholding food from a dying person would be unacceptable. But even the notion of what it means to "provide food" isn't as easily understood as it once was. "Providing food" through the insertion of feeding tubes might be considered a medical treatment and thus not necessarily "routine."[1]

Jewish texts do make it clear that "hastening a patient's death" is forbidden, while "removing an impediment" to death is permitted. Even so, the distinction between these two concepts is not always obvious, and some rabbinic texts actually seem to condone euthanasia.

Liberal Jewish perspectives would include individual autonomy as a valid "ingredient" in making decisions (i.e., "I should have the liberty to decide what happens to my own body"). In Israel, where Jewish values and democratic values both complement and compete with each other, a precedent was set in the 1990s when an individual with a terminal disease was allowed by the court to refuse life sustaining treatment, including artificial respiration and artificial feeding.

The extent to which we can assist a *gosays* (a moribund patient whose death is imminent) through the last stages of life is debatable. Some would agree that administering increasing amounts of pain relieving morphine is acceptable, though it likely will hasten death. There is more consensus concerning the removal of an impediment to death. Our tradition is more definitive about cases involving a non-*gosays* — someone for whom death is not imminent. Assisting in the suicide of a relatively healthy person diagnosed with a disease carrying a bleak prognosis, such as multiple sclerosis, would be forbidden.

General Perspectives

In the world at large, the question of whether euthanasia or assisted suicide is ever justified is most controversial. Patients, families, and care providers all have consciences and religious/spiritual commitments that influence end of life decisions. Some rationales in favor of assisted suicide include release from pain and suffering, giving patients more of a sense of control over their situation, not abandoning patients when nothing else medically can be done, and helping patients avoid certain medical technologies that only seem to prolong their suffering.[2]

Compelling arguments opposing assisted suicide might include not knowing for sure that a so-called terminally ill patient has no chance for recovery, that what seems to be a suicide request may really be more of a general cry for help, that permitting assisted suicide may encourage us to divert resources away from research in palliative (pain relief) care, and that patients may feel coerced to die (that they should agree to an assisted suicide because that's what other people seem to want). Furthermore, especially vulnerable members of a society — the poor, the disabled, the elderly, and the very young — could be singled out as candidates for death.[3]

Assisted Suicide: Opinions on Legal Distinctions

In 1997, the U.S. Supreme Court decided a significant case — Vacco v. Quill — and upheld a New York law making physician assisted suicide illegal. The Court distinguished between withdrawing life sustaining treatment and assisted suicide, contending that when a patient refuses life support, he/she dies because the disease has run its natural course. However, if a patient self-administers lethal drugs, his/her death results from that medication. The Court also distinguished between the physician's intention in both scenarios — ending futile treatment and suffering versus hastening death.

Proactive Decision Making

The American Medical Association encourages proactive efforts in medical decision making. It recommends that patients exercise as much control as possible over end of life decisions through:

1. creating living wills
2. appointing durable powers of attorney (to make medical decisions if we are unable to do so)
3. advance directives (making surrogate decision makers aware of our wishes).

Summary of the Overview

The paragraphs below summarize key considerations regarding euthanasia and assisted suicide:

1. Life is precious, a gift from God. The value of life is immeasurable. Human beings should not hasten death in any way, for God bestows life and determines when life should end.

2. Loving another person as yourself (Leviticus 19:18) includes choosing an easy death for him/her (*Sanhedrin* 45a). To prolong the suffering of those who have clearly begun the dying process — for whom continued aggressive medical therapy would be futile — may detract from life's sanctity and reduce a person's dignity.[4] We must do whatever we can to alleviate a person's pain, including accepting a patient's decision to refuse life sustaining treatments.

3. The technological/medical advances of the last 50 years have prolonged life and extended the dying process. Due to improved methods available for supporting respiration and heart function, it has become difficult to recognize when death is imminent. These factors have created a new urgency and difficulty in dealing with the spiritual and moral dimensions of care and decision making at the end of life.

Scenarios: How Things Have Changed

There are a number of factors which make euthanasia and assisted suicide particularly complicated in our day: the ability to prolong life with artificial life support, medical advances which have increased our understanding of the prognosis of certain illnesses, and improvements in palliative care (pain relief). Yet determining how to make end of life decisions in the contemporary world remains a great challenge.

Below are two imaginary scenarios followed by questions intended to stimulate thought and spark discussion. Read each scenario and reflect, either individually or in a group discussion, on the questions in the "For Thought and Discussion" section that follows. Then continue on to the "Text Study" section to see what Jewish sources have to say on the subject. Finally, you may wish to come back and discuss the questions a second time, to see if your views have changed.

Scenario I: 1150 C.E.

Shlomo ben Shlomo had shown a decline in health in recent years, related to a growing weakness in his muscles. One day, Shlomo was bathing in a river. As he emerged from the water, he lost his footing, fell back into the water, and knocked his head on a large rock. Nearby, a fisherman, who had observed this incident, ran to Shlomo's aid. But the damage had been done. The fisherman leaned over Shlomo's face. No breath could be discerned. Shlomo was dead.

Scenario II: "Nowadays"

Sheldon had declined in health in recent years, due to a disease causing progressive muscle deterioration. One day, Sheldon was walking by the river, two blocks from where Main Street intersects Central Avenue. It was so hot that he decided to wade in and splash his face with some cool water. As he emerged from the water, he lost his footing, fell back, and knocked his head on a large rock. He stopped breathing. Nearby, a fisherman, who had observed this incident, grabbed his cell phone, immediately dialed 911, and summoned help. Sheldon was taken to the hospital. As he was unable to breathe on his own, he was put on a respirator. Within a few hours, his breathing returned to normal. However, because of his illness, doctors decided to keep him at the hospital for a few days in order to monitor his condition. By the end of the week, Sheldon felt well enough to return home.

For Thought and Discussion:

How does Scenario II offer a different approach toward death than Scenario I?

Do you think Sheldon's resuscitation was for the best given his illness, which will progress?,

Text Study

As we have seen, the issues of euthanasia and assisted suicide are quite complicated. Jewish sources provide many opinions, yet these often highlight the tension between seemingly opposing considerations. The chart below poses a number of questions and offers two opposing points of view. Text sources supporting each of these points of view follow.

1. **Is preserving life always the highest priority in medical settings?**

   On the One Hand:

   Life is sacred. Euthanasia and assisted suicide are murder.

   A. I [God] bring death, bestow life, I wound and I myself heal (Deuteronomy 32:39).

Making Ethical Decisions about Euthanasia and Assisted Suicide: Questions to Consider

The Question	On the One Hand	On the Other Hand
1. Is preserving life always the highest priority in medical settings? (see page 33)	Life is sacred. Euthanasia and assisted suicide are murder.	To forcibly sustain the physical body under all circumstances is a distortion of the definition of life.
2. What is a physician's primary responsibility? (see page 35)	Physicians have a responsibility to preserve and protect life.	Physicians have a responsibility to alleviate pain and suffering.
3. Are there traditional Jewish sources sympathetic toward euthanasia and assisted suicide? (see page 35)	Intentionally causing another person harm is condemned.	Insisting that a person endure unrelenting pain when there is a way out is harmful.
4. To what extent should we rely on medical prognoses? (see page 36)	There can be errors in diagnosis.	There can be strict guidelines regarding second and third opinions before decisions are made concerning termination of treatment.
5. Do we offer sufficient treatment and care to those who are dying or who are in pain? (see page 37)	By increasing access to euthanasia, there is less motivation to research pain control medications or to pursue alternative ways of offering comfort and care to the dying (e.g., spiritual or psychological support).	Dying people often express a clear wish to continue or discontinue treatment. We can persist in researching and offering "alternatives," but ultimately the choice of how one's life ends should be up to the patient.
6. Will easing restrictions on euthanasia lead to abuses? (see page 38)	Those without a strong advocate — the poor, young, elderly, mentally disabled — could be exploited.	Legal scholars could come up with safeguards so that all are protected equally under the law.
7. Isn't choosing euthanasia or assisted suicide an expression of a person's free will? (see page 39)	Those suffering with illnesses could be coerced to die, either blatantly or subtly. Even mentioning euthanasia to dying patients compromises the notion that they would be choosing to die of their own free will.	It is appropriate to be honest with people who are dying about all of their options.
8. How do we compare "hastening a person's death" to "removing an impediment?" (see page 39)	"Hastening a person's death" is equivalent to murder.	"Removing an impediment" to death is permitted.

B. Behold, all souls are Mine (Ezekiel 18:4).

C. You shall not murder (Exodus 20:13, see also Genesis 9:6, Exodus 21:14, Leviticus 24:17 and 24:21, Numbers 35:30, and Deuteronomy 5:17).

D. One who closes the eyes of a dying person while the soul is departing sheds blood (*Shabbat* 151b. See also Text Study #8 below).

On the Other Hand:

To forcibly sustain the physical body under all circumstances is a distortion of the definition of life.

a. And it came to pass in the morning when the wine was gone out of Nabal, that his wife told him these things, and his heart died within him, and he became as a stone. And it came to pass about ten days later, after the Eternal smote Nabal, that he died (I Samuel 25:37).

What Do You Think?

The texts make it clear that giving and taking of life are solely God's responsibility. Do you agree or disagree with this perspective based on what you read above? Why?

If a person becomes a "stone," he/she is not a living organism any longer. Does Text #1a offer a sufficient foundation for developing the case for euthanasia (under specific circumstances)?

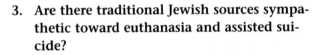

2. **What is a physician's primary responsibility?**

On the One Hand:

Physicians have a responsibility to preserve and protect life.

A. The sages in the school of Rabbi Ishmael taught: "And to heal he shall heal" (Exodus 21:19). From this verse we infer that permission has been given [by God] to the physician to heal (*Brachot* 60a).

On the Other Hand:

Physicians have a responsibility to alleviate pain and suffering.

a. When a person is led out to be executed, the person is given a goblet of wine containing a grain of frankincense in order to numb the person's senses (*Sanhedrin* 43a).

b. Behold Rabbi Nachman said in Rabbah ben Abbuha's name: Scripture says, "Love your neighbor as yourself" — choose an easy death for him/her (*Sanhedrin* 45a).

What Do You Think?

Do you think one of the above described responsibilities of physicians outweighs the other? Which one and why?

How do a physician's responsibilities extend beyond physical care?

3. **Are there traditional Jewish sources sympathetic toward euthanasia and assisted suicide?**

On the One Hand:

Intentionally causing another person harm is condemned.

A. One who strikes a person so that the person dies is to be put to death, yes, death (Exodus 21:12).

On the Other Hand:

Insisting that a person endure unrelenting pain when there is a way out is harmful.

a. When [Judah Ha-Nasi] was dying, the rabbis declared a public fast and offered prayers that God have mercy on him [i.e., spare his life] . . . Rabbi's maid went up to the roof and prayed: "The angels want rabbi [to join them in heaven] and the people want him to remain with them. May it be God's will that the people overpower the angels." However, when she saw how many times he had to use the bathroom, each time painfully taking off his *tefillin* and putting them on again, she prayed, "May it be God's will that the angels overpower the people." But the rabbis did not cease imploring God's mercy [to allow rabbi to live]. She, then, took a vase and threw it off the roof. [The rabbis] stopped praying [because they were startled by the noise], and the soul of rabbi departed (*Ketubot* 104a).

b. There is a story of a woman who grew very old. She came before Rabbi Yosi ben Halafta. She said to him, "Rabbi, I have gotten too old. Life is repugnant to me — I can neither taste food nor drink. I would like to depart from this world." He said to her, "How is it that you have lived so long?" She answered, "Every day, I am accustomed to go early to the synagogue even if I must stop doing something I like." He said to her, "Refrain for three successive days from going to the synagogue." She went and did this. On the third day, she became ill and died (*Yalkut Shimoni* 2, 943).

What Do You Think?

Do you agree with the lessons taught in texts #3a and #3b? Why or why not?

Would you say that Texts #3a and #3b are sufficient proof that Judaism is sympathetic to euthanasia? To assisted suicide? Explain your position.

———◆———

4. **To what extent should we rely on medical prognoses?**

On the One Hand:

There can be errors in diagnosis.

A. [Elisha] went in, shut the door behind the two of them and prayed to the Eternal. Then he mounted [the bed] and placed himself over the [seemingly dead] child. He put his mouth on its mouth, his eyes on its eyes, and his hand on its hands, as he bent over. And the body of the child became warm. He stepped down, walked once up and down the room, then mounted and bent over him. Thereupon, the boy sneezed seven times, and the boy opened his eyes (II Kings 4:33-35).

On the Other Hand:

There can be strict guidelines regarding second and third opinions before decisions are made concerning termination of treatment.

a. The following are excerpts from The Oregon Death with Dignity Act (1994, implemented 1997). Under this Act, a mentally competent adult resident of Oregon who is terminally ill (likely to die within six months) may request a prescription for a lethal dose of medication to end his or her life. The practice of a physician prescribing medication to end a patient's life (assisted suicide) departs from what would be acceptable from most Jewish points of view.

Section 3.01: attending physician responsibilities

The attending physician shall:

(1) Make the initial determination of whether a patient has a terminal disease, is capable, and has made the request voluntarily;

(2) Inform the patient of;

(a) his or her medical diagnosis;

(b) his or her prognosis;

(c) the potential risks associated with taking the medication prescribed [to end one's life in a humane and dignified manner];

(d) the probable result of taking the medication to be prescribed;

(e) the feasible alternatives, including, but not limited to, comfort care, hospice care, and pain control.

(3) Refer the patient to a consulting physician for medical confirmation of the diagnosis, and for determination that the

patient is capable and acting voluntarily;

(4) Refer the patient for counseling if appropriate pursuant to section 3.03;

(5) Request that the patient notify next of kin;

(6) Inform the patient that he or she has an opportunity to rescind the request at any time and in any manner, and offer the patient an opportunity to rescind at the end of the 15 day waiting period . . . ;

(7) Verify, immediately prior to writing the prescription for medication under this Act, that the patient is making an informed decision;

(8) Fulfill the medical record documentation requirements . . .

(9) Ensure that all appropriate steps are carried out in accordance with this Act prior to writing a prescription for medication to enable a qualified patient to end his or her life in a humane and dignified manner.

3.02 Consulting Physician Confirmation

Before a patient is qualified under this Act, a consulting physician shall examine the patient and his or her relevant medical records and confirm, in writing, the attending physician's diagnosis that the patient is suffering from a terminal disease, and verify that the patient is capable, is acting voluntarily and has made an informed decision.

3.03 Counseling Referral

If in the opinion of the attending physician or the consulting physician a patient may be suffering from a psychiatric or psychological disorder, or depression causing impaired judgment, either physician shall refer the patient for counseling. No medication to end a patient's life in a humane and dignified manner shall be prescribed until the person performing the counseling determines that the person is not suffering from a psychiatric or psychological disorder, or depression causing impaired judgment.

What Do You Think?

Do you agree it is possible to create a sufficient means of verification in diagnosing patients (physically, psychologically, emotionally, spiritually)? Does the Oregon Death With Dignity Act do so? If not, what is missing?

What would be your greatest concern(s) in creating guidelines for ascertaining correct diagnoses?

5. Do we offer sufficient treatment and care to those who are dying or who are in pain?

On the One Hand:

By increasing access to euthanasia, there is less motivation to research pain control medications or to pursue alternative ways of offering comfort and care to the dying (e.g., spiritual or psychological support).

A. It is a clearly documented fact that those asking for assisted suicide almost always change their minds once we have their pain under control. We undermedicate terribly in American medicine (Dr. Kathleen Foley, a pain specialist at Memorial Sloan-Kettering Cancer Center in New York, as quoted in "Of Life and Death: A Jewish Response to Doctor Assisted Suicide" by Asher Lipner, in *Viewpoint: National Council of Young Israel*, Winter, 1996, a paper posted on the web-site of the Institute of Jewish Medical Ethics, www.ijme.org, 2001).

On the Other Hand:

Dying people often express a clear wish to continue or to discontinue treatment. We can persist in researching and offering "alternatives," but ultimately the choice of how one's life ends should be up to the patient.

a. As a punishment for teaching Torah, Rabbi Hananiah is to be burnt at the stake by the Romans. His disciples encourage him to open his mouth so that he will die more quickly and endure less suffering. They say to him, "Rabbi . . . open your mouth that the fire may enter [and you will die]." [Rabbi Hananiah] said to them, "It is better that God who gave my soul should take it and let no one harm himself." The executioner asked him, "Rabbi, if I intensify the fire and remove the mats from your body, will you bring me in to the World to Come?" He said, "Yes." "Swear to me" [said the executioner]. He swore to him. [The executioner] immediately removed the mats and increased the flames. [Hananiah's] soul speedily departed. Then [the executioner] leaped up and fell into the fire. A heavenly voice [*bat kol*] went out and proclaimed, "Rabbi Hananiah and the executioner are prepared for the Life-to-Come." Rabbi [Judah Ha-Nasi] wept and said, "Some may attain their world in but one moment while others may take many years" (*Avodah Zarah* 18a).

What Do You Think?

How should Dr. Kathleen Foley's concern in Text #5A be integrated into ethical decision making regarding euthanasia?

Refer to the story of Hananiah's execution in Text #5a. Why do you think the heavenly voice (*bat kol*) said that both Rabbi Hananiah and his executioner are prepared for the Life-to-Come? Do you agree?

———◆◇◆———

6. **Will easing restrictions on euthanasia lead to abuses?**

On the One Hand:

Those without a strong advocate — the poor, young, elderly, mentally disabled — could be exploited.

A. You shall not mistreat any widow or orphan. If you do mistreat them, I will heed their outcry as soon as they cry out to Me, and My anger shall blaze forth and I will put you to the sword, and your own wives shall become widows and your children orphans (Exodus 22:21-23).

B. When strangers reside with you in your land, you shall not mistreat them. Strangers who reside with you shall be to you as your own citizens; you shall love them as yourself, for you were strangers in the land or Egypt; I the Eternal am your God (Leviticus 19:33-34).

C. I bring heaven and earth to witness that the Divine Spirit rests upon a non-Jew as well as upon a Jew, upon a woman as well as upon man, upon a maidservant as well as a manservant (*Yalkut Shimoni*, on Judges, section 42).

On the Other Hand:

Legal scholars could come up with safeguards so that all are protected equally under the law.

See Text Study #4a, excerpts from the Oregon Death with Dignity Act, plus the following summary of its provisions:

a. • The request must be voluntary.
   • No doctor would be forced to comply.
   • The patient must be an adult who is terminally ill and mentally competent.
   • The request must be an enduring one; a 15-day waiting period is required.
   • An examination by a mental health professional may be required.
   • The request must be made orally and in writing and witnessed.
   • All alternatives would be explained to the patient.
   • The patient would receive a prescription for a lethal dose of medication which would be self-administered.
   • The patient may change his or her mind at any time.
   (Source: The Hemlock Society USA)

What Do You Think?

Do the passages in the first group of texts make a strong argument against assisted suicide? Why or why not?

Is it reasonable to believe that a legal document can prevent exploitation of the poor, young, elderly, and mentally disabled? Can such a document be effective in providing protection against economic or family pressures?

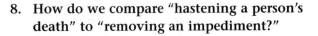

7. Isn't choosing euthanasia or assisted suicide an expression of a person's free will?

On the One Hand:

Those suffering with illnesses could be coerced to die, either blatantly or subtly. Even mentioning euthanasia to dying patients compromises the notion that they would be choosing to die of their own free will.

A. Any act performed in relation to death should not be carried out until the soul has departed (*Tur, Yoreh Deah,* 339).

B. Not only are physical acts on the patient . . . forbidden, but one should also not provide a coffin or prepare a grave or make other funeral or related arrangements lest the patient hear of this and his death be hastened. Even psychological stress is prohibited (Fred Rosner, *Modern Medicine and Jewish Ethics,* Hoboken, NJ: KTAV Publishing House, Inc., New York: Yeshiva University Press, 1991, p. 207).

C. A doctor who suggests assisted suicide as an option to a patient, or relatives who respond too readily to a patient's mention of euthanasia, send a powerful message that they believe the patient should not continue to live. In such cases we are not dealing with autonomy or the patient's right to die but with the will of the doctor and the relatives and their right to influence the ending of a life that has become a burden, or that they think is not worth living (*Seduced by Death* by Herbert Hendin, M.D., p. 185).

On the Other Hand:

It is appropriate to be honest with people who are dying about all of their options.

a. Those who deal deceitfully shall not live in My house; those who speak untruth shall not stand before My eyes (Psalms 101:7).

b. Teach your tongue to say, "I don't know, " lest you be caught in a lie (*Brachot* 4a).

c. If I lie, may I incur the eternal wrath of God and God's angel Raphael, and may nothing in the medical art succeed for me according to my desires (Amatus Lusitanus, a Jewish physician, included in a section on honesty toward the patient, in *Lying: Moral Choice in Public and Private Life* by Sisela Bok, New York: Pantheon Books, a Division of Random House, 1978, p. 76).

What Do You Think?

Which grouping of texts makes the stronger argument about euthanasia? Why?

Do you think it is ever appropriate to mention euthanasia to a person who has a terminal and painful disease?

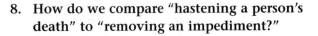

8. How do we compare "hastening a person's death" to "removing an impediment?"

On the One Hand:

"Hastening a person's death" is equivalent to murder.

A. One who is in a dying condition is regarded as a living person in all respects. It is not permitted to bind the person's jaws, to stop up the organs of the lower extremities, or to place metallic or cooling vessels upon the person's navel in order to prevent swelling. The person is not to be rubbed or washed, nor is sand or salt to be put upon the person until the person expires. Anyone who touches the person is guilty of shedding blood. To what may this person be compared? To a flickering flame, which is extinguished as soon as one touches it. Whoever closes the eyes of the dying while the soul is about to depart is shedding blood. One should wait a while; perhaps the person is only experiencing a fainting spell (Maimonides, *Mishneh Torah, Hilchot Avel* 4:5).

On the Other Hand:

"Removing an impediment" to death is permitted.

a. If there is anything which causes a hindrance to the departure of the soul, such as the presence near the patient's house of a knocking noise, such as wood chopping, or if there is salt on the patient's tongue, and these hinder the soul's departure, it is permissible to remove them from there because there is no act involved in this at all but only the removal of the impediment (*Rema* on *Shulchan Aruch, Yoreh Deah* 339:1)

b. In truth, one cannot truly call the "removal of the impediment" a passive action: one must go to the woodchopper to tell him to stop and one must reach into the patient's mouth to remove the salt. There is certainly an "act" involved! . . . If at this moment, the sounds and the salt are keeping the patient alive, then stopping the one and removing the other, either "allow the patient to die" or "kill the patient" depending on sensibility. Like the prayers affected by the maid's dropped pot (see Text #3a above), that process . . . which has maintained the patient's life has been interrupted and the patient dies. How would this be essentially different from disconnecting a moribund patient's oxygen line? . . . Nowadays the patient is connected by tubing to the oxygen pipes which are in the walls of the hospital room: to disconnect the tubing one has to do something and that is active euthanasia . . . the acting or not acting is a function of technology not morality . . . I think that the issue of euthanasia must be re-thought. For as a liberal Jew, texts of the past have votes but not vetoes; however, the texts adduced as we have seen, do not vote for what people have said they vote for . . . Euthanasia, we have said, applies to one who is in the process of dying and who is suffering; we must be sure of the first and unable to control the second. If that person be lucid and not wish the battle for life to

continue, then his/her wishes should be followed as to when and how the end should come, whether that end comes by not doing something or by doing something . . . (Dr. Leonard Kravitz, "Euthanasia" in *Death and Euthanasia in Jewish Law,* 1995).

What Do You Think?

Is Dr. Kravitz's objection to differentiating between "hastening a death" and "removing an impediment" valid?

After studying the passages in the "Text Study" section, name what you believe are the greatest hazards in liberalizing laws having to do with euthanasia and assisted suicide.

Related Middot and Mitzvot

Practicing these virtues and commandments will help infuse our end of life decisions with Jewish values:

Anavah (Humility): In making decisions about medical treatment, all involved must maintain great humility. While we should try to make wise choices, we should appreciate the complexity of the situation, listen to each other, and avoid the arrogance of asserting the absolute rightness of our preference.

Eino Samayach BeHora'ah (Not Delighting in Rendering Decisions): Acknowledge and appreciate the gravity of making end-of-life decisions.

Emunah (Trustworthiness): The physician-patient relationship must be built on trustworthiness. Patients need to believe that their physician will truly listen to them and advocate for their needs. The same holds for family and friends — patients should be able to trust that their loved ones have their best interests in mind always. Furthermore, patients should be able to trust that the laws of society will protect them from potential abuses.

Ohev et HaMakom (Loving God): Taking care of others reflects our love for God.

Ohev veKavod et HaBriyot (Loving and Respecting Creation): Taking care of others reflects our love and respect for other human beings.

Rachamim (Compassion): The suffering patient should be treated compassionately.

Rofeh Cholim (Healing the Sick): We have a duty to do whatever we can to bring healing to those who are suffering from illness.

Talmud Torah: (Study Jewish Sources): Learn what Jewish tradition says about the value of life, compassion, treatment of the dying, and the definition and determination of death. Also look for any examples of euthanasia, suicide, or assisted suicide in Jewish texts. Read contemporary responsa on the subject, plus research how the secular courts in Israel are handling matters of this nature.

Where Do I Go From Here?

Euthanasia, like all of the hot topics, is an issue that extends far beyond the classroom. Your teacher will present you with activities that will help you further explore how the issue affects real people's lives. You will continue to see how all of the different angles on euthanasia apply, and you will, hopefully, begin to form your own beliefs about euthanasia and assisted suicide, informed by what you have read in the texts and what you do in the classroom.

We've barely scratched the surface of this complex and challenging issue, and you may wish to explore further on your own. Following is a list of suggested resources that you may find helpful.

Books and Articles

Address, Richard F. *Making Sacred Choices at the End of Life.* Woodstock, VT: Jewish Lights Publishing, 2000.

Borowitz, Eugene B., and Frances Weinman Schwartz. *The Jewish Moral Virtues.* Philadelphia, PA: The Jewish Publication Society, 1999.

Dorff, Elliot. "End Stage Medical Care: A Halachik Approach." *Conservative Judaism* 43, no. 3 (Spring 1991).

Foley, Kathleen, and Herbert Hendin, eds. *The Case against Assisted Suicide: For the Right to End-of-Life Care.* Baltimore, MD: Johns Hopkins University Press, 2002. See also, Sherwin B. Nuland's review of this book: "The Principle of Hope," in *The New Republic*, May 27, 2002, pp. 25-30.

Freeman, Susan. *Teaching Jewish Virtues: Sacred Sources and Arts Activities.* Denver, CO: A.R.E. Publishing, Inc., 1999.

Friedman, Dayle A., ed. *Jewish Pastoral Care: A Practical Handbook from Traditional and Contemporary Sources.* Woodstock, VT: Jewish Lights Publishing, 2000.

Hendin, Herbert. *Seduced by Death: Doctors, Patients, and Assisted Suicide.* New York: W.W. Norton & Company, Inc., 1998.

Herring, Basil F. *Jewish Ethics and Halakhah for Our Time: Sources and Commentary.* Hoboken, NJ: KTAV Publishing House, Inc. and New York: Yeshiva University Press, Volume I, 1984, Volume II, 1989.

Kadden, Barbara Binder, and Bruce Kadden.. *Teaching Jewish Life Cycle: Traditions and Activities.* Denver, CO: A.R.E. Publishing, Inc., 1997.

———. *Teaching Mitzvot: Concepts, Values, and Activities.* Rev. ed. Denver, CO: A.R.E. Publishing, Inc., 2003.

Rosner M.D., Fred. *Modern Medicine and Jewish Ethics.* Hoboken, NJ: KTAV Publishing House, Inc. and New York: Yeshiva University Press, 1991.

Sinclair, Daniel B. *Tradition and the Biological Revolution: Application of Jewish Law To the Treatment of the Critically Ill.* Edinburgh, Scotland: Edinburgh University Press, 1989.

Snyder, Carrie. *Death and Dying: Who Decides?* Farmington Hills, MI: Gale Group, Information Plus Reference Series, 2001.

Tendler, Moshe, and Fred Rosner. "Quality and Sanctity of Life in the Talmud and Mishnah". In *Tradition*, vol. 28, no. 1 (Fall 1993).

Wahrman, Miriam Z. *Brave New Judaism: When Science and Scripture Collide.* Waltham, MA: Brandeis University, 2002.

Web Sites

Euthanasia.com: www.euthanasia.com
> *Information for research on euthanasia, physician assisted suicide, living wills, mercy killing. Committed to the fundamental belief that the intentional killing of another person is wrong.*

Exit's Fast Access: www.aez61.dial.pipex.com/index.html
> *This site contains hundreds of pages of material explaining the arguments for and against euthanasia. It is promoted by Exit (formerly the Scottish Voluntary Euthanasia Society), which campaigns for a change in British law to promote individual patient choice, and strategies for improved palliative care and other resources at the end of life.*

International Anti-Euthanasia Task Force: www.internationaltaskforce.org
> *An organization opposing euthanasia and assisted suicide.*

Euthanasia Research and Guidance Organization: www.finalexit.org

The Hemlock Society of America: www.hemlock.org
> *Two organizations most sympathetic toward euthanasia and assisted suicide.*

Religious Tolerance: www.religioustolerance.org/euthanas.htm
> *An organization that seeks to provide balanced information about euthanasia and assisted suicide.*

Films

The following commercial films deal with issues of euthanasia and assisted suicide in a frank and mature manner. Some may not be appropriate for younger students — check with teachers or parents before viewing.

Whose Life Is It Anyway? (1981, 118 minutes, rated R)
> An artist, paralyzed from his neck down, goes to trial to be allowed to die.

Peaceful Exit (1995, 50 minutes, no rating)
> Left brain damaged after an operation, two-year-old Ian Stewart is in pain day and night and not expected to reach his teens. His parents, who have sacrificed their careers to care for Ian, feel his quality of life is negligible. This film records both their tragic situation and the moral dilemma they face: is euthanasia the answer?

Glossary

Euthanasia

Literally, "a good death;" an act of inducing death painlessly, sometimes called "mercy killing."

Voluntary Euthanasia

The patient asks to die or agrees with the physician's recommendation that he/she die.

Nonvoluntary Euthanasia

A surrogate agrees, on the patient's behalf, with the physician's recommendation that the patient die.

Involuntary Euthanasia

Someone other than the person involved performs an intentional act to terminate life without the consent of the person involved.

"Passive Euthanasia"

Involves the withholding and withdrawing of life support, and is not technically euthanasia since the patient dies of the underlying disease.

Physician-assisted Suicide

Intentional assistance given by a physician to enable a person to terminate his/her own life upon that person's request. Prescribing a lethal dose of medicine for the patient would be a typical method.

Double Effect

Pain-relief (or palliative) treatment given to a patient to reduce suffering may have the "double effect" of hastening a patient's death. The intent is to reduce suffering, not to end life. However, the patient's death may be a side effect of the treatment, and one that could be predicted. Administering increasing amounts of morphine is an example — this drug helps to relieve pain, but slows down the functioning of the body in a way that could bring death more quickly.[5]

Gosays

A moribund patient whose death is imminent.

CHAPTER 4

HARMFUL BEHAVIORS:
SMOKING, ALCOHOL ABUSE, AND OVER/UNDEREATING

Note: You may notice that the format of this chapter is a little different from the others, more suitable for our topic.

Overview

Judaism teaches us that we should do what we can to avoid harm. We are to take care of ourselves to the best of our ability. Our oldest Jewish sources warn against being careless or intentionally doing things that could hurt ourselves or others. In recent years, we have become more aware of the dangers of widespread behaviors such as smoking, drinking alcohol, and over/undereating. We begin our study of this topic with an overview of Judaism's teachings on caring for the body. Then, we focus on what makes smoking, drinking, and over/undereating potentially harmful, why people engage in these behaviors, and how to evaluate their risks.

Once we learn general facts and theories about smoking, drinking, and over/undereating, we will better understand how Jewish guidance and wisdom can be helpful to us. We will seek practical advice: For example, is the specified behavior allowed or not? We will also raise spiritual questions: For example, what unfulfilled yearnings, brokenness of spirit, or painful feelings of emptiness might lead us to engage in practices that eventually hurt us? We will conclude by looking at ways of coping with harmful behaviors.

On Taking Care of Your Body and Avoiding Dangerous Practices

We might say that the essence of Judaism is about sanctifying life. To do so, we are to cherish our existence and avoid danger and harm. Taking care of ourselves shows respect to God, in whose image we were created (Genesis 9:6).

Over the ages, Jewish sages have discussed cleanliness, safety, adequate medical care, proper eating, and other health-related issues. Especially important is avoiding danger: we are not to take chances, and deliberately causing harm to oneself is prohibited. If we choose to engage in risky behaviors, we can't count on miracles to save us.

Current understanding of harmful behaviors recognizes the complexity of addictions (whether alcohol, nicotine, or drugs) and eating disorders. Sometimes we lose control of our behavior. We no longer feel we are making choices about what we're doing; rather, our bad choices seem to have taken us over. We feel our problems have gotten too big for us to handle on our own. Such a scenario requires the attention of those who can help us heal. An important Jewish teaching reminds us, "If you're in pain, go to a physician" (*Baba Kamma* 46b).

What Makes a Behavior Harmful?

Defining Use, Abuse, and Addiction: Smoking and Drinking

No one can say for sure when moderate use of a substance becomes abuse, and when abuse becomes addiction or dependency. Patterns of abuse and addiction can vary from person to person and from substance to substance. Abuse is indicated by compulsive use, meaning a person feels obsessed by and driven to use a particular substance. More extreme patterns of abuse are called addiction or dependency. Addicts generally develop physical tolerance to a substance, needing increasingly higher doses to experience the same effect. They may become powerless to emerge from their problems without help.

Defining Harmful Eating Behaviors

When individuals become deeply unhappy with their body image, their eating habits may become compulsive and harmful. These habits can include "binge eating" (consuming huge quantities of food over a short period of time), "purging" (using laxatives or vomiting as a misguided means of controlling weight), and the use of steroids — a dangerous drug — in order to build muscle. Certain eating behaviors are so far outside the spectrum of reasonable eating habits that they require thoughtful intervention and may be treated as mental disorders.

The Effects of Smoking: What Research Says

The nicotine in cigarettes is highly addictive and the long-term effects alarming. Smoking can cause serious health damage — heart attacks, strokes, and other cardiovascular disorders, as well as cancer, and other ailments. Smokers not only damage their own health: pregnant smokers expose their unborn children to dangers such as low birth weight, and "second-hand" smoke exposes other people to health hazards such as lung cancer and respiratory ailments.

Despite the dangers, smoking is widespread and affects countless millions of people around the globe. In its extensive study, the World Bank reports that the only two causes of death that are huge and growing worldwide are AIDS and tobacco-related illnesses. The Centers for Disease Control and Prevention expects tobacco to become the biggest killer in most developing countries within the next 20 years, causing more deaths than AIDS, malaria, tuberculosis, automobile crashes, homicides, and suicides combined. By the year 2030, tobacco is projected to be the single biggest cause of death worldwide, accounting for about 10 million deaths per year.[1]

The Effects of Alcohol Consumption: What Research Says

Excessive alcohol consumption over a period of time can lead to physical addiction and to numerous health problems. Because of its effect on the brain and central nervous system, alcohol is considered a drug. It is teenagers' drug of choice: in a 1999 study, 73.8 percent of high school seniors had used alcohol in the previous 12 months and 51 percent in the last 30 days.[2]

Since alcohol consumption impairs concentration and reaction time, driving while under the influence of alcohol is very risky and often leads to tragic accidents. The brain has difficulty processing information such as speed, distance, curves in the road, and even the difference between the gas and brake pedals. Motor vehicle crashes are the leading cause of death for Americans under the age of 21. Yet a 1999 study found that in the month prior to a survey given, 13.3 percent of students reported they had driven a vehicle after drinking alcohol. Another 33.1 percent admitted riding with a driver who had been drinking alcohol.[3]

Besides the dangers of drinking and driving, frequent drinking can have serious emotional and interpersonal consequences. Alcohol is a major factor in many cases of murder, violent crime, child and spouse abuse, and suicide.[4] A person who drinks heavily is less inhibited, becoming more susceptible to fighting, engaging in offensive behavior, and physically or verbally abusing others.

The Effects of Harmful Eating Habits: What Research Says

Eating disorders such as anorexia (self-starvation) and bulimia (bingeing and purging) are a serious and often fatal problem. The American Anorexia and Bulimia Association estimates that every year one million women develop eating disorders, and 150,000 die from anorexia. Anorexia has the highest death rate for any psychiatric disorder — approximately 5 to 15 percent die.[5]

Poor eating habits, leading to excessive weight gain, are also problematic. One third of American adults are classified as obese (about 20 percent over their optimal weight)[6], as are roughly 12 percent of children ages 6 to 17. The number of obese children is about double what it was in 1974. Overweight children often become overweight adults, and are at an increased risk for many chronic medical conditions including coronary heart disease, hypertension, diabetes, gallbladder disease, respiratory disease, some cancers, and arthritis.[7] Though regular physical activity is a key component of weight control, a large number of American adults trying to lose weight do not participate in any such activity.[8]

On the other hand, the emphasis that our culture places on thinness is worrisome as well. While about 12 percent of children are overweight, nearly a third think they are overweight.[9] Such attitudes can lead to useless, unhealthful dieting. On and off dieting, fad diets, crash diets, and "failed" diets are hard on the body and often cause mental and emotional anguish.

The "Cost"

Besides harming the addict him/herself, addictions usually take a toll on loved ones as well. The high cost of cigarettes, alcohol, and "bingeing" food may strain the financial resources of individuals and/or their families. In addition, treatment costs for psychological therapy, medical care, or residency in a treatment center are often expensive. And unfortunately, in a desperate quest for a cure to their problems, some people are duped into futilely spending huge amounts of money on unsubstantiated herbal remedies or fad diet books.

Why Do People Do Harmful Things to Their Bodies?

General Factors to Consider

There are no easy answers as to why people use, abuse, or become dependent on nicotine or alcohol or develop eating disorders. Physiological, social, and emotional reasons all can contribute to why people do harmful things to their bodies. Psychological pressures and emotional factors may originate from an inner emptiness akin to spiritual suffering. More details follow in the next three sections.

Smoking and Drinking

Drugs — which include nicotine and alcohol — have physical effects, such as stimulating feelings of pleasure and/or release from pain. These physical effects are temporary and offer no enduring relief from problems, but the "side effects," as we have seen, can be quite damaging.

Research suggests that risks for developing addictions tend to run in families. Studies seem to indicate that a genetic component is at work, though no one responsible gene has been identified. Still, parents who smoke influence their children's habits, and alcoholism occurs at much higher rates among the relatives of alcoholics than in the general population.

The acceptability of smoking or drinking in certain communities and cultures reinforces the legitimacy of these behaviors. Many young people begin to use harmful substances for social reasons — to experiment with something they see as fun, to act grown up, to be one of the crowd, or to rebel.[10] Once substance use becomes dependence, psychological and emotional factors are usually involved. Smokers may rely on nicotine to moderate mood shifts brought on by stressful situations. People who abuse alcohol often drink to overcome difficulties coping with problems, to deaden pain and alleviate stress, or to loosen up in social situations. Yet abusing alcohol ultimately does not solve troubles or enhance social skills. In the long run, problems usually get worse.

Overeating and Undereating

Social, cultural, psychological, and emotional factors may contribute to harmful eating behaviors. So much of our socializing happens around food. Learning good habits and listening to our bodies can be difficult when we are besieged by tantalizing advertisements for food products, oversized portions, readily available "junk" (low nutrition) and instant foods, plus social opportunities that highlight food consumption.

Contemporary culture may influence the development of eating problems, especially in its projections of body-image ideals. Messages in TV, movies, magazines, and fashion advertisements encourage girls to compare their bodies to unhealthful thin "ideals." Boys especially are bombarded with images of unnaturally muscle-bound "hunks." Popular fashion styles don't account for varieties in body types, making it impossible for some young dressers to "fit in." Pressures to conform can be stressful, and for some leads to a sense of loathing for their bodies.

A number of other significant factors can influence eating habits, among them other cultural values, peer and parental influence, physiology/genetics, and individual circumstances and personality characteristics. There may also be spiritual reasons for overeating and undereating. With these behaviors, perhaps we fill ourselves up with negativity (or extraneous, unhealthful food) rather than with what would nourish us most. Whatever the causes, understanding a person's internal motivations for engaging in problematic eating behaviors is crucial for treating and trying to reverse damaging eating patterns. With supportive guidance, harmful eating behaviors can be overcome. They do not have to be disabling for life.

Is There an Acceptable Level of "Risk" for Smoking?

General Perspectives

The overwhelming popular view is that when it comes to smoking only abstinence works. When a person begins to smoke, he/she may intend to limit the habit, but we have seen that the progression from initial use to addiction is elusive. There is no sure means for preventing casual use of nicotine from becoming serious dependence.

Jewish Perspectives

When tobacco first came into use in the Jewish community, there was a sense that it was beneficial for the body. Some 200 years later, tobacco's harmful effects came more into focus. The highly esteemed 20th century halachist Rabbi Moshe Feinstein faced a difficult dilemma — how to reconcile the growing evidence of the dangers of smoking with the fact that the habit was widespread, having become a popular practice. While Rabbi Feinstein did not encourage smoking, he would not prohibit it outright.

As the dangers of tobacco use have become ever more apparent, Jewish leaders increasingly are taking harsher stances on smoking. Rabbi Moshe Zemer, in his book *Evolving Halachah: A Progressive Approach to Traditional Jewish Law*, summarizes the current consensus of halachic opinion:

1. Smoking near anyone who may be disturbed or harmed by smoke is prohibited.

2. It is forbidden to harm oneself by smoking. Accordingly, smokers who cannot break the habit "cold turkey" must make every effort to cut back gradually or receive professional help until they are weaned of their addiction.

3. It is forbidden for children and adolescents to begin or to become accustomed to smoking. Adults may not help or encourage them to acquire the habit.

4. Encouraging smokers in their habit, by offering them a cigarette or light, is prohibited.

5. Elected officials and spiritual leaders should sponsor serious educational campaigns to convince the public of the extreme danger of smoking.[11]

Is There an Acceptable Level of "Risk" for Alcohol Consumption?

General Perspectives

The use of alcohol or drinking in moderation (by those of a legal age) tends to be acceptable in American culture. Drinking more than moderate amounts, to a harmful degree is abuse. Abuse of any drug, alcohol included, is unsafe, presenting dangerous risks to oneself and others.

No simple formula exists for calculating risk-free drinking, though there are useful guidelines. One such guideline comes from the BAC (blood alcohol content) test, measuring the ratio of alcohol to blood in drinkers. An average size woman will become legally impaired after two drinks, and an average man, after three drinks. (A "drink" consists of three to five ounces of wine, 12 ounces of beer, or one ounce of hard liquor.) If one does drink, some ways of reducing the risks include eating something before or while drinking, sipping drinks rather than gulping them, avoiding drinking and driving, avoiding using alcohol within a few hours of using any other drug, avoiding drink when the body is in a vulnerable state (i.e., sick or tired), avoiding drinking during pregnancy (which can harm the fetus), and avoiding drinking as a way of solving or escaping from problems.

Jewish Perspectives[12]

References to alcohol consumption in Jewish sources suggest a continuum of attitudes — from acceptable to problematic. Jewish celebrations and rituals often include drinking alcohol (for example, wine for Kiddush on Shabbat and holidays and as part of life cycle events). Certain festivities such as the Passover Seder with its four cups of wine and the Purim celebration tolerate or even encourage consumption of more than "moderate" amounts of alcohol.

However, Judaism does recognize a problematic side of drinking. Drinking beyond moderate amounts has consequences. For instance, a drunk person is constrained from fully participating in communal life. Princes, judges, priests, teachers, and ritual slaughterers must remain sober in order to carry out their duties properly.[13] Any individual who has been drinking faces restrictions in joining in communal prayer (*Yerushalmi Terumot* 1:4).

Jewish sources, like secular law, specify legal consequences for causing harm or damage during an episode of drunkenness. A community should do whatever it can to prevent situations in which citizens abuse alcohol and cause serious harm. In our day, there are laws against underage drinking and against driving while intoxicated. Individuals who have committed crimes while under the influence of alcohol must often participate in a rehabilitation program.

While using alcohol in moderation and on special occasions is permissible, abuse is problematic and is to be avoided. Modern understandings of the dangers of alcoholism lead us to conclude that complete abstention is necessary for individuals addicted to alcohol. It is a matter of life and death.

Are the Risks of Dieting or Overeating Ever Worth Taking?

General Perspectives
If we were to condense the best advice on eating into one rule (with few exceptions) this would be it: Only eat when you're hungry, and when you are hungry, always eat. To do otherwise is to risk obesity or eating disorders.

This does not mean that it is never appropriate to make modifications in our eating behavior. Changes in diet and lifestyle are advisable in specific instances, but should always be guided by recognized healthful guidelines and the consultation of a professional. Certain weight-loss strategies such as using appetite suppressants, fasting, going on very restrictive diets, and relying on diet formulas usually fail and can present health risks. Extreme "modifications" of eating habits — such as binging, purging, or starving oneself (i.e., bulimia or anorexia) — are abusive to the body and may indicate a serious disorder for which professional help is required.

Jewish Perspectives
There are times during the year for feasts and fasts, as part of holiday observances or life cycle events. But these occasions are exceptions to what should be our every day eating habits. Eating in moderation is the Jewish ideal.

The medieval scholar Maimonides reminds us to avoid whatever is injurious to our bodies, overeating included. His recommendations for moderate eating and engagement in exercise are quite consistent with currently accepted recommendations.

Avoiding injury to the body includes being careful not to overeat or undereat. Someone who has become dependent or addicted to damaging patterns of eating behaviors — such as self-starvation (anorexia) or binging and purging (bulimia) — is vulnerable to potentially life threatening risks. Getting help is an urgent priority.

When We're "In Over Our Heads"

Do I Have a Problem?
Sometimes it's obvious to us when we're "in over our heads." But this is not always the case. Judging just how serious our habits are can be confusing. Our habits may have become such a part of our daily lives that we don't even notice the toll they've taken both on us and on those around us.

Questions to Ask about Substance Use (Nicotine, Alcohol, or Other Drug)
One way to judge the seriousness of our habits is to closely examine our behavior. Following are some questions to ask about substance abuse (nicotine, alcohol, or other drugs):

- Has someone close to you sometimes expressed concern about your substance use?

- Do you use a substance as a way of avoiding or coping with problems?

- Are you sometimes unable to meet home or work responsibilities because of substance use?

- Has use of a substance caused any problems in your relationships with family, friends, or coworkers?

- Do you rely on a substance to get you going in the morning?

- Do you find you have to take increasing amounts of a substance to achieve the same effects?

- Have you had distressing physical or psychological reactions when you've tried to stop the habit?

- Have you ever required medical attention as a result of your substance use?

- Have you often failed to keep the promises you have made to yourself or others about controlling or cutting out your substance use?

- Do you ever feel guilty about your use of a substance or try to conceal it from others?[14]

- Are you in pain (physical, emotional, or spiritual)?

Questions to Ask about Eating Disorders

- Has someone close to you sometimes expressed concern about your eating habits?

- Do you engage in harmful eating behaviors as a way of avoiding or coping with problems?

- Does your eating behavior have a negative impact on your home, school, or work responsibilities?

- Has your eating behavior caused any problems in relationships with family, friends, or co-workers?

- Has the intensity of your eating problems increased over time?

- Have you had distressing physical or psychological reactions when you've tried to stop engaging in a harmful eating habit?

- Have you ever required medical attention as a result of your eating behavior?

- Have you often failed to keep the promises you have made to yourself or others about controlling problematic eating patterns?

- Do you ever feel guilty about what you're doing or try to conceal it from others?[15]

- Are you in pain (physical, emotional, or spiritual)?

Getting Help

Answering yes to any of the questions in either category above signals the need for help. Harmful use of substances and problematic eating behavior significantly interferes with life. These habits can damage physical health, hurt relationships, and hamper school or other work. Answering yes also is a signal to pay attention to and take care of one's spiritual well-being. When we're "in over our heads," we cannot deal with our problems alone. But with guidance and support, we can overcome incapacitating despair and negativity.

Caring for the Spirit

Spiritual issues may be tied in to our experience of pain and our efforts to recover. We may wish to explore spiritual concerns with a rabbi, close friend, and/or through meditation, study, and prayer. *Teshuvah* (repentance and return) teaches that we can "return" to taking care of our bodies, reentering the community, and working to improve strained relationships. We also can turn and return to God, as God is merciful and accepts us even when we are vulnerable and broken-hearted.

Summary: The Key Points

The following points summarize the key Jewish considerations regarding harmful behaviors:

1. Judaism teaches us to take care of our bodies and avoid dangerous practices.

2. Smoking, excessive alcohol consumption, and certain eating/dieting practices can be hazardous to our health and well-being. Sometimes we take risks without wholly understanding our motivations or fully realizing the potential for harmful consequences. There can be physical, psychological, social, and/or spiritual reasons for beginning or for continuing with a specific habit. Genetic patterning and/or cultural values also may influence us toward a self-destructive behavior.

3. It can be difficult to judge what is an acceptable level of risk for using potentially harmful substances (i.e., cigarettes or alcohol) or for engaging in potentially harmful practices (i.e., dieting, fasting, or bingeing). The potential for serious harm varies from individual to individual, from substance to substance, and from behavior to behavior.

4. If we find we are "in over our heads" in substance use or other self-destructive practices,

we will need care and support from others — from doctors, therapists, clergy, teachers, family members, friends, and/or support groups. Besides professional assistance, renewed attention to our spiritual lives can help us to manage our pain and to overcome a dependence on the things that hurt us.

Scenarios: How Things have Changed

Avoiding danger is as important today as it ever was. However, new dangers and modern understandings of familiar dangers challenge us with their complexity. Jewish texts and traditions can provide important insights for coping with potentially harmful behaviors.

Below are two imaginary scenarios, one set in the late 1800's and the other set in contemporary times. They are intended to raise questions and spark discussion. Read each scenario and reflect, either individually or in group discussion, on the questions in the "For Thought and Discussion" section that follows. Then continue on to the "Text Study" section to see what Jewish and other sources have to say on the subject. Finally, you may wish to come back and answer the questions a second time, to see if your views have changed.

Scenario I: Russia in the Late 1800's

A rabbi is concerned for the residents of his village. Lately, bands of marauders have come through, destroying property. Neighboring villages are reporting worse violence, including rapes and murders. The rabbi decides he must address his community and insist they do whatever possible to avoid the dangers in their midst. In planning his comments, he realizes that the *parashah* (Torah reading) for the week is *Va'etchanan*. In the reading God urges the Israelites to "take heed, take exceeding care of yourself . . . take good care of your lives" (Deuteronomy 4:9, 15).

The rabbi weaves together a *drash* (sermon), invoking the words from the *parashah*. He also refers to teachings from the Talmud and Maimonides about avoiding danger. Though the circumstances of his community are different, he

plans to get his point across by applying the earlier teachings to the threats of his own times. He warns of being out alone or going to desolate areas. However, he knows that the marauders have no compunction about entering a village in broad daylight and mounting great devastation. Therefore, he also urges the community to be proactive, to create hidden safe havens wherever they can, such as in a basement, entered through a concealed opening.

Scenario II: America in the Early 21st Century

In their Confirmation class, a group of young people has gotten into a heart-to-heart conversation about problems they see concerning kids their age. They note how a lot of kids they know are unhappy or depressed; some seem angry all the time. Some kids do things which are really dangerous — drinking and driving, doing drugs, eating huge amounts and then making themselves throw up. Two kids from their high school were killed last month because they had been drinking and driving. It's scary and upsetting. Even so, some of the students admit they're curious about smoking, drinking, and drugs. A few have "experimented" with various substances. But they worry about going too far.

As the "heart-to-heart" unfolds, students talk about all the mixed messages they hear — from parents, friends, teachers, the media, and popular culture. They complain about how so many values get distorted. Advertisements try to make smoking and drinking seem glamorous. Only the most beautiful bodies are shown in ads, or in movies and magazines. And "beautiful" is almost always way too thin for women, plus the men's bodies are equally unrealistic. The whole media scene makes kids feel ugly and inadequate. The really sensitive kids have an especially hard time dealing with so many expectations of how they should look and how they should act. Everyone feels stressed out enough as it is! And the conversation continues.

As part of their Confirmation coursework, some of the students have recently been studying Jewish views of health and care for one's body. They were particularly intrigued by a verse from *parashat Va'etchanan*, an admonition to "take heed, take exceeding care of yourself . . . take good care of your lives" (Deuteronomy 4:9, 15). The students decide to make taking care of yourself the theme of their Confirmation presentation.

From their studies, observations of peers, and own experiences, the students have become concerned about the dangers of abuse and addiction. In their presentation they urge people to get help if they become dependent on a harmful behavior. They conclude by expressing a commitment to working with the administration of the local high school to create a peer support group for students coping with addictions. In addition, they ask the synagogue Board to welcome "Anonymous" groups (i.e. Alcoholics Anonymous, Narcotics Anonymous, Overeaters Anonymous, JACS — Jewish Alcoholics and Chemically Dependent persons) to meet in the building and to sponsor a crisis hotline. The hotline would be for anyone in their community who is overwhelmed by a harmful behavior or for "standers by" who are concerned for loved ones.

For Thought and Discussion:

What concerns does the rabbi face in Scenario I?

Is the rabbi's response to the concerns appropriate? Explain.

What concerns do the students face in Scenario II?

Is the students' response to the concerns appropriate? Explain.

How is the students' situation like that of the villagers? How is it different?

Text Study

Jewish textual sources provide significant guidance regarding the challenges of harmful behaviors. Modern sources complement Jewish ideas and further clarify some of the issues. (Unlike the other chapters in this book, the texts here are presented in a straightforward format. Presenting opposing points of view is not a relevant approach for understanding harmful behaviors.)

1. **On Taking Care of Your Body and Avoiding Dangerous Practices**

   A. "Take heed, and guard your soul diligently . . . Take good care of your lives" (Deuteronomy 4:9, 15).

   B. Rabbi Akiba said, "A person is not permitted to harm him/herself" (*Baba Kamma* 90a).

   C. The Sages forbade many things that involve mortal danger. Anyone who does these things and says, "I am endangering myself and what does it matter to others," or "I don't care" is to be flogged [by the rabbinical court] (Maimonides, *Mishneh Torah, Hilchot Rotzayach,* 11:5).

   D. One should aim to maintain physical health and vigor, in order that the soul may be upright, in a condition to know God. For it is impossible for one to understand sciences and meditate upon them, when one is hungry or sick, or when any of one's limbs is aching (Maimonides, *Mishneh Torah, Hilchot De'ot,"* 3:3).

   What Do You Think?

   Do you agree with the rationale Judaism proves for taking care of your body?

   In Text #1C what does Maimonides believe the response should be to those who choose to endanger themselves?

   What is behind Maimonides' thinking? Do you agree with him?

   What should our response be today to someone who says, "It's my business what I do with my body" or "I don't care?"

What does it say in Text #1D about "sickness" and our relationship with God? Some might argue that during sickness people often draw closer to God. How do you think abusive or addictive behaviors would affect a person's relationship with God?

—◆◆◆—

2. On Smoking

A. One should certainly take care not to start smoking, and to take proper care in desisting. But should one conclude that it is forbidden as an activity dangerous to one's health? The answer is that because the multitude are accustomed to smoking, and the Gemara [part of the Talmud] in such a case invokes the principle that "the Eternal will protect the foolish" (*Shabbat* 129b and *Niddah* 31a, [reflecting Psalms 116:6]), and in particular since some of the greatest Torah scholars of present and past generations do or did smoke [there is no prohibition] (Moshe Feinstein, *Iggerot Moshe, Yoreh Deah*, 2:49).

B. One must avoid anything that may be injurious to one's well being and do everything that maintains and strengthens good health . . . Since smoking has been proven, beyond any shadow of a doubt, to be injurious to health and dangerous to life, one should do one's utmost to avoid it. According to some authorities, smoking is (in light of present medical knowledge) an offense prohibited by the Torah. If, as a consequence of smoking, we become ill and are thereby prevented from studying Torah or performing mitzvot, we are not considered as those who are exempt because of extraneous circumstances which prevent them from doing so. On the contrary, we are judged as those who willfully desist from Torah study or from performing mitzvot.

One may not smoke in public places since cigarette smoke has been proven to be injurious also to those in the vicinity of the smoker who inhale it (Compilation of

rabbinic views by Abraham S. Abraham, adapted from *The Comprehensive Guide to Medical Halachah*, Jerusalem: Feldheim Publishers, 1996, p. 25).

What Do You Think?

Who do you think makes the more compelling argument — Rabbi Feinstein or Rabbi Abraham? Why?

Do you believe smoking — since we know it harms the body — is the equivalent to a violation of other mitzvot?

—◆◆◆—

3. On Alcohol Consumption

A. When the wine goes in, intelligence takes its leave. Wherever there is wine there is no intelligence. When the wine enters, the secret (*sod*) comes out; the numerical total of wine (*yayin*) is seventy and the total of *sod* is seventy (Numbers *Rabbah* 10:8).

B. A drunkard (*shikur*) who has become as drunk as Lot (*shikur k'Lot*) — his judgment is like that of an idiot . . . (*Shulchan Aruch, Yoreh Deah* 1:8).

C. If a [drunk person] (*shikur*) committed a transgression involving the penalty of death, that person is to be executed; and if [a drunk person] committed one involving flogging, that person is to be flogged . . . Rabbi Chanina said: This applies only to one who did not reach the stage of Lot's drunkenness, but one who did reach such a stage is exempt from all responsibilities (*Eruvin* 65a).

D. The benefits of wine are many if it is taken in the proper amount, as it keeps the body in a healthy condition and cures many illnesses.

But the knowledge of its consumption is hidden from the masses. What they want is to get drunk, and drunkenness causes harm . . .

The small amount that is useful must be taken after the food leaves the stomach. Young children should not come close to it because it hurts them and causes harm to their body and soul . . . (Maimonides, *The Preservation of Youth*).

E. Do not take drugs because they demand periodic doses and your heart will crave them. You will also lose money. Even for medicinal purposes, do not take drugs if you can find a different medicine that will help (Rashbam, lived 1085-1158, commentary on *Pesachim* 113a).

What Do You Think?

Suppose these texts were all the information you had about Jewish views on alcohol consumption. How then would you summarize the "Jewish position?" In what ways do the texts reflect a permissive viewpoint; in what ways a restrictive one? What are the "gray areas?"

In Text #3C how does Rabbi Chanina's position differ from the majority opinion? What are the pros and cons of abiding by Rabbi Chanina's position? How do modern opinions compare with those expressed in this text?

What standard of responsibility should we impose for those who drink — fully responsible for their actions, somewhat responsible, not responsible at all? Explain.

What would Maimonides (Rambam) and Rashbam (Texts #3D and #3E) say are the greatest dangers of alcohol consumption? Do you agree with them? What does Maimonides mean (in Text #3D) when he says that alcohol hurts children, that it causes harm to their body and soul?

Have you witnessed situations in which drugs or alcohol seemed to have harmed someone's "soul?" Explain.

4. **On Eating**

A. Have you found honey? Eat so much as is sufficient for you, lest you be filled with it and vomit it (Proverbs 25:16).

B. If a man would take care of his body as he

takes care of the animal he rides on, he would be spared many serious ailments. For you will not find a man who would give too much hay to his animal, but he measures it according to its capacity. However, he himself will eat too much without measure and consideration. Man is very attentive to his animal's movement and fatigue in order that it should continue in a state of health and not get sick, but he is not attentive to his own body . . . We should eat only when justified by a feeling of hunger, when the stomach is clear and the mouth possesses sufficient saliva. Then we are really hungry. We must not drink water unless we are truly justified by thirst. This means that if we feel hungry or thirsty we should wait a little, as occasionally we are led to feel so by a deceptive hunger and deceptive thirst (Maimonides, *Mishneh Torah*, "Hilchot De'ot" 4).

C. It is our duty to avoid whatever is injurious to the body; therefore food should not be taken to repletion. We should not be gluttons, but eat food conducive to health; and of such food we should not eat to excess; we should not be eager to fill our stomachs, like those who gorge themselves with food and drink until the body swells. Overeating is like a deadly poison to any constitution and is the principal cause of all diseases. Most maladies that afflict humankind result from bad food, or are due to the patient filling the stomach with an excess of foods even though these be (in themselves) wholesome" (Compilation of rabbinic views by Abraham S. Abraham, adapted, *The Comprehensive Guide to Medical Halachah*. Jerusalem: Feldheim Publishers, 1996, p. 26).

What Do You Think?

Drawing from these three texts, define the Jewish ideal in eating habits. How do you think modern ideals in eating habits have departed from the ideals presented above?

On a scale from 1 to 10, how would you rate

"being attentive" as an important factor in good eating habits? Explain.

5. **When We're "In Over Our Heads"**

   A. "If you're in pain, go to a physician" (*Baba Kamma* 46b).

   B. Those who have become slaves to habit are no longer their own masters, and cannot act differently, even if they should want to do so. Their will is held in bondage by certain habits which have become second nature to them (Moses Hayyim Luzzatto, *The Path of the Upright*, p. 122).

   C. Select a master-teacher for yourself; acquire for yourself a friend. When you assess people, tip the balance in their favor (*Pirke Avot* 1:6).

   D. Seeking forgiveness from others (*teshuvah*), turning to God (*tefilah*), and reaching out to others in need (*tzedakah*) temper judgment's severe decree (High Holiday *Machzor*).

   E. Those whose anger is strong and their wrath intense are not far from the demented. And those who are given to anger, their life is no life (*Pesachim* 113b).

   F. You support all who are falling, lift up all who are bowed down . . . You are near to all who call upon You, to all who call upon You in earnest (Psalms 145:14, 18).

   G. Though I walk through a valley of deepest darkness, I fear no harm, for You are with me, Your rod and Your staff — they comfort me (Psalms 23:4).

What Do You Think?

How can we glean suggestions to help us when we're in over our heads from these texts?

Which text (or message) do you think is most important for a person coping with a harmful behavior to pay attention to? Why?

What suggestions would you give to your best friend if he/she became overwhelmed by something going on in his/her life? Would you be prepared to take the same advice that you would give others? Explain.

Related Middot and Mitzvot

Practicing these virtues and commandments will help us to cope with harmful behaviors in a manner informed by Jewish values:

Anavah (Humility): Admitting feelings of powerlessness over an addiction is a humbling, but necessary first step in our efforts to make changes.

Chochmah (Wisdom): We will make wiser decisions when we heed the insights of our sages and the advice gleaned from contemporary experience.

Emunah (Trust, Faith): When we put our trust in God, our faith in ourselves grows.

Kabbalat HaYisurin (Acceptance of Suffering): Everyone encounters pain at times. In acknowledging this, we can learn to cope with our pain in healthy, compassionate ways.

Ma'akeh (Preventing Accidents): Accidents are more prone to happen when one uses alcohol or other drugs — they can impair judgment, decrease alertness, diminish coordination, plus lead to less self-control and fewer inhibitions.

Ometz Lev (Courage): If we find ourselves dependent on a harmful behavior, we will need courage to take the necessary steps to reverse the course our lives have taken.

Shmiat HaOzen (Attentiveness, Being a Good Listener): To make the healthiest choices we can, we must pay careful attention to the signals our bodies give us and listen closely to our feelings and thoughts. Listening deeply to others will alert us to when others may need help.

Shmirat HaGuf (Taking Care of Your Body): This includes avoiding abuse of dangerous substances and being mindful of eating behavior.

Simchah (Joy and Happiness): Nurturing joy and happiness helps displace the negativity that feeds self-destructive behaviors. Feelings of optimism, vibrancy, and well-being are nourishing for body and soul.

Teshuvah (Returning, Repentance, Making Amends): Restoring care for our bodies, healing relationships with others, and turning to God are ways of "returning" from the confusion and pain of addiction.

Where Do I Go From Here?

These harmful behaviors may seem remote, or they may be something you have already dealt with on some level. Hopefully, your exploration of this chapter will prepare you not only to recognize situations in which harmful behaviors might arise and avoid them, but also to have more insight into how to deal with such behaviors in your family, friends, or yourself if they do arise. Judaism offers much insight into these behaviors. Look to the tradition for help and guidance.

Following is a list of suggested resources that you may find helpful as you explore further the issues raised by smoking, drinking, and under/overeating.

Jewish Sources

Abraham, Abraham S. *The Comprehensive Guide To Medical Halachah.* Jerusalem: Feldheim Publishers, 1996.

Brazen, Judith, and Susan Freeman. "Intervening in the Life of an Alcoholic" (1989). In *Reform Jewish Ethics and the Halakhah,* edited by Eugene B. Borowitz. Springfield, NJ: Behrman House, Inc., 1994, pp. 79-95.

Dorff, Elliot N. "Preventing Illness." In *Matters of Life and Death: A Jewish Approach to Modern Medical Ethics.* Philadelphia, PA: The Jewish Publication Society, 1998, pp. 245-254.

Freeman, Susan. *Teaching Jewish Virtues: Sacred Sources and Arts Activities.* Denver, CO: A.R.E. Publishing, Inc., 1999.

Goldwasser, Dovid. *Starving to Live: An Inspirational Guide To Eating Disorders.* New York: Judaica Press, 2000.

Herring, Basil F. "Smoking and Drugs." In *Jewish Ethics and Halakhah for Our Time: Sources and Commentary, Volume I.* Hoboken, NJ: KTAV Publishing House, Inc. and New York: Yeshiva University Press, 1984, pp. 221-243.

Kadden, Barbara Binder and Bruce Kadden. *Teaching Mitzvot: Concepts, Values, and Activities.* Rev. ed. Denver, CO: A.R.E. Publishing, Inc., 2003.

Olitzky, Kerry M., and Stuart A. Copans. *Twelve Jewish Steps to Recovery: A Personal Guide To Turning from Alcholoism and Other Addictions.* Woodstock, VT: Jewish Lights Publishing, 1991.

Rosner, Fred. "Cigarette and Marijuana Smoking." In *Modern Medicine and Jewish Ethics.* Hoboken, NJ: KTAV Publishing House, Inc. and New York: Yeshiva University Press, 1991, pp. 391-403.

Ross, Allen, and Stuart Copans. "A Jewish Way of Eating." In *Where We Stand: Jewish Consciousness on Campus.* Edited by Allan L. Smith. New York: UAHC Press, 1997.

Zemer, Moshe. *Evolving Halachah: A Progressive Approach To Traditional Jewish Law.* Woodstock, VT: Jewish Lights Publishing, 1999, p. 345-350.

On Smoking

Books and Articles

Boston Women's Health Collective. *The New Our Bodies Ourselves.* New York: Simon & Schuster, 1992.

Quiram, Jacquelyn, et al, eds. *Alcohol and Tobacco: America's Drugs of Choice.* Wylie, TX: Information Plus, 1999.

Krogh, David. *Smoking: The Artificial Passion.* New York: W.H. Freeman and Company, 1991.

Web Sites

Antismoking Master Support Site: www.mindconnection.com/interests/ antismoking.htm
  "A page for those who want to put an end to the destruction smoking wreaks on our loved ones and on ourselves."

Films

The Insider (1999, rated R, 158 minutes)
True story of tobacco executive-turned-whistle-blower Jeffrey Wigand and his relationship with "60 Minutes" producer Lowell Bergman.

Secrets Through the Smoke (2001, 55 minutes)
Documentary featuring former tobacco scientist Jeffrey Wigand (protagonist in The Insider) talking to teens about smoking. It also has skits, people talking about their smoking problems, and several non-smoking advertisements that have been on television.

The Teen Files: "Smoking: Truth or Dare" (1998, 52 minutes)
Obtain purchase information from www.aimsmultimedia.com.

On Alcohol

Books and Articles

Alcoholics Anonymous: The Story of How Many Thousands of Men and Women Have Recovered from Alcoholism. New York: Alcoholics Anonymous World Services, Inc. 1976.

Berg, Steven L., comp. *Jewish Alcoholism and Drug Addiction: An Annotated Bibliography.* Westport, CT: Greenwood Press, 1993.

Boston Women's Health Collective. *The New Our Bodies Ourselves.* New York: Simon & Schuster, 1992.

Quiram, Jacquelyn, et al, eds. *Alcohol and Tobacco: America's Drugs of Choice.* Wylie, TX: Information Plus, 1999.

Web Sites

Dream Inc. (Developing Resources for Education in America, Inc.): www.dreaminc.org
A source for materials and information to aid in the fight against drug and alcohol abuse.

Jewish Alcoholics, Chemically Dependent Persons and Significant Others: www.jacsweb.org
This site gives information about retreats and programs, and also has a helpful bibliography of support materials, including ones with Jewish spiritual guidance.

Mothers Against Drunk Driving (M.A.D.D.): www.madd.org
MADD's mission is to stop drunk driving, support the victims of this violent crime, and prevent underage drinking.

The National Clearinghouse for Alcohol and Drug Information: www.health.org
An information resource run by the Substance Abuse & Mental Health Services Administration, an agency of the U.S. Department of Health and Human Services.

National Council on Alcoholism and Drug Dependence: www.ncadd.org
The NCADD fights the stigma and the disease of alcoholism and other drug addictions.

Students Against Destructive Decisions (also known as Students Against Driving Drunk and S.A.D.D.): www.saddonline.com
S.A.D.D. is a peer leadership organization dedicated to preventing destructive decisions, particularly underage drinking, other drug use, impaired driving, teen violence, and teen depression and suicide.

Films

Bright Lights, Big City (1988, 110 minutes, rated R)
A young man from Kansas moves to New York to work on a magazine and gets caught up in a world of drinking and drugs.

My Name Is Bill W. (1989, 100 minutes, unrated)
Based on the true story of a successful stock broker who must come to grips with his alcoholism. He forms a support group that would evolve into Alcoholics Anonymous.

Shattered Spirits (1986, 93 minutes, rated PG-13)
A dedicated middle-class family man has his life shattered by his uncontrolled drinking.

On Eating Issues

Books and Articles

Boskind-White, Marlene, and William C. White. *Bulimia/Anorexia: The Binge/Purge Cycle and Self-Starvation.* New York: W.W. Norton & Company, 2000. (Includes excellent bibliography)

Boston Women's Health Collective. *The New Our Bodies Ourselves.* New York: Simon & Schuster, 1992.

Friedman, Sandra Susan. *When Girls Feel Fat: Helping Girls through Adolescence.* New York: Firefly Books, 2000. (Includes excellent bibliography)

Hall, Lindsey, and Leigh Cohn. *Anorexia Nervosa: A Guide To Recovery.* Carlsbad, CA: Gurze Books, 1998.

————. *Bulimia: A Guide To Recovery.* Rev. ed. Carlsbad, CA: Gurze Books, 1999.

————. *Self-Esteem: Tools for Recovery.* Rev. ed. Carlsbad, CA: Gurze Books, 1990.

Schwartz, Rosie. *The Enlightened Eater: A Guide To Well-Being through Eating.* Toronto, Canada: Macmillan, 1998.

Web Sites

Anorexia Nervosa and Related Disorders: www.anred.com
> *Explains the science of the disease and describes various eating disorders, their causes, and sources for treatment.*

Gurze Books: www.gurze.com
> *Eating disorders resources and links to other sites.*

InnerSolutions: www.innersolutions.net
> *Loving, non-diet approach to healing, food, weight, and body-image issues.*

National Association of Anorexia Nervosa and Associated Disorders: www.altrue.net/site/anadweb/
> *Provides counsel to eating disorder sufferers and their families, and referrals to specialists.*

National Eating Disorders Association: www.nationaleatingdisorders.org
> *A prevention and advocacy organization providing information, sponsoring school programs, and offering a referral page for local eating disorder specialists.*

Films

The Teen Files: "The Truth about Body Image" (2001, 21 minutes)
> Obtain purchase information from www. aims-multimedia.com

Full (2001)
> A Canadian short film exploring a young man's eating disorders. Difficult to find.

The Karen Carpenter Story: A CBS TV Movie (1988, 97 minutes)
> Story of the meteoric rise and sudden fall of Karen Carpenter, who became a famous singer while battling anorexia and bulimia.

Nova: Dying to Be Thin (2000)
> A powerful PBS documentary on eating disorders. Each of the eight short episodes are available for viewing online at www.pbs.org/ wgbh/nova/thin/program.html

Glossary

The definitions below are adapted from the 1994 Fourth Edition of the American Psychiatric Association's Diagnostic and Statistical Manual of Mental Disorders.

Anorexia Nervosa

A. Refusal to maintain body weight at or above a minimally normal weight for age and height (e.g., weight loss leading to maintenance of body weight less than 85 percent of that expected, or failure to make expected weight gain during a period of growth, leading to body weight less than 85 percent of that expected.).

B. Intense fear of gaining weight or becoming fat, even though underweight.

C. Disturbance in the way in which one's body weight or shape is experienced, undue influence of body weight or shape on self-evaluation, or denial of the seriousness of the current low body weight.

D. In postmenarcheal females, amenorrhea; i.e., the absence of at least three consecutive menstrual cycles.

Bulimia Nervosa

A. Recurrent episodes of binge eating. An episode of binge eating is characterized by both of the following:

   (1) eating, in a discrete period of time (e.g., within any two-hour period), an amount of food that is definitely larger than most people would eat during a similar period of time and under similar circumstances

   (2) a sense of lack of control over eating during the episode (e.g., a feeling that one cannot stop eating or control what or how much one is eating)

B. Recurrent inappropriate compensatory behavior in order to prevent weight gain, such as self-induced vomiting; misuse of laxatives, diuretics, enemas, or other medications; fasting; or excessive exercise.

C. The binge eating and inappropriate compensatory behaviors both occur, on average, at least twice a week for three months.

D. Self-evaluation is unduly influenced by body shape and weight.

E. The disturbance does not occur exclusively during episodes of Anorexia Nervosa.

Substance Abuse

An abnormal pattern of recurring use that leads to significant impairment or distress marked by one or more of the following in a 12-month period:

- Failure to fulfill major obligations at home, school, or work (for example, repeated absences, poor performance, or neglect).

- Use in hazardous or potentially hazardous situations, such as driving a car or operating a machine while impaired.

- Legal problems, such as arrest for disorderly conduct while under the influence of the substance.

- Continued use in spite of social or interpersonal problems caused by the use of the substance, such as fights or family arguments.

Substance Dependence (Addiction)

Present when three or more of the following occur in a 12-month period:

- Increasing need for more of the substance to achieve the desired effect (tolerance), or a reduction in effect when using the same amount as previously.

- Withdrawal symptoms if the use of the substance is stopped or reduced.

- Progressive neglect of other pleasures and duties.

- A strong desire to take the substance or a persistent but unsuccessful desire to control or reduce the use of the substance.

- Continued use in spite of physical or mental health problems caused by the substance.

- Use of the substance in larger amounts or over longer periods of time than originally intended or difficulties in controlling the amount of the substance used or when to stop taking it.

- A lot of time spent in obtaining the substance, using it, or recovering from its effects.

PART II

Civil and Political Issues

Ethics of Business

The Death Penalty

School Violence

Ethics of War

CHAPTER 5
ETHICS OF BUSINESS

Overview

In business interactions, we face constant temptations for tainting honesty and integrity. "If I just cheat a little bit, no one will know, no one will really suffer that much . . . " "I could encourage this millionaire seeking my advice to invest in such-and-such company. What does it matter if I don't mention how her investment will benefit me personally . . . " "I don't have to tell this customer that the gold in the ring he plans to purchase from me is mixed with another metal. It looks genuine enough . . . " Even if no such thoughts have passed through our own minds, we easily can imagine how they might.

Each player in a business transactions brings different needs and goals to the table. For instance, the merchant wants to sell at the highest price possible; the buyer wants to purchase at the lowest price possible. Because of competing needs and goals, everyone involved in business transactions needs protections: employers and employees, merchants and customers, business owners and their neighbors, developers and community members.

While people should be able to run their businesses in ways they believe are most effective, there need to be safeguards against exploitation. Moral principles must guide business practices. Business ethics seek to ensure that no one is cheated, misled, taken advantage of, or otherwise treated unfairly.

Jewish Perspectives

Underlying Principles

The Talmud tells us that the first thing a person is asked in the world to come is, "Have you been honest in business?" (Shabbat 31b). Judaism charges us to live in a sanctified manner, and living in a sanctified manner includes being honorable in business. Specific principles underlying the ethics of business include not stealing, not coveting, not dealing deceitfully or falsely with one

another, and not oppressing.

Our tradition insists that we consider not only the question, "What am I legally allowed to do?" but also, "What is the right thing to do?" If what we're about to do is not moral – that is, if our intentions are not respectful, honorable, and dignified — then what we're about to do is not legal, not allowed. Jewish sources disallow not only explicit robbing and stealing, but stress that we must not exploit, misrepresent, coerce, conceal the truth, or in any other way intentionally put others at an unfair disadvantage.

Categories of Concern

Jewish sources distinguish several categories of unethical behavior, applicable in business as well as in our personal lives:

G'nayvah: (Thievery) This means stealing from others in secret, without their knowledge. Examples of *g'nayvah* include shoplifting, hotwiring a car, pickpocketing, or using another's credit card to acquire goods. Maintaining accurate weights and measures are a must for avoiding *g'nayvah.* Customers should get exactly what they think they are paying for.

Less obvious examples of *g'nayvah* are tax evasion, padding business expense accounts, and private use of an employer's materials or facilities.[1]

G'zaylah (Robbery): This means taking from others through force, coercion, or deceit. Examples of *g'zaylah* include using physical force to take something, exploiting a worker, denying the discovery of a lost article, abusing one's position, misusing power, or misapplying strength.

Specific mitzvot form the basis for prohibitions related to *g'zaylah.* These include returning a robbed article, returning a lost article, not robbing, not oppressing, not coveting, not desiring what belongs to someone else, and not ignoring a lost article.[2]

Ona'ah (Exploitation, overreaching). Examples of *ona'ah* include wronging others by withholding important information, selling items for more than their real worth, or overcharging by more than 1/6th of an item's worth.

Just as sellers have obligations to avoid exploitation, so too do buyers. Thus, buyers are not to purchase items for less than their real worth.

Ona'at Devarim (Verbal exploitation) This includes the avoidance of causing others needless mental anguish. The Mishnah gives the example of a customer who asks the price of an object but has no intention of buying the item, falsely raising the hopes of the seller.

G'nay-vat Da'at (Stealing another's mind) This means misrepresenting or concealing the truth so as to put another person at a disadvantage, or giving any impression that we are acting to benefit others when such benefits are either absent or unintended. Examples of *g'nay-vat da'at* include flattery, inconsistencies between what we say and what we're really thinking, and all manner of verbal deception. A characteristic practice of *g'nay-vat da'at* is knowingly giving the wrong impression, but making no attempt to clear things up (such as a shop owner who doesn't correct a customer's mistaken notions of an item's quality).

Some would include as *g'nay-vat da'at* the practice of luring customers into a shop using special treats and gifts, or other "bonus enticements." Hiding the true quality of merchandise is a clear example of *g'nay-vat da'at*. Less obvious instances of giving mistaken impressions are repeatedly inviting a guest knowing that the guest will not accept, or offering a gift knowing it will not be accepted.

Lifnay Evare (Not putting a stumbling block in the path of the blind) In business, one party is "blind" to the full consequences of a transaction or to another's deceitful motivations. Examples of *lifnay evare* include selling weapons to a known criminal or selling stolen goods to an unsuspecting buyer. Some might even include in this category anyone selling guns, cigarettes, or pornography. Other instances of *lifnay evare* are giving misleading advice or not disclosing a conflict of interest — as Rashi wrote, "One must not tell another to sell a field and buy a donkey when one wishes to buy a field and sell a donkey." (*Sifra* to *Vayikra* 19:4).

Neighbors and Others in the Community

So far, we have focused our presentation of business ethics primarily on the relationship between merchants and customers. The broader community also needs protections. Community members need protections from pollution, noises, smells, and any other detrimental effects of business practice.

Still, business people should be entitled to make a living. Just as members of the community need protections, so too do individuals conducting business need protections.

In our day, with the development of "megabusinesses," new issues have arisen. One of these, which Jewish sources also address, is fair competition. Ensuring fair competition is a concern affecting all members of a community.

Employer-Employee Relations

Employers have many obligations to their employees. These include paying wages in a timely fashion and fulfilling the standards of local customs (for example, working hours and meal breaks).

Workers have responsibilities, too. These include not idling away time, being punctual, and not engaging in practices in off-hours that will affect the quality of work during employed hours. Employees become vulnerable to dismissal by committing crimes, for not being competent, or for improper behavior outside the workplace.[3]

Dina d'Malchuta Dina — "The Law of the Land is the Law"

In business, this phrase expresses the Jewish idea of valuing and following local custom. Note, however, that in places where unethical business practices are common, we must be wary of distorting this principle as a way of justifying dishonesty. For instance, even if everyone "cuts corners," an ethical Jew still must not do so.

Balancing Competing Considerations

Realizing our own dreams and goals (business or otherwise) cannot involve trampling on others along the way. While we may strive to maximize earnings and profits, we are not to exploit or oppress others while doing so. Society must impose rules and guidelines to protect everyone's interests, to make certain business is practiced fairly.

General Perspectives

Comparing Jewish and General Perspectives

Jewish and general discussions of business ethics share many concerns. These include balancing the needs of all those involved in business transactions, negotiating issues of freedom versus restraint (the free market versus the regulated market), preserving free competition, protecting the environment, and respecting local custom.

In Judaism, legality and morality always stand together. In general business practice, this is not necessarily the case. For instance, Judaism tends to be more restrictive in *Ona'at Devarim*, verbal exploitation, and in *G'nay-vat Da'at*, "stealing another's mind" or deception. In America and elsewhere, business regulations do not go to the extent Judaism does to protect citizens from emotional manipulation and mental deception.

The High Stakes of Business Today

Today, businesses are rapidly developing new technologies of transportation, communication, and information. These technologies lead to new ethical challenges, especially in the realms of fair competition, expected product quality, worker protections, and environmental policy.

In addition, our world is becoming increasingly enmeshed in a "global economy." Global economy implies business practices with far-ranging interests and involvements across the globe. This reality raises new ethical challenges for business, including:

Diffusion of responsibility — that is, who is responsible for poor or irresponsible business practices?

Multinational corporations — that may have more resources and power than governments of individual countries.

Monopolies — challenging fair competition.

Publicly-owned companies – which can confuse our understanding of employer-employee relations.

High stakes litigation — with potential for far-ranging economic impact.

In today's world a single business decision can affect the lives and livelihoods of thousands. With the stakes so high, the marketplace requires proactive efforts for preserving honesty and fairness.

Summary of the Overview

The paragraphs below summarize key considerations regarding business ethics as discussed in the Overview.

1. We are not to cheat, mislead, take advantage of one another, or otherwise treat others unfairly.

2. Some unethical business practices are most comparable to stealing, as they lead to outright losses to another individual. Other practices deceive in more subtle ways, such as through withholding important information, concealing the truth, false flattery, misrepresentation, and so on. Judaism condemns both types of practices.

3. Judaism lays down basic ground rules for ethical business practice. Yet, the parameters of acceptable versus unacceptable business interactions always take local custom into account.

4. An emphasis on the immorality of mental deception is one of the distinguishing factors in Judaism's approach to business ethics.

5. A "global economy" increasingly characterizes our world today. This reality raises new ethical challenges for business.

Scenarios: How Things have Changed

The ethics of business have been a concern since ancient times. Our texts are rich with laws, debates, and discussions regarding fair and honorable expectations in a variety of business relationships. Below are two imaginary scenarios, one set in ancient days, and one set in contemporary times. These scenarios are intended to raise questions and spark discussion. Read each one and answer the questions that follow. Then continue on to the "Text Study" section to see what Jewish and other sources have to say on the subject. Finally, you may wish to come back and answer the questions a second time, to see if your views have changed.

Scenario I: "Back Then"

Yosi is an apprentice hired by Reb Moshe, the sandal maker. Yosi is to show up every day at 8:00 A.M. He works until 10:30 A.M. when Reb Moshe, his employer, gives Yosi a 15-minute break. Reb Moshe provides Yosi with a light snack of pita bread and sweetened mint tea. Yosi usually sits in the courtyard during these breaks and enjoys the company of other apprentices. The other apprentices, in accord with local custom, also take a break each day at 10:30. At 1:00 P.M., Yosi returns to his family where he eats a full meal, takes a rest, and helps with chores. At 4:00 P.M., Yosi returns to Reb Moshe's shop where he works until 7:00 P.M. Before Yosi leaves, Reb Moshe hands him a few coins, Yosi's wages for the day.

Scenario II: "Nowadays"

Josephine is a web site designer for footwear companies. As a single mother, she can't start her workday until her two children leave for school at 8:00 A.M. After rushing through household chores, Josephine sits down at her computer to work at 8:30 A.M. At 10:30, she takes a five minute break to brew a cup of coffee that she brings back to her desk to sip while continuing her work. Because competition has become so fierce in her field, Josephine feels she cannot lose a minute of valuable work time. Thus, she continues to work without stopping until 3:15 P.M. when her children come home. She fixes a snack for the children and pops a frozen meal for herself into the microwave oven (since she didn't have lunch). The family spends time together until 4:00 P.M. when the teenager from next door arrives. The teenager will stay until 6:30 P.M. Josephine returns to her computer work.

At 6:30, Josephine fixes the family a pasta dinner. After cleaning up and putting her children to bed, she returns a few phone calls while exercising on the stationary bike. In one of her phone calls, Josephine complains to a friend. She used to be able to count on a little extra income from doing web design for people in the community. But because those clients came to her home, some of her neighbors objected. The neighborhood is not zoned for private businesses.

Josephine returns to her computer at 9:00 P.M. She continues working until 11:00 P.M., then washes up and collapses into bed. Though she knows she has put in a hard day's work, she tosses and turns for a long time. She is unsure of whether the work she has done will bring in enough money to support her family.

For Thought and Discussion:

What would you imagine to be most challenging to Yosi in his work?

What would you imagine to be most challenging to Josephine in her work?

How might the community infrastructure support or detract from Yosi's or Josephine's ability to succeed in their work? Consider such issues as financial success, benefits (health care, retirement, personal time), support of family and friends (child care, etc.).

Text Study

Judaism holds honorable business practices in high esteem. Torah, Talmud, Mishnah, and scholars through the ages have all addressed the proper conduct of business in great detail. There are many difficult questions to consider regarding sellers and buyers; business people and their neighbors; and employers and employees. Jewish textual sources provide many answers, but these sometimes highlight the tensions between seemingly opposing considerations. In addition Jewish resources have been "stretched" to respond to some of the new ethical challenges we face today. The chart on page 67 poses questions and offers two points of view. Text sources supporting each of these points of view follow.

1. **How do the objectives of sellers and buyers differ?**

   On the One Hand:

   Sellers aim to maximize profits.

Ethical Business Practices: Questions to Consider

The Question	On the One Hand	On the Other Hand
1. How do the objectives of buyers and sellers differ? (see page 66)	Sellers aim to maximize profits.	Buyers want to purchase for the lowest price possible.
2. What are fair strategies for sellers to use in promoting their merchandise? (see page 68)	Sellers are entitles to make merchandise attractive and desirable to potential customers.	Buyers must not be deceived. Sprucing up items is acceptable; disguising the inferior quality of items is not.
3. How should sellers interact with potential customers? (see page 68)	Impressing, enticing, and luring customers are all effective strategies for increasing business.	It is unethical to misrepresent, allow mistaken impressions to stand, or sell under false pretenses.
4. Are certain businesses unethical by their very nature? (see page 69)	If they'll buy it, you can sell it.	Selling harmful items or stolen items is prohibited. So is stockpiling basic commodities, then selling at inflated prices.
5. What should employers and employees expect of each other? (see page 70)	Employers want to get as much work as they can from employees. They rightly expect employees to be competent, diligent, and scrupulous.	Employers must not oppress or treat their employees unfairly. They are in an advantageous position in relation to their employees.
6. What might developers/ business people and local citizens demand of each other? (see page 70)	Developers and other business people should be able to run their enterprises in ways they feel are most effective.	The impact on neighbors, community members, and the environment must be taken into account.

Judaism considers both overcharging and underpaying to be *ona'ah*, a type of fraud. The rabbinic tradition understands the following verse from Leviticus to refer to monetary exploitation.

A. When you come to sell, you shall not wrong (*lo tonu*) one another (Leviticus 25:14).

B. It is forbidden to defraud one's fellow person, whether in buying or in selling. Whoever of them [the parties to the transaction] does so, whether buyer or seller, transgresses a negative commandment [see verse from Leviticus above] (*Shulchan Aruch, Choshen Mishpat, Hilchot Mekach u'Memkar*, 227:1).

On the Other Hand:

Buyers want to purchase for the lowest price possible.

To avoid inflated or deflated prices, the buyer and seller must know the exact quality and quantity of the product(s) they're dealing with. Any type of stealing is forbidden, and accurate weights and measures are essential. (An *ephah* and *hin* are ancient measurements.)

a. You shall not steal (Exodus 20:13).

b. Just balances, just weights, a just *ephah*, and a just *hin* shall you have. I am the Eternal your God, who brought you out of the land of Egypt (Leviticus 19:36).

What Do You Think?

Judaism condemns both overcharging and underpaying. What might be the damaging repercussions of such practices?

The concept of *ona'ah* comes from *lo tonu* or "do not oppress." What is the connection?

Have you had any personal experiences related to *ona'ah*? How did you handle the situation(s)?

2. **What are fair strategies for sellers to use in promoting their merchandise?**

On the One Hand:

Sellers are entitled to make merchandise attractive and desirable to potential customers.

A. Samuel permitted fringes to be put on a cloak. Rabbi Judah permitted a gloss to be put on fine cloth. Rabbah permitted hemp cloths to be beaten [to appear of finer texture]. Rava permitted arrows to be painted. Rabbi Pappa permitted baskets to be painted . . . (*Baba Metzia* 4:12).

B. It is permitted to sift pounded beans [to remove the refuse, make them look better, and presumably raise their price] . . . [For the continuation of this text see #2b below.] (Maimonides, *Mishneh Torah, Hilchot Mechirah* 18, based on *Baba Metzia* 4:12).

On the Other Hand:

Buyers must not be deceived. Sprucing up items is acceptable; disguising the inferior quality of items is not.

a. Painting new utensils is permitted, whereas old ones [to make them appear new] is forbidden (*Baba Metzia* 4:12).

b. It is permitted to sift pounded beans — but not when the sifting is only at the top of the bin, because [sifting only at the top of the bin] serves to deceive the eye into thinking that the whole container is similarly sifted (Maimonides, *Mishneh Torah,*

Hilchot Mechirah 18, based on *Baba Metzia* 4:12).

What Do You Think?

Do these texts provide sufficient guidance as to the allowances and limits of enhancing items for sale?

What other strategies might you add that would be fair to both sellers and buyers?

3. **How should sellers interact with potential customers?**

On the One Hand:

Impressing, enticing, and luring customers are effective strategies for increasing business.

A. A shopkeeper may distribute parched corn or nuts to children and maidservants to accustom them to frequent his store. And he may reduce the price to increase his customer share. His competitors cannot prevent this for it does not constitute deception (Maimonides, *Mishneh Torah, Hilchot Mechirah* 18 and *Baba Metzia* 4:12).

On the Other Hand:

It is unethical to misrepresent, allow mistaken impressions to stand, or sell under false pretenses.

a. You are not to steal, you are not to lie, you are not to deal falsely with each other (Leviticus 19:11).

b. There are seven categories of fraud: the first among them is to misrepresent oneself to others [*gonev da'at ha-briyot*], one who insincerely invites another to his home, one who plies another with gifts that he knows the other will not accept, one who impresses his guest by opening a barrel of wine that is already sold to a vendor [thus the guest will believe that his host has on his account risked a financial loss, given that an open barrel of wine might spoil until such a time as a vendor comes along to purchase it], one who has improper measures, one who lies regarding his weights, and one who adulterates his merchandise . . . " (*Mechilta, Mishpatim,* chapter 13, *Tosefta, Baba Kamma* 7:3).

c. When one knows that there is some defect in one's merchandise, one must so inform the purchaser (Maimonides, *Mishneh Torah, Hilchot Mechirah* 18).

d. It is forbidden to accustom oneself to smooth speech and flatteries. One must not say one thing and mean another. The inward and outward self should correspond; only what we have in mind should we utter with the mouth. We must deceive no one, not even an idolater . . . Even a single word of flattery or deception is forbidden. A person should always cherish truthful speech, an upright spirit, and a pure heart freed of all pretense and cunning (Maimonides, *Mishneh Torah, Hilchot De'ot* 2:6).

What Do You Think?

Do these texts provide sufficient guidance as to the allowances and limits of impressing, enticing, and luring customers? Do you disagree with any of them? What are limits might you add?

Have you ever had an experience in which you felt the merchant misrepresented his/her merchandise? How did you handle the matter? After reading the texts above, is there a better way you could have handled it?

———◆◇◆———

4. **Are certain businesses unethical by their very nature?**

On the One Hand:

If they'll buy it, you can sell it.

Jewish sources do not suggest this model of business.

On the Other Hand:

Selling harmful items or stolen items is prohibited. So is stockpiling basic commodities, then selling at inflated prices.

a. Everything that is forbidden to sell to non-Jews is similarly forbidden to sell to Jewish robbers, because by doing so, one strengthens the hands of the evildoers and leads them astray [if they would not be able to buy the weapons perhaps they would not rob. Similarly, without weapons, aggression becomes more difficult.] So, too, anyone who misleads others who are blind [who are not aware or knowledgeable], causing them to sin, and those who give others advice, which they themselves know is to the others' detriment [not only in money matters but even in referring to ways of travel, etc.], or those who strengthen the hands of evildoers who are actually so blinded by lust and desire that they are unwilling to see the true path — all these types transgress a negative commandment, as it is written, "You shall not place a stumbling block in the path of the blind" (Leviticus 19:14). (Maimonides, *Mishneh Torah, Hilchot Rotzayach u'Shmirat Hanefesh,* 12:14, bracketed commentary by Meir Tamari, p. 102)

b. It is forbidden to buy stolen goods from a thief. This is a grievous sin, since it strengthens the hands of those who transgress and causes them to steal again, because if they would not find a buyer, they would not steal (*Shulchan Aruch, Hilchot G'nayvah,* 356:1).

c. While Jewish sources limit profits from the sale of basic commodities, there are less restrictions in marketing luxury-type items.

> The *beit din* (court) is obligated to fix prices and to appoint overseers to implement them. This applies only to basic goods, like wine, oil, and vegetables. But special goods like spices and similar articles do not have fixed prices, so everyone may earn what they wish (Maimonides, *Mishneh Torah, Hilchot Mechirah,* 14:1, 2).

Do these sources outline reasonable expectations for business owners? Why or why not?

Selling weapons to robbers or buying stolen goods from thieves are examples of *lifnay evare*, placing a stumbling block before the blind. What other examples can you think of that fit this category of unacceptable commerce? Pornography? Cigarettes? Anything else?

Also in the category of *lifnay evare* is giving ill-suited advice and advice based on a conflict of interest. What are specific examples of giving ill-suited business advice?

Relating to the question of making profits on basic commodities, should the government control or set prices on basic goods (flour, rice, etc.)?

5. **What should employers and employees expect of each other?**

On the One Hand:

Employers want to get as much work as they can from employees. They rightly expect employees to be competent, diligent, and scrupulous.

A. Just as the employer is enjoined not to deprive poor workers of their wages or withhold wages from them when they are due, so are workers enjoined not to deprive employers of the benefit of their work by idling away time, a little here and a little there, thus wasting the whole day deceitfully. Indeed, workers must be very punctual concerning time (Maimonides, *Mishneh Torah, Hilchot Sechirut* 13:7).

B. Workers must not work at night at their own work and then hire themselves out during the day. [Nor are workers] to plow with their ox in the evenings and then hire the animal out in the mornings. Nor should workers go hungry and afflict themselves in order to feed their children — for by doing so, they steal labor from their employer (*Tosefta, Baba Metzia* 8:2).

C. Any [worker] who causes an irretrievable loss is liable to be dismissed immediately (*Baba Batra* 21b).

On the Other Hand:

Employers must not oppress or treat their employees unfairly. They are in an advantageous position in relation to their employees.

a. You shall not abuse needy and destitute laborers, whether they be your fellow citizens or sojourners in one of the communities of your land. You must pay them their wages on the same day, before the sun sets, for they are needy and urgently depend on it; else they will cry to the Eternal against you and you will incur guilt (Deuteronomy 24:14-15).

b. Whoever withholds an employee's wages, it is as though they have taken the person's life away (*Baba Metzia* 112a).

c. If an employer hires laborers and asks them to work in the early morning or late evening, at a place where it is not the local custom to work early or late at night, the employer cannot force the laborers to do so. Where it is customary to provide food for workers, the employer must do so. If it is customary to give them dessert, the employer must do so — it all depends on local custom (*Baba Metzia* 7:1).

What Do You Think?

What do these texts define as the key responsibilities of the employer and employee?

Would you say that these responsibilities are the most important? What other responsibilities do you think employers and employees owe each other?

6. **What might developers/business people and local citizens demand of each other?**

On the One Hand:

Developers and other business people should be able to run their enterprises in ways they feel are most effective.

A. This text comes from the secular world of business:

> There is one and only one social responsibility of business: to use its resources and engage in activities designed to increase its profits so long as it stays within the rules of the game, which is to say, engage in open and free competition without deception or fraud (Milton Friedman, "The Social Responsibility of Business," in *The Essence of Friedman*, edited by Kurt R.Leube [Stanford, CA: Hoover Institution Press, 1987], p. 42).

On the Other Hand:

The impact on neighbors, community members, and the environment must be taken into account.

a. [If a person wished to open] a store in a courtyard, [the neighbors] can protest against the person, saying, "I cannot sleep because of the noise of those entering and leaving. An artisan may make utensils [at home] and go about and sell them in the marketplace. The others cannot protest . . . " (*Baba Batra* 2:3).

b. Carcasses, cemeteries, and tanneries must be kept at fifty cubits distance from a town [because of the bad odor]. A tannery must be established on the east side of town [because the east wind is gentle and will not carry the stench to town] (*Baba Batra* 2:9).

What Do You Think?

What is the essence of what Milton Friedman says? Do you agree with him?

The Mishnah gives some examples of what people in its day could justifiably protest concerning neighboring businesses. What kinds of things might you or others protest about today?

Related Middot and Mitzvot

Practicing these virtues and commandments supports ethical business practices.

Bal Tashchit ("Not Destroying," Preserving the Earth): Businesses need to be responsible about their impact on the environment.

Emet (Truth): Speaking and acting truthfully is a key underlying value of business ethics.

Histapkut (Contentedness): If you're continually dissatisfied with your material lifestyle, you may be more likely to engage in questionable business practices, to cheat to get ahead.

K'vod et HaBriyot (Respecting Others): Treating others with dignity means not taking advantage of them in any manner.

Lo Tachmod (Not Coveting): Envy feeds greed and possibly underhanded competitiveness. Controlling envy is an important component of maintaining moral business standards.

Malachah (Work/Industriousness): Being dependent on others when you are able to work or living in poverty can be demoralizing. Engaging in business can provide a suitable way to live a secure and honorable life.

Nedivut (Generosity): Generous people are less likely to want to take advantage of others. Generous employers will take to heart their employees' welfare and the community's well-being and act accordingly.

Yirah (Awe and Reverence): We are not to oppress, but are to have yirah or "fear God" (Leviticus 25:17). If we deceive others in our day-to-day business interactions, it's not as if no one knows. God knows and God sees. Doing wrong will catch up with us one way or another.

Where Do I Go From Here?

The realm of business ethics, as you have begun to explore, extends far beyond businesses themselves. In class, you will participate in activities that illuminate the texts you have studied and emphasize the roles of communities, investors, and employees, as well as the business owners themselves. When you finish this unit, you should begin to look at the business world in a new way, with Jewish eyes that see all of the angles. Remember these angles when you are faced with business-related decisions.

Books and Articles

Blumberg, Paul. *The Predatory Society: Deception in the American Marketplace*. New York: Oxford University Press, 1989.

Glazer, Myron Peretz, and Penina Migdal Glazer. *The Whistleblowers: Exposing Corruption in Government and Industry*. New York: BasicBooks, a division of HarperCollins Publishers, 1989.

Herring, Basil F. "Truth in the Marketplace." In *Jewish Ethics and Halakhah for Our Time, Volume II*. Hoboken, NJ: KTAV Publishing House, Inc. and NY: Yeshiva University Press, 1989.

Levine, Aaron, and Moses Pava, eds. *Case Studies in Jewish Business Ethics*. Hoboken, NJ: KTAV Publishing House, Inc. and NY: Yeshiva University Press, 2000.

Pava, Moses L. *Business Ethics: A Jewish Perspective*. Hoboken, NJ: KTAV Publishing House, Inc., and New York: Yeshiva University Press, 1997.

Pomerantz, Gayle, and David Stern. "Employee Rights in a Situation of Dismissal." In *Reform Jewish Ethics and the Halakhah*, ed. by Eugene B. Borowitz. New Jersey: Behrman House, Inc., 1988.

Reich, Robert B. *The Future of Success*. New York: Alfred A. Knopf, 2001.

Repa, Barbara Kate. *Your Rights in the Workplace*. Berkeley, CA: Nolo Press, 1999.

Straus, Livia Selmanowitz. "Jewish Business Ethics: Teaching toward Moral Living." In *Jewish Education News* 20, No. 1, Spring 1999.

Tamari, Meir. *The Challenge of Wealth: A Jewish Perspective on Earning and Spending Money*. Northvale, NJ: Jason Aronson Inc., 1995.

———. *In the Marketplace: Jewish Business Ethics*. Southfield, MI: Targum/Feldheim, 1991.

———. *With All Your Possessions*. Northvale, NJ: Jason Aronson Inc., 1998.

Web Sites
Sites related to business ethics:

Business Ethics – Corporate Social Responsibility Report: www.business-ethics.com
> *A magazine promoting ethical business practices. Publishes an annual list of the 100 best Corporate Citizens.*

Corporate Social Responsibility News: www.csrnews.com
> *An international news service dedicated to the publication and distribution of corporate social responsibility news.*

Department of Labor (of the United States Government): www.dol.gov
> *The Department of Labor fosters and promotes the welfare of all workers through a wide range of programs and policies.*

International Business Ethics Institute (IBEI): www.business-ethics.org
> *"Fostering Global business practices which promote equitable economic development, resource sustainability, and just forms of government."*

International Labor Organization: www.ilo.org
> *A United Nations agency which seeks the promotion of social justice and internationally recognized human and labor rights.*

Environmental organizations that have concerns that relate to business ethics:

Clean Water Action: www.cleanwater.gov
> *A government organization responsible for restoring and protecting America's watersheds.*

Environmental Defense Fund: www.edf.org
> *A leading national nonprofit organization linking science, economics, and law to create innovative, equitable, and cost-effective solutions to our society's most urgent environmental problems.*

Environmental Protection Agency: www.epa.gov
The U.S. governmental agency whose mission is to protect human health and safeguard the natural environment — air, water, and land — on which life depends.

Greenpeace: www.greenpeace.org
Greenpeace is an international non-profit organization that focuses on the most crucial worldwide threats to our planet's biodiversity and environment.

Films

Some sections of the following films may be valuable for illustrating certain aspects of the Ethics of Business, but other parts may not be appropriate. Check with teachers or parents before viewing.

A Civil Action (1998, 115 minutes, rated PG-13)
The true story of a lawyer who brings a case against two large corporations for their polluting practices. Available from video stores.

Erin Brockovich (2000, 130 minutes, rated R)
The true story of a legal assistant who almost single-handedly brings down a California power company accused of polluting a community's water supply. Available from video stores.

The Insider (1999, 157 minutes, rated R)
The true story of Jeffrey Wigand, who after being fired from his top level job with a tobacco company, turns whistle-blower, claiming his employers lied about the dangers of cigarettes. Available from video stores.

Norma Rae (1979, 114 minutes, rated PG)
The story of a southern textile worker employed in a factory with intolerable working conditions. She struggles to unionize the workers in order to protect their rights. Available from video stores.

Silkwood (1983, 131 minutes, rates R)
The true story of Karen Silkwood, a worker in a nuclear power facility who might have been murdered to prevent her from exposing dangerous conditions at the power plant. Available from video stores.

Wall Street (1987, 125 minutes, rated R)
A young and impatient Wall Street stockbroker is willing to do anything to get to the top. Available from video stores.

Glossary

Dina de'Malchuta Dina
"The law of the land is the law."

Efah
Ancient weight measurement. (Merchants must insure weights are accurate.)

G'nay-vah
Thievery; taking in secret

G'nay-vat Da'at
"Stealing another's mind;" deception.

G'zay-lah
Robbery; taking by force.

Hin
Ancient weight measurement. (Merchants must ensure weights are accurate.)

Lifnay Evare
"In front of a blind person" (Leviticus 25:36). One party provides the means to sin or gives unsuitable advice to someone who is "blind" to the full consequences or implications of a transaction. (The means to sin or unsuitable advice are kinds of "stumbling blocks.")

Ona'ah
Exploitation; withholding important information.

Ona'at Devarim
Verbal exploitation.

CHAPTER 6
THE DEATH PENALTY

Overview

Can people do something so wrong, so horrifying that they deserve to die? Those who support the death penalty would say yes. People who commit a violent, murderous act may forfeit their life. Society demands and victims' families deserve this response. In addition, within many religious traditions, including Judaism, one can find support for the death penalty.

Death penalty opponents believe a government should not punish criminals by executing them. Abolitionists (death penalty opponents) argue against the death penalty on several fronts, including the general immorality of killing, especially when there are alternative punishments. They claim the death penalty does not realize many of its intended objectives, such as deterring other would-be offenders or providing "closure" for grieving family members. Furthermore, grave injustices exist.

Jewish abolitionists say death penalty supporters interpret our religious sources too narrowly. That is, necessary conditions for a death sentence effectively eliminated the possibility that such a penalty would ever take place.

It might seem the ethical choice is this: You are either for the death penalty or against it. That is, you either believe it is permissible to punish another person by executing him/her or you believe that killing criminals is wrong. However, a compromise perspective may exist. This position would forbid the death penalty except in the rarest of instances, for the most heinous of crimes.

Jewish Perspectives

What Offenses Warrant the Death Penalty?

Biblical law mandated the death penalty for 36 offenses, including murder, kidnapping, adultery, incest, certain instances of rape, idol worship, public incitement to apostasy (worshiping other gods), disrespecting parents, and desecrating

Shabbat. Over the centuries, however, Judaism has severely restricted death sentences and they were rarely carried out.

Why Punish and Why the Death Penalty?

The objectives of punishment are what a community intends to gain or accomplish through imposing a particular sentence. Jewish attitudes toward various objectives have continually evolved, but have included, at various periods of time, the realignment of God with creation, retribution, deterrence,[1] restoring the moral order of society, and "special prevention." Each of these objectives will be discussed in the following five sections.

Realignment of God with Creation

God demands that human beings behave in certain defined ways. Criminal acts transgress God's will, God's blueprint for an ethical society. From the Bible's perspective, executing violators of God's laws helps make amends, helps "realign us" with God. Being "realigned with God" means we recommit as a society to living rightly.

Additionally, the Bible taught that besides offending God, a murderer "offended" the land itself. Executing a "blood spiller" made expiation for contaminating the land: "The land will not be purged of the blood that has been shed upon it except through the blood of the one who shed it" (Numbers 35:33).

Today, many find this objective to be an unconvincing justification for executions, and most Jews recognize that we can fulfill the objective of realigning God with creation through other punishments. Effective courts of justice can mark certain crimes as abhorrent by imposing stiff prison sentences, fines, and other non-lethal punishments.

Retribution

"An eye for an eye" retribution is known as *lex talionis*. This objective maintains that people should get what they deserve. The basic logic is this: If I inflict on you the same injury that you inflicted on me, we're "even." Rabbis in the post-biblical period allowed monetary compensation for injuries (e.g., a fine rather than an actual eye for an eye). With murder, as opposed to injury, "making things even" gets more complicated. According to Jewish sources, in the case of murder it is more difficult to accept compensation. As we read in Genesis, "Whoever sheds the blood of humankind, by humankind shall that one's blood be shed, for in God's image did God make humankind" (Genesis 9:6). Still, the Rabbis made it very difficult to carry out the death penalty, imposing conditions that seem nearly impossible to fulfill (see "By What Authority — A Sentence of Death?" below).

Deterrence

In several instances, after pronouncing a death penalty for a particular offense, the Bible adds, "All will hear and be afraid." (Deuteronomy 17:13, 19:20, and 21:21). The objective of deterrence is preventing others from committing offenses. That is, if you know so-and-so was executed for a crime, and you're thinking of committing a similar act, you won't do it since you could be executed for such a crime, as well. In reality, however, deterrence is a faulty justification for the death penalty as the claim that capital punishment deters other would-be offenders has not been proven.

Restoring the Moral Order of Society

Judaism holds that living according to God's will reinforces the moral order of the universe. Unlawful acts, such as murder, threaten the moral order. Too much crime can undermine and unravel civilization. The Bible declares, "Put away evil from your midst" (Deuteronomy 17:7, 12; 19:19; 21:21; 22:24; 22:27). Most Jews today agree that punishing criminals can help restore the moral order of society, but question the necessity of killing a criminal to realize this objective. Other punishments can be equally as effective and ethically more justifiable.

Special Prevention

Special prevention means cutting off known criminals before they strike again, possibly in more lethal ways. In other words, by executing "mid-level" criminals, such as burglars, we prevent them from committing further and possibly worse crimes, such as murder. A death sentence decisively prevents an offender from committing future crimes. Mainstream Jewish thinkers today do not support killing individuals for crimes they may or may not commit in the future. Rather than putting criminals to death, we can restrain them in alternate ways.

By What Authority — A Sentence of Death?

These were necessary conditions for imposing a death sentence in the days of the Temple:

1. A case was decided by a court of twenty-three judges.
2. The offender had to receive a warning before committing the crime (hatra'ah).
3. Two eyewitnesses had to observe the offender in the act (edut mechuvenet).
4. Witnesses had to be impeccably qualified and able to withstand severe cross-examination.[2]

Alternatively, the king could pass a death sentence. This might happen if the courts were unable or unwilling to impose capital punishment, even when overwhelming evidence pointed to the suspect's guilt.

Since the days of the Mishnah, Sages have debated the legitimacy of death sentences. Some claim that today, without the Sanhedrin and the unbroken chain of ordained judges, or without a king, a death sentence is no longer a permissible response to murder.[3] Others suggest today's judicial authorities have sufficient credentials for declaring death sentences.

In short, these are three possibilities, given the modern societies in which Jews live:

1. Permitting only the highest, most scrupulous courts to pronounce death sentences.
2. Banning the death penalty under all circumstances.
3. Imposing alternative sentences.

(The second and third possibility are not mutually exclusive. That is, we could ban the death penalty, but still impose an alternative sentence.)

The Death Penalty in America and Israel

Those dedicated to Judaism's values and laws cannot support frequent and liberal use of the death penalty. In rare instances, a Jewish opinion may legitimately defend a particular death sentence imposed by the American courts. But overall, mainstream Jewish leaders and scholars criticize the death penalty in America as being terribly flawed and misguided.

The modern state of Israel, in the first 50 years of its existence, carried out one death sentence. The offender was the Nazi master of genocide, Adolf Eichmann. In 1954, Israel passed the Penal Law Revision (Abolition of the Death penalty for Murder). The country retained the death penalty, however, for crimes of genocide and for treason committed in times of actual warfare.

General Perspectives

What Offenses Warrant the Death Penalty?

As of the early part of the 21st century, Federal courts and most, but not all, American states allowed death sentences. In contrast, most democracies around the world, including Canada, Australia, and the nations of the European Union, have abolished the death penalty. In American states that do allow the death penalty, various types of homicide may be considered capital crimes: murder carried out during the commission of a felony (e.g., while robbing a store); murder of a peace officer, corrections employee, or firefighter engaged in the performance of official duties; murder by an inmate serving a life sentence; and murder for hire (contract murder).[4]

Abolitionists are those who oppose executions, believing that no offense warrants the death penalty. Some countries, including Israel, are abolitionist for ordinary crimes only (such as murder, kidnapping, and rape). They allow the death penalty, but only for very limited crimes.

Why Punish and Why the Death Penalty?

As we learned above, some democratic societies retain the death penalty. We elaborate on these objectives in the following five sections: retribution, "closure," deterrence, restoring the moral order of society, and special prevention.

Retribution

People in favor of the death penalty do not see execution as "murder" but as punishment. They consider retribution a justifiable objective, and distinguish it from revenge. Revenge is associated with a desire that the wrongdoer truly suffer for his/her evil act. While retribution is a desire to uphold society's values.

Death penalty opponents, on the other hand, believe that capital punishment is an extreme response to crime. Thus, by its very nature, executing someone is as much about revenge as retribution.

Closure

The logic of "closure" is that when a murderer is put to death, family members and living victims will breathe a sigh of relief, knowing that the criminal is dead. The problem is that the closure objective often falls short. Victims may feel some satisfaction when the criminal dies, but an execution doesn't make grief and pain simply disappear. While death penalty supporters may invoke "closure" as a worthy objective, death penalty opponents choose to focus on reducing violence and offering support to those who grieve for their lost loved ones.

Deterrence

In theory, the logic of deterrence is reasonable: We'll execute this one really bad guy and make sure everyone hears about it. The horror of being put to death will be such a frightening prospect that would-be killers will think twice about getting involved in crime. Better yet, they will realize that a life of crime is not worth it and will turn to more productive ways of living.

The problem with deterrence is there is no reliable evidence of its effectiveness. States with the death penalty have higher crime rates than those without. Democratic countries that have abolished the death penalty have lower crime rates than does the United States, which has retained it. No significant changes in crime and murder rates appear when states either abolish capital punishment or institute it.[5] And police chiefs asked to rank the factors that, in their judgment, reduce the rate of violent crime, put the death penalty last. Law enforcement professionals often favor such other deterrents to violent crime as curbing drug use, putting more officers on the street, longer sentences, and gun control.

Restoring the Moral Order of Society

Advocates of the death penalty may claim it helps us define and commit to what our society holds to be right, moral, and lawful. With capital punishment we are making the important statement that we distance ourselves from evil, embrace civilized values, and affirm an uncompromising dedication to justice and order.

Abolitionists, on the other hand, view executions as violent public spectacles. They believe governments should not encourage official homicide as the solution to social problems.

Special Prevention

The death penalty conclusively prevents a proven criminal from ever again becoming a menace to society. But a relatively new sentencing provision in which a convicted murderer is sentenced to "life without parole" may fulfill the same objective. Many who might support death penalty would opt instead for "life without parole" when this alternate sentence is available.

Who Gets the Death Penalty and By What Authority?

Statistics show the death penalty is ridden with inconsistencies, prejudices, and mistakes. The American judicial system has imposed the death penalty disproportionately upon those whose victims are white, upon offenders who are people of color, and upon people who are poor and uneducated.[6] Furthermore, some question the policies of jury selection. Allowing the execution of minors and mentally retarded people is especially controversial.

Most troubling are cases of mistaken convictions. One study of the death penalty in America found that over a 23-year period the national error rate in death penalty cases was 68%. That means two out of three convictions were problematic. Incompetent representation and prosecutorial misconduct were the most common errors.[7] No

one can correct or undo the consequences of the death penalty — they are final and irreversible.

Staking Out Positions

A defensible position exists within Judaism that accepts the death penalty in principle. However, most Jewish communities, for most of Jewish history, did not apply the death penalty. Thus, in practice, capital punishment rarely took place. Though the death penalty remains legal in 21st century America, an abolitionist movement is strengthening. The likelihood of fulfilling many commonly cited death penalty objectives is highly questionable.

For modern nations, two death penalty positions are consistent with Jewish thinking: One is that it should be wholly abolished. The other is that it should happen only on the rarest of occasions, by impeccably thorough courts, and for the most heinous of crimes (such as genocide).

Summary of the Overview

- A defensible position exists within Judaism that accepts the death penalty *in principle*.

- However, most Jewish communities, for most of Jewish history, did not apply the death penalty. Thus, *in practice*, capital punishment rarely took place.

- Today, the likelihood of fulfilling many commonly cited death penalty objectives is highly questionable.

- For modern nations, two death penalty positions are consistent with Jewish thinking: One is that it should be wholly abolished. The other is that it should happen only on the rarest of occasions, by impeccably thorough courts, and for the most heinous of crimes (such as genocide).

Scenarios: How Things Have Changed

For centuries, the death penalty question has been fraught with controversy. Do we really fulfill our intended objectives with the death penalty? Can we justify responding to violent crime by executing the offenders? These are difficult philosophical questions, and those on both sides of the debate hold strong opinions and deep convictions.

Below are two imaginary scenarios, one set in ancient days, and the other in contemporary times. They are intended to stimulate thought and spark discussion. Read each scenario and reflect, either individually or in group discussion, on the questions in the "For Thought and Discussion" secdtion that follows. Then continue on to the "Text Study" section to see what Jewish and other sources have to say about our topic. Finally, you may wish to come back and answer the questions a second time to see if your views have changed.

Scenario I: Adapted from the Talmud, Sanhedrin 37b, around 500 C.E.

A shepherd sat under a tree, on the side of a hill, tending his flock of sheep. Suddenly two men ran past. Ya'akov was chasing another man. The chase led the two men into some ruins. The shepherd got up and quickly followed them. By the time the shepherd got to the entrance of the ruin, Yaakov was coming out. In his hand he held a bloody sword. Just inside the ruins, on the ground was the other man, wounded and writhing, taking his last breaths of life.

The shepherd exclaimed to Ya'akov, "How wicked you are! Who slew this man? It is either me or you. Obviously, you're the murderer! Yet you know the courts won't be able to convict you since two witnesses didn't actually see you kill him" (Deuteronomy 17:6).

The shepherd continued, "But God knows what you did, Ya'akov. The courts might not be able to get you, but God will set things right. A killer eventually gets what he deserves."

The shepherd began to turn away from the murderer to go get help when a snake appeared. It bit the murderer so that he died.

Scenario II: Nowadays

The court was called to order to try Ms. Jackson for murder. A witness stood for questioning. She was asked to explain what she had seen regarding an incident that left a woman dead.

The witness explained: "I was sitting in my car outside QuickStop, a gas station with a convenience store. My friend and I had stopped to pick up a few things. Before we left, my friend decided to run across the street to buy a doughnut. So, I was alone in my car. As I looked out, I saw the gas station attendant with the defendant, Ms. Jackson. It looked as if the attendant was helping Ms. Jackson with one of the gasoline pumps. Suddenly, Ms. Jackson seemed to be pushing the attendant back toward the store. I looked closer; Ms. Jackson had a knife in her hand. I quickly dialed 911 on my cell phone, then got out of my car. As I took a few steps toward the store, Ms. Jackson was running out with a bloodied knife in her hand. The attendant lay just inside the doorway. She had a huge wound across her chest and was dying."

The trial continued with prosecutors presenting a few other important pieces of testimony against Ms. Jackson. These included the absence of an alibi for her whereabouts at the time of the murder, and documentation of a recent knife purchase she made. Still, the QuickStop witness's testimony was the central evidence against Ms. Jackson. The jury returned a guilty verdict. A sentencing jury would decide the punishment. Because the murder took place in a state that allows death penalty, jury members could consider it if sufficient aggravating circumstances were found.

For Thought and Discussion:

What does Ya'akov's crime seem to be?

Could a Jewish court convict Ya'akov and impose the death sentence? Explain.

What does Ms. Jackson's crime seem to be?

Would it be appropriate for a modern Jewish court to convict Ms. Jackson and impose the death sentence? Explain.

Text Study

The ethics of the death penalty raise many difficult questions. Jewish and other textual sources provide helpful responses, but these responses often highlight tensions between opposing considerations. The chart below poses the questions and offers two opposing points of view. Text sources supporting each of these points of view follow.

1. **Is the death penalty a legitimate punishment?**

On the One Hand:

It is appropriate to consider capital punishment for the perpetrator of certain crimes.

A. The Bible is the earliest Jewish source to mention death penalty, with biblical law mandating death penalty for thirty-six offenses. Rabbinic and later sources add provisions and restrictions.

> He that strikes a man, so that he dies, is to be put to death, yes, death . . . When a man schemes against his neighbor, to kill him with cunning, you shall take him away from My altar, to die (Exodus 21:12, 14).

B. Authorities could defend the death penalty because of the "needs of the time" (*Sanhedrin* 46a):

> A court may execute one not subject to the death penalty. This would not be in violation of the Torah but to protect it. Thus, if the court recognizes that the people willfully ignore the law, the court may issue special decrees to strengthen the law as it sees fit. This is by way of a temporary decree, not as a permanent statute for all generations . . . Such was the case of the man who rode a horse on the Sabbath . . . and was stoned, and such was the case when [*Sanhedrin* 45b] Shimon ben Shetach hanged eighty women on one day, even though there was no proper cross-examination, warning, or unequivocal evidence. He acted by way

of a temporary measure as he saw fit (Maimonides, *Mishneh Torah, Hilchot Sanhedrin* 24:4).

C. If there are murderers who are not subject to the death penalty, then an Israelite king may execute them by his royal prerogative and by reason of societal need, if he so wishes. Likewise if a court wishes to execute such a person as a temporary measure, it may do so if such are the needs of the hour (Maimonides, *Mishneh Torah, Hilchot Rotzayach* 2:4).

On the Other Hand:

The death penalty is so severe, so final that to carry it out should be very difficult, if not impossible.

a. A Sanhedrin that passes the death penalty once in seven years is called a violent court. Rabbi Eleazar ben Azariah says that this is true of a court that passes such a sentence even once in seventy years. Rabbi Tarfon and Rabbi Akiva say, "Had we been members of the Sanhedrin, no one would ever have been executed" (*Makkot* 1:10).

b. If anyone kills a person, the murderer may be murdered only on the evidence of witnesses; the testimony of a single witness against a person shall not suffice for a sentence of death (Numbers 35:30).

c. A death sentence passed by a court of twenty-three judges required full compliance with due process. Necessary conditions included *hatra'ah*, i.e., warning the culprit before the crime, and *edut mechuvenet*, i.e., impeccably qualified witnesses able to withstand severe cross-examination. (Basil F. Herring, *Jewish Ethics and Halakhah for Our Time*, p. 155. See Text Study #8b below for a related passage):

> Once the witnesses say, "We gave him due warning and we know him," the court gives [the witnesses] a solemn charge [regarding the gravity of their position] (Maimonides, *Mishneh Torah, Hilchot Sanhedrin* 12:3).

Evaluating the Death Penalty: Questions to Consider

The Question	On the One Hand	On the Other Hand
1. Is the death penalty a legitimate punishment? (see page 80)	It is appropriate to consider capital punishment for the perpetrator of certain crimes.	The death penalty is so severe, so final, that to carry it out should be very difficult, if not impossible.
2. Can we enforce the death penalty meaningfully and effectively? (see page 82)	There are procedures and methods for executing criminals.	Whatever the method, the fact is that executions turn the state into a killer.
3. Is retribution a legitimate objective for the death penalty? (see page 83)	The death penalty is retributive justice — giving criminals what they deserve (i.e., *lex talionis* or "an eye for an eye . . . ")	The death penalty only aggravates cycles of crime as it feeds a culture of violence.
4. Is the death penalty a deterrent for those who would consider committing violent crimes? (see page 84)	The possibility of receiving the death penalty will deter those who would commit violent crimes.	There is no evidence that the death penalty deters criminals from unlawful acts.
5. Does the death penalty help communities identify and recommit to moral values? (see page 85)	The death penalty restores the moral order of society, realigns the community with God, and lifts a vile contamination from the land.	Alternative punishments can achieve the same goals.
6. Does the process preceding and surrounding an execution contribute to teshuvah (restitution and repentance)? (see page 86)	Being put to death serves as expiation (compensation) for a murderer.	The death penalty prevents rehabilitation and thwarts teshuvah (restitution and repentance).
7. How are the victims' loved ones affected by the execution of the offending criminal? (see page 87)	Once the perpetrator is executed, the victim's family finally can experience a well-deserved sense of "closure" to their tragedy.	Putting the criminal to death won't bring back a loved one.
8. Do democracies that continue to enforce the death penalty have reliable standards? (see page 88)	The American judicial system requires reasonable standards for imposing the death penalty.	Mistakes, unreliable witnesses, incompetent lawyers and judges, biased juries, and racial and economic discrimination make the death penalty a gross distortion of justice.

d. They used to examine [the witnesses] with seven inquiries: In what Sabbatical year [of the Jubilee did the crime occur]? In what year [of the seven year cycle]? In what month? On what date of the month? On what day [of the week]? In what place [was the suspect observed committing the crime]? Rabbi Yosi says: [They need only ask] on what day, in what hour, and in what place. [Also witnesses were asked]: Do you know him? Did you warn him? Is he an idolater? Whom does he worship? What is the manner of his worship?

The more [a judge] examines, the more praiseworthy he is. It once happened that ben Zakkai probed the evidence regarding the stalks of fig trees (*Sanhedrin* 5:1-2).

e. It is a Scriptural decree that the court shall not put a man to death or flog him on his own admission (of guilt) (Maimonides, *Mishneh Torah, Hilchot Sanhedrin* 18:6).

f. "You shall do no unrighteousness in judgment" (Leviticus 19:15). This refers to the judge who perverts judgment, acquits the guilty, and condemns the innocent. It also refers to the judge who delays judgment, who discusses at undue length things that are obvious in order to annoy one of the parties to the suit. He too is included among the unrighteous. (Maimonides, *Mishneh Torah, Hilchot Sanhedrin* 20:6)

g. It is clear that with such a procedure [restrictions and provisions imposed by the Rabbis], conviction in capital cases was next to impossible, and that this was the intention of the framers of the rules is equally plain (George Foot Moore, *Judaism*, Harvard University Press, 1927, Vol. II, p. 186).

What Do You Think?

Many Jewish texts discuss the conditions necessary for imposing the death penalty. However, if we were to consult only the texts above, what would we find the Jewish attitude toward death penalty to be — in favor, not in

favor, somewhere in between? Explain.

Once the death penalty is "on the books" (as it is in the Bible), authorities must decide how and when to apply it. Do you agree with the decisions presented in the texts above? Why or why not?

2. **Can we enforce the death penalty meaningfully and effectively?**

On the One Hand:

There are procedures and methods for executing criminals.

A. And you shall come unto the priests, the Levites, and unto the judge that shall be in those days; and you shall inquire and they shall declare unto you the sentence of judgment (Deuteronomy 17:9).

B. Bat Tali, the daughter of a priest, had illicit sexual relations. Rabbi Chama bar Tuvia wrapped her in branches and burned her to death. Said Rabbi Joseph, "Rabbi Chama thereby erred doubly. He contradicted Rabbi Matna [in using that particular mode of execution], and he contradicted the Beraita that says . . . that capital punishment occurs only when there is a priest [and Sanhedrin functioning in the Temple] (*Sanhedrin* 52b).

C. See also Text Study #1b-e above.

On the Other Hand:

Whatever the method, the fact is that executions turn the state into a killer.

a. In all the lands of my acquaintance, the death penalty is not practiced, except here in Spain. When I arrived here, I was most surprised that this was done without a Sanhedrin. I was told that it was by way of a royal dispensation utilized by the Jewish court to save lives that would be lost were they to be left to Gentile courts. And while I permitted them to maintain this practice, I never agreed with their taking of life in such a fashion (Rosh, *Responsum* 17:8).

b. In the late 1990's SueZann Bosler declared that if the state killed the man who killed her father.

> We become murderers, too. We become just like him. I don't want to be like him. I don't want his blood on my hands (Robert Jay Lifton and Greg Mitchell, *Who Owns Death*, p. 212).

(For a related passage from a Jewish source, see Text Study #8b below.)

c. See also Text Study #3e below.

What Do You Think?

How would the authors of each of the texts above respond to the statement that the death penalty turns the state into a killer? What do you believe?

Which argument from the texts do you find most compelling? Why?

⇒◆⇐

3. **Is retribution a legitimate objective for the death penalty?**

On the One Hand:

The death penalty is retributive justice — giving criminals what they deserve (i.e., *lex talionis* or "an eye for an eye . . . ")

A. But if harm should occur, then you are to give life in place of life — eye for eye, tooth for tooth, hand for hand, foot for foot, burnt-scar for burnt-scar, wound for wound, bruise for bruise (Exodus 14:23-25).

B. Certain crimes constitute such outrageous violation of human and moral values that they demand retribution. It was to control the natural human impulse to seek revenge and, more broadly, to give expression to deeply held views that some conduct deserves punishment, that criminal laws, administered by the state, were established. The rule of law does not eliminate feelings of outrage but does provide controlled channels for expressing such feelings . . . The death penalty's retributive function thus vindicates the fundamental moral principle that a criminal should receive his or her just desserts. Through the provision of just punishment, capital punishment affirms the sanctity of human life and thereby protects it (Statement of Paul G. Cassell, Associate Professor of Law, University of Utah, Salt Lake City, before the Senate Judiciary Committee, April 1, 1993).

On the Other Hand:

The death penalty only aggravates cycles of crime as it feeds a culture of violence.

a. Forty years prior to the destruction of the Second Temple, the Sanhedrin moved from the Temple and met in the marketplace, so as not to judge capital cases. What was the reason? Because they recognized the proliferation of capital crimes which they were unable to judge properly, thus they relocated so as not to pass the death sentence (*Avodah Zarah* 8b).

b. The Bible is clear: *midah keneged midah*, measure should be met with like measure. Yet a lifetime sentence without probation, which is appropriate for murder in the first degree, provides a severe enough punishment that can be equated with the death penalty. After all, money can never replace an eye either, yet for the sake of justice our rabbis were willing and able to make moral equivalencies (Elie Spitz, "The Jewish Tradition and Capital Punishment" in *Contemporary Jewish Ethics and Morality*, p. 344, 346-347).

c. Some would argue that the death penalty will teach society at large the seriousness of crime. Yet we say that teaching people to respond to violence with violence will, again, only breed more violence. (A Joint Statement, To End the Death Penalty, by the National Jewish/Catholic Consultation [co-sponsored by the National Council of Synagogues and the Bishops' Committee for Ecumenical and Interreligious Affairs of the National Conference of Catholic Bishops], December 3, 1999).

d. Executions are bad for our minds because of their effect on our violent and vengeful impulses . . . Capital vengeance, the principle of "a death for a death," sustains and legitimates those violent impulses. It encourages us to remain "stuck" in them rather than transforming them into constructive advocacies and actions (Robert Jay Lifton and Greg Mitchell, *Who Owns Death*, p. 236).

e. With each new death penalty statute enacted and each execution carried out, our executive, judicial, and legislative branches, at both the state and federal level, add to a culture of violence and killing. With each person executed, we're teaching our children that the way to settle scores is through violence, even to the point of taking a human life (Statement of Senator Russell Feingold, on introducing the Federal Death Penalty Abolition Act of 1999 [S. 1917] before the Senate, November 10, 1999).

What Do You Think?

Which of these texts, in your opinion, most accurately articulates the advantages of making the punishment equal in gravity to the crime? What about the disadvantages?

To what extent should retribution ("getting back at the bad guy") be a consideration in coming up with an appropriate punishment for a criminal?

⇒◆⇐

4. **Is the death penalty a deterrent for those who would consider committing violent crimes?**

On the One Hand:

The possibility of receiving the death penalty will deter those who would commit violent crimes.

A. See passage #1a above. That passage continues with these words:

> Rabbi Shimon ben Gamaliel says, "[By

avoiding all capital punishment, as do Rabbi Tarfon and Rabbi Akiva] they would have caused a proliferation of murderers in Israel" (*Makkot* 1:10).

B. If those who testified are false witnesses, if they have testified falsely against their fellow, you shall do to them as they schemed to do to their fellow. Thus you will sweep out evil from your midst; others will hear and be afraid, and such evil things will not again be done in your midst. Nor must you show pity: life for life, eye for eye, tooth for tooth, hand for hand, foot for foot (Deuteronomy 19:18-21).

C. Whether or not capital punishment will deter others, it definitely will prevent the offender him/herself from committing further crimes. (This idea is known as "special prevention.")

> As for a "stubborn and rebellious son" (Deuteronomy 21:18-21) he must be put to death because of what he will become, for necessarily he will murder later on. "He that kidnaps" (Exodus 21:16) likewise must be punished in this manner, for he exposed him to death. Also "he that comes breaking in" (Exodus 22:1), for he too is prepared to kill, as [the Sages], may their memory be blessed, have explained. These three, I mean a stubborn and rebellious son, a kidnapper, and a thief, will become shedders of blood (Maimonides, *Guide of the Perplexed*, 3:41).

D. If the death penalty can deter one murder of an innocent life or if it can make a statement to the community about what will and will not be tolerated, then it is justified (Statement of James C. Anders, Solicitor, Fifth Judicial Circuit of South Carolina, before the Senate Judiciary Committee, September 19, 1989).

On the Other Hand:

There is no evidence that the death penalty deters criminals from unlawful acts.

a. In a climate of increasing crime, the Sanhedrin moved its meeting site away from where it could proclaim death sentences. The court wasn't prepared to put so many people to death. Perhaps they understood that executing criminals does not necessarily deter other would-be offenders. Such punishments may only add to an environment of violence. (See also #3a above.)

b. Some would argue that the death penalty is needed as a deterrent to crime. Yet the studies that lie behind our statements over the years have yet to reveal any objective evidence to justify this conclusion. Criminals tend to believe they will escape any consequences for their behavior, or simply do not think of consequences at all, so an escalation of consequences is usually irrelevant to their state of mind at the time of the crime (A Joint Statement, To End the Death Penalty, by the National Jewish/Catholic Consultation [co-sponsored by the National Council of Synagogues and the Bishops' Committee for Ecumenical and Interreligious Affairs of the National Conference of Catholic Bishops], December 3, 1999).

c. Following the logic of death penalty supporters who believe it's a deterrent, you would think that our European allies, who don't use the death penalty, would have a higher murder rate than the United States. Yet, they don't and it's not even close. In fact, the murder rate in the United States is six times higher than the murder rate in Britain, seven times higher than in France, five times higher than in Australia, and five times higher than in Sweden. [In America] during the period 1995-1998, Texas [the highest-percentage death penalty user] had a murder rate that [was] nearly double the murder rate in Wisconsin [death penalty-free for nearly 150 years] (Statement of Senator Russell Feingold, on introducing the Federal Death Penalty Abolition Act of 1999 [S. 1917] before the Senate, November 10, 1999).

d. I have inquired for most of my adult life about studies that might show that the death penalty is a deterrent. And I have not seen any research that would substantiate that point (Attorney General Janet Reno, at a Justice Department news briefing, 2000).

What Do You Think?

Which texts do you find more convincing: those that would claim death penalty deters others from criminal acts, or those what would disagree with that conclusion?

Is proven deterrence an important justification for death penalty? Is proven deterrence a necessary justification? Explain.

---

5. **Does the death penalty help communities identify and recommit to moral values?**

On the One Hand:

The death penalty restores the moral order of society, realigns the community with God, and lifts a vile contamination from the land.

A. You are not to corrupt the land that you are in, for the blood — it will corrupt the land, and the land will not be purged of the blood that has been shed upon it except through the blood of the one who shed it (Numbers 35:33).

B. Punishment (which includes the death penalty) expresses the emotions of the society wronged, the anger and outrage felt, and it solidifies and reinforces the goals, values, and norms of acceptable behavior in the society . . . (Statement of James C. Anders, Solicitor, Fifth Judicial Circuit of South Carolina, before the Senate Judiciary Committee, September 19, 1989).

On the Other Hand:

Alternative punishments can achieve the same goals.

a. There is an established procedure, one which we follow in practice, whereby a person who is guilty of a crime for which the punishment is death is instead excommunicated and whipped, and never given an opportunity for pardon. The reason is that today we no longer carry out the death penalty (Maimonides, Commentary on the Mishnah, *Chullin* 1).

b. There are three overarching objectives for punishment to be found in the Bible: the realignment of God with creation, retribution, and deterrence . . . We live in a time with a punitive option which our tradition lacked, namely, prisons. This new factor plus [several] practical considerations constitute a moral challenge to the death penalty in our current U.S. penal system . . . Prisons today do meet the three goals of execution in the Bible (Elie Spitz, "The Jewish Tradition and Capital Punishment" in *Contemporary Jewish Ethics and Morality,"* p. 344, 346-347).

c. See also Text Study #3b above.

What Do You Think?

Do the texts about alternative punishments convince you that they achieve the same goal as the death penalty? Why or why not?

Do you agree with the statement that the death penalty restores the moral order of society, realigns the community with God, and lifts a vile contamination from the land? Explain.

6. **Does the process preceding and surrounding an execution contribute to teshuvah (restitution and repentance)?**

On the One Hand:

Being put to death serves as expiation (compensation) for a murderer.

A. When he was about ten cubits from the place of stoning they would say to him: "Make confession," for it was the custom of those condemned to death to make confession, and all who confess have a share in the World To Come . . . And if the condemned does not know how to make confession, they say to him, "Repeat these words: 'May my death be an atonement for all my sins.'" Rabbi Yehudah says, "If he knew he had been sentenced through false evidence, he says, 'Let my death be an atonement for all my sins except this sin.'" [The Sages] said to [Rabbi Yehudah], "If that were what he would say, then every convicted criminal would say likewise to exonerate himself" (*Sanhedrin* 6:2).

B. Notwithstanding the high regard for humanity, the cherished value of every unique individual, and the great love that we have for every individual made in the image of God, even those condemned to death . . . nonetheless an evil person cannot be permitted to remain alive, for by his death he gains atonement, even as he is removed from life (Rabinowitz-Teomim, *Mishpetei Nefashot*, p. 48-49 as quoted by Basil Herring, Jewish *Ethics and Halakhah for Our Time,* p. 157).

On the Other Hand:

The death penalty prevents rehabilitation and thwarts teshuvah (restitution and repentance).

a. Judaism expects a person to make ongoing efforts to repent. Traditionally, a Jew recites the "Amidah" prayer three times each weekday. The prayer includes these passages:

> Our Parent, bring us back to Your Torah. Our Ruler, draw us near to Your service. Lead us back to You, truly repentant. Praised are You, Eternal who welcomes repentance.

> Forgive us, our Parent, for we have sinned; pardon us, our Ruler, for we have transgressed, for You forgive and pardon. Praised are You, Eternal who is gracious and forgiving.

> Behold our affliction and deliver us.

Redeem us soon because of Your mercy, for You are the mighty Redeemer. Praised are You, Eternal, Redeemer of the people Israel.

b. Justice didn't do a thing to heal me. Forgiveness did . . . I've seen mankind's idea of ultimate justice. I have more faith in God's . . . I want people to know that our hope for healing is not in the legal system (Debbie Morris, a woman raped and nearly murdered when she was sixteen, quoted in *Who Owns Death* by Robert Jay Lifton and Greg Mitchell, p. 207).

What Do You Think?

Do these texts provide a convincing argument that remaining alive provides worthwhile opportunities for a violent criminal to repent?

What do you believe is the most valuable way a murderer might receive expiation for his/her crime?

———◆———

7. **How are the victims' loved ones affected by the execution of the offending criminal?**

On the One Hand:

Once the perpetrator is executed, the victim's family finally can experience a well-deserved sense of "closure" to their tragedy.

A. We victims need a closure to our grief. I did not rejoice when Wallace Norrell was executed July 13, 1990, for murdering [my daughter] Quenette, but I certainly felt relief . . . (Statement of Miriam Shehane, State President, Victims of Crimes and Leniency, Montgomery, Alabama, before the Senate Judiciary Committee, April 1, 1993).

B. A mother in Ohio who had waited fifteen years for the killer of her two daughters to die claims:

[I would have] no problem injecting him (with lethal poison) myself. I could lie down and have a good night's sleep, knowing that justice had

been done (Robert Jay Lifton and Greg Mitchell, *Who Owns Death*, p. 199).

On the Other Hand:

Putting the criminal to death won't bring back a loved one.

a. See the passage written by Marie Deans, founder of Murder Victims' Families for Reconciliation above, in "Why Punish and Why the Death Penalty?" in the "General Perspectives" section above, page 77.

b. Betty Slusher refused to attend the execution of the killers of her husband in South Carolina in 1998:

I thought when this day came that I wouldn't be sad, that I would be happy, but I am sad. Let's face it, we're taking two men's lives (Robert Jay Lifton and Greg Mitchell, *Who Owns Death*, p. 202).

c. The words of a mother of a young girl murdered in Pennsylvania:

The gaping wound will never heal. And it is because of this intense pain that I have come to know that I would not, and could not, inflict it on another mother . . . Justice would only be served if, in taking his life, Aimee could come back to life, and that is impossible (Robert Jay Lifton and Greg Mitchell, *Who Owns Death*, p. 204).

d. The strongest argument [for death penalty] is the deep pain and grief of the families of victims and their quite natural desire to see punishment meted out to those who have plunged them into such agony. Yet it is the clear teaching of our traditions that this pain and suffering cannot be healed simply through the retribution of capital punishment or by vengeance. It is a difficult and long process of healing, which comes about through personal growth and God's grace. We agree that much more must be done by the religious community and by society at large to solace and care for the grieving families of the victims of violent crime (A Joint Statement, To End the Death Penalty, by the National Jewish/Catholic Consultation [co-sponsored by the National Council of Synagogues and the Bishops' Committee for Ecumenical and Interreligious Affairs of the National Conference of Catholic Bishops], December 3, 1999).

What Do You Think?

What do you think "closure" means as it relates to the death penalty? Look to the texts for guidance.

Why do you suppose families of victims might feel they would experience "closure" if the offender were executed?

Do you feel that the closure argument justifies the death penalty?

8. **Do democracies that continue to enforce the death penalty have reliable standards?**

On the One Hand:

The American judicial system requires reasonable standards for imposing the death penalty.

A. The Fifth Amendment provides that "no persons shall be held to answer for a capital crime, unless on a presentment of indictment of a Grand Jury . . . nor be deprived of life . . . without due process of law." This clearly permits the death penalty to be imposed and establishes beyond doubt that the death penalty is not one of the "cruel and unusual punishments" prohibited by the Eighth Amendment (From Justice Antonin Scalia's concurring opinion in the Supreme Court decision "Callins v. James" [510 U.S. 1141, 1994], denying review of the death penalty case (in response to Justice Blakmun's dissent).

B. The system imposes a vast array of due process protections to assure that no innocent person is convicted of a crime (Statement of Paul G. Cassell, Associate Professor of Law, University of Utah, Salt Lake City, before the Senate Judiciary Committee, April 1, 1993).

C. Lest we forget, in addition to the extensive appeals of the courts, every state with a capital punishment statute has a procedure for executive clemency . . . (Statement of Miriam Shehane, State President, Victims of Crimes and Leniency, Montgomery, Alabama, before the Senate Judiciary Committee, April 1, 1993).

On the Other Hand:

Mistakes, unreliable witnesses, incompetent lawyers and judges, biased juries, and racial and economic discrimination make the death penalty a gross distortion of justice.

a. You shall have one standard for stranger and citizen alike: for I the Eternal am your God (Leviticus 24:22).

b. In capital cases, authorities were to impress upon witnesses the gravity of their position. If witnesses' testimony were to cause an injustice:

> The blood of the accused and his unborn offspring stain the perjurer forever. Thus, in the case of Cain, Scripture says, "The voice of the bloods of your brother call to Me." Observe that the text reads in the plural — not "blood" but "bloods". For Abel's blood and that of his unborn seed were alike involved. It is for this reason that God created only one human in the beginning, a token to humanity that if one destroys one life, it is as though one had destroyed all humankind; whereas if one preserves one life, it is as though one had preserved all humankind (*Sanhedrin* 4:5).

c. Some would argue that our system of justice, trial by jury, can ensure that capital punishment will be meted out equitably to various groups in society and that the innocent will never be convicted . . . Statistics, however weighted, indicate that errors are made in judgment and convictions. Recent scientific advances, such as DNA testing, may reveal that persons on death row, despite seemingly "overwhelming" circumstantial evidence, may in fact be innocent of the charges against them. Likewise, suspiciously high percentages of those on death row are poor or people of color. Our legal system is a very good one, but it is a human institution. Even a small percentage of irreversible errors is increasingly seen as intolerable. God alone is the author of life (A Joint Statement, To End the Death Penalty, by the National Jewish/Catholic Consultation [co-sponsored by the National Council of Synagogues and the Bishops' Committee for Ecumenical and Interreligious Affairs of the National Conference of Catholic Bishops], December 3, 1999).

d. On January 11, 2003, Governor George Ryan commuted 167 Illinois death sentences to prison terms for life. The following are excerpts from his remarks explaining this action:

> You are five times more likely to get a death sentence for first-degree murder in the rural areas of this state . . .
>
> Half . . . of the nearly 300 capital cases in Illinois had been reversed for a new trial or resentencing. How many . . . professionals can get by with 50 percent accuracy?
>
> Thirty-three of the death row inmates were represented at trial by an attorney who had later been disbarred or at some point suspended from the practice of law. Of the more than 160 death row inmates, 35 were African-American defendents who had been convicted or condemned to die not by a jury of their peers, but by all-white juries (Governor George Ryan, "Excerpts From Governor's Speech on Commutations" in the New York Times, Sunday, January 12, 2003, "National" section, p. 22).

What Do You Think?

In your opinion, which of these texts make the most compelling arguments for or against the death penalty?

Regarding the death penalty, is the American justice system trustworthy?

If we believe that "God alone is the author or life" (Text Study #8c above), does that mean the courts should never impose the death penalty?

Related Middot and Mitzvot

We should keep these virtues and commandments in mind as we evaluate the ethics of the death penalty.

Anavah (Humility): Taking anyone's life, even a criminal's, is a momentous action. We must be extremely humble as we weigh justification of the death penalty.

Ayd Shahkeyr (Not Bearing False Witness): Any level of falsity in accusing a suspect could contribute to him/her wrongly being put to death. We must do everything possible to prevent such a tragic scenario.

Charatah (Regret): Expressions of regret on the part of the offender sometimes help shift the angry emotions of the victim's family and society so that they are more willing to consider alternatives to the death penalty.

Emet (Truth): No sentence should be pronounced upon the suspect without certainty of the truth of the accusations.

Lo Tikom (Not Taking Revenge): Revenge is not an acceptable objective of punishment.

Lo Tirtzach (Not Murdering): Even if we say that executing a criminal is an exception to this commandment, we must recognize the gravity of purposefully killing any human being.

Mishpat Echad (One Standard of Justice for All): Any justice system that discriminates against the poor or against a particular race of people is corrupt and has no right ever to enact a death penalty sentence.

Salchanut (Forgiveness): To forgive a violent criminal may be too much to ask of those harmed by his/her actions. Even so, striving for forgiveness helps many victims (and victims' families) to begin healing. Aspiring toward forgiveness is a difficult but worthy struggle.

Teshuvah (Repentance): Some say a criminal's death will atone for his/her wrongs. We must weigh such a belief against the atonement that could happen if a person worked to make amends on this side of life.

Where Do I Go From Here?

The death penalty is an issue that is discussed and debated all the time. You are sure to come across the issue in the future, so make sure that your opinion on the matter counts. Form it thoughtfully, with the insights gained from the material you have studied in this chapter. Continue to watch the newspapers and television for additional information, interesting case studies, and new legal precedents as the laws pertaining to the death penalty evolve.

Following is a list of suggested resources that you may find helpful as you continue your exploration of the complex issues that surround the death penalty.

Books and Articles - Jewish Sources

Blidstein, Gerald J. "Capital Punishment — The Classic Jewish Discussion." In *Contemporary Jewish Ethics*, edited by Menachem Marc Kellner. New York: Sanhedrin Press, 1978.

Borowitz, Eugene B., and Frances Weidman Schwartz. *The Jewish Moral Virtues*. Philadelphia, PA: The Jewish Publication Society, 1999.

Cytron, Barry D., and Earl Schwartz. *When Life Is in the Balance*. New York: United Synagogue, 1986.

"Capital Punishment." *Encyclopedia Judaica.* Jerusalem, Israel: Keter Publishing House Jerusalem Ltd., 1974.

Freeman, Susan. *Teaching Jewish Virtues: Sacred Sources and Arts Activities*. Denver, CO: A.R.E. Publishing, Inc., 1999.

Herring, Basil F. *Jewish Ethics and Halakhah for Our Time*, Vol 1. New York: KTAV Publishing House, Inc., and Yeshiva University Press, 1984.

Kadden, Barbara Binder and Bruce Kadden. *Teaching Mitzvot: Concepts, Values, and Activities*. Rev. ed. Denver, CO: A.R.E. Publishing, Inc., 2003.

Kazis, Israel J. "Judaism and the Death Penalty." In *Contemporary Jewish Ethics*, edited by Menachem Marc Kellner. New York: Sanhedrin Press, 1978.

Miller, Judea B. "Capital Punishment." In *Where We Stand: Jewish Consciousness on Campus*, edited by Allan L. Smith. New York: UAHC Press, 1997.

"Punishment." *Encyclopedia Judaica*. Jerusalem, Israel: Keter Publishing House Jerusalem Ltd., 1974.

Spitz, Elie. "The Jewish Tradition and Capital Punishment." In *Contemporary Jewish Ethics and Morality*, edited by Elliot N. Dorff and Louis E. Newman. New York and Oxford: Oxford University Press, 1995.

Books and Articles - General Sources

Ferro, Jeffrey. *Prisons and Jails: A Deterrent To Crime?* Farmington Hills, MI: Gale Group, 2002.

Lifton, Robert Jay, and Greg Mitchell. *Who Owns Death?: Capital Punishment, the American Conscience, and the End of Executions*. New York: HarperCollins Publishers, 2000.

Prejean, Helen. *Dead Man Walking*. New York: Vintage Books, 1993.

Rein, Mei Ling. *Capital Punishment: Cruel and Unusual?* Farmington Hills, MI: Gale Group, 2000.

Web Sites

American Civil Liberties Union: www.aclu.org.
A longtime activist organization pursuing individual rights.

Citizens United for Alternatives to the Death Penalty: www.cuapd.org.
Campaigns for public education and the promotion of tactical grassroots activism.

Death Penalty Focus: www.deathpenalty.org.
Dedicated to the abolition of capital punishment.

Death Penalty Information Center: www.deathpenaltyinfo.org
A non-profit organization that provides comprehensive information on the death penalty.

Equal Justice USA: www.quixote.org/ej/
A faith-based organization coordinating a campaign for a moratorium on death penalty.

Jewish Law — Articles: www.jlaw.org
Examines halachah, Jewish issues, and secular law.

The Justice Project; www.thejusticeproject.org
Educates about the flaws of capital punishment in the American justice system.

Moratorium 2000: www.moratorium.org
A global petition drive for a moratorium on the death penalty.

Murder Victims Families for Reconciliation: www.mvfr.org
Works to abolish the death penalty while supporting programs that address the needs of victims.

National Center for Victims of Crimes: www.ncvc.org
Information and support for crime victims.

National Coalition to Abolish the Death Penalty: www.ncadp.org
Coalition of individuals and organizations dedicated to the abolition of the death penalty.

Pro Death Penalty: www.prodeathpenalty.com
Information and arguments in favor of the death penalty.

Religious Action Center of Reform Judaism: www.rac.org
Builds a case against the death penalty, drawing on analysis of the American legal system and Jewish values.

The Religious Organizing Against the Death Penalty Project: www.deathpenaltyreligious.org.
Provides people of faith with tools and resources for becoming effective advocates for abolition. Site coordinated by the American Friends Service Committee.

Films

The following films deal with the death penalty in a frank and sometimes graphic way. Check with parents and teachers before viewing.

Dead Man Walking (1995, 122 minutes, rated R)
The true story of a caring nun who struggles with the moral and spiritual issues of comforting a death row inmate awaiting execution. Based on the book by Sister Helen Prejean (New York: Vintage Books, 1993). Available from video stores.

The Executioner's Song (1982, 136 minutes, unrated)
The true story of Gary Mark Gilmore, the first man to be executed in the United States after the death penalty was reinstated in 1976. The film spans the last nine months of his life. Available from video stores.

The Green Mile (1999, 188 minutes, rated R)
The story of the lives of Death Row prison guards in the 1930s, leading up to the execution of a wrongly accused man. Available from video stores.

The Life of David Gale (2003, 130 minutes, rated R)
An advocate for the abolishment of capital punishment is falsely convicted of rape and murder, and finds himself on death row. Available for purchase online at www.amazon.com. Available from video stores.

Glossary

Edut Mechuvenet

Impeccably qualified witnesses able to withstand severe cross-examination.

Hatra'ah

Warning the culprit before the crime.

Lex Talionis

Translates as, "The Law of the Talon/Claw." "An eye for an eye" type of punishment.

Sanhedrin

A court, made up of Sages.

CHAPTER 7
SCHOOL VIOLENCE

Overview

School violence is an increasingly problematic issue in our society. There are schools in which students and teachers fear for their safety. In addition, some schools that "feel" safe unwittingly harbor students on the verge of causing great harm. The general mission of schools is to educate children. We understand that schools cannot fulfill every personal need a child has, but everyone can agree that our children should not be hurt at school. Learning cannot happen at an optimal level, if at all, when violence at schools is a threat.

In this chapter we will look at several general questions regarding school violence: What is responsible for the increase in violence? How should we deal with it? Who should take charge of implementing strategies for change?

As a point of clarification, we will use the English definition for the word violence found in *Webster's Third New International Dictionary*: "exertion of any physical force so as to injure or abuse." All kinds of incendiary words and actions can hurt another person. Though we will look at many problematic behaviors throughout this chapter, we reserve the word "violence" for the specific problem of physical assault.

Jewish Perspectives

Traditional Jewish texts do not speak directly to the phenomenon of school violence as we witness it today. However, various *halachic* concepts, ethical principles, and *middot* (Jewish virtues) provide us with insightful guidelines for approaching this complex problem.

The Ben Sorer U'Moreh: "The Stubborn and Rebellious Child"

The *ben sorer u'moreh* is a wayward child who doesn't listen to his parents, and is a glutton and a drunkard (Deuteronomy 21:18). Teachings on this subject provide insights on how to cope with youth who deviate from the standards of civility we expect in our communities.

The recommended punishment for the "stubborn and rebellious child" is severe – stoning! Even so, scholars so narrowly define such a child that they essentially eliminate the possibility of ever labeling a child a *ben sorer u'moreh*. They conclude that the prescribed punishments never actually happened or will happen. This conclusion is significant. No child should be considered irredeemable, nor wholly evil. The community should not give up on problematic children — the potential for good and for evil exists in every one of us.

A rebellious child's family does not bear the total brunt of coping with the problematic situation. In the case described in the Bible, the elders of the town, all the men of the town, and to some degree all Israel have a role in responding to the child's unacceptable behavior. The lesson is that broad responsibility exists. That is, much of the community must become involved in handling volatile situations in its midst.

Though we don't always have clear-cut answers to what causes acts of violence, one thing is clear from the teachings of the *ben sorer u'moreh*. We are to resist responding to violence with violence.

The Rodef: "The Pursuer"

Another area of Torah-based law concerns the *rodef*, or "pursuer." From teachings on the *rodef*, we learn the principle that we must do what we can to help a fellow person whose life is in jeopardy, who is being "pursued" by someone who appears to have evil intentions. We learn in Leviticus 19:16, "Do not stand idly by the blood of your fellow." Applying these concepts to school violence means protecting school community members from (being "pursued" by) potentially violent youths.

In short, we are to protect the pursued. But we need to mention an additional duty: we are to "protect" the pursuer, that is, to save the pursuer from doing wrong. When potentially violent individuals are in our midst, we must help them to help themselves. We must do whatever we can to prevent them from becoming criminals.

In the case of school violence, just who is the *rodef* may be cause for debate. Sometimes those who appear to be dangerous pursuers feel vulnerable and threatened themselves. They believe they were the ones being pursued in the first place. They may have felt subjected to bullying, taunts, and other humiliations. Thus, before becoming "pursuers," these volatile individuals experienced threatening situations. From their perspective, becoming a "pursuer" is an act of self-defense. While humiliation is not a justification for becoming violent, Judaism recognizes it as a legitimate grievance.

Here, as in the case of the *ben sorer u'moreh*, it is clear that the community bears responsibility for protecting people who are at risk of being harmed. The concept — *mipnay darkay shalom*, for the sake of peace — reminds us that our concerns must expand to include all people. We are to uphold the dignity of all individuals, because all people are created in the image of God (*ha-adam nivra b'tzelem Elohim*).

Who Is Responsible for a Crime? What We Learn from the Eglah Arufah

The term *eglah arufah* refers to an elaborate ritual concerning a slain man found in a field between two cities, whose murderer is unknown. When such a body is found, the elders slaughter a calf (the *eglah arufah*) to purge the community of the crime. As part of the cleansing ritual, they say, "Our hands did not shed this blood, our eyes did not see!" (Deuteronomy 21:7). Though not suspects in the murder, the elders must proclaim their innocence because of the question of indirect causation of the death (*Sotah* 9:6). That is, it is possible that the crime happened because a hungry man was not able to find food or because an unescorted traveler entered a danger zone. Such circumstances require a response by the community leadership. The *eglah arufah* reminds a community's leaders that they are responsible for ensuring a safe and healthy community infrastructure. They must answer for circumstances that

lead to such tragedy as murder, and commit themselves to whatever changes are necessary to improve the fabric of the community.

In our day, providing for vital needs includes ensuring safety. Safety guarantees require an examination of access to guns, influence of media violence, school security procedures, parental/adult supervision of teens, and school cultures that condone bullying and exclusion. In addition, society must protect individuals from falling so deeply into poverty, despair, and degradation that they feel pressed to engage in criminal acts. The leadership of the community must assume responsibility for committing to necessary changes to improve the fabric of the society.

Jewish Values and Virtues

Many Jewish values and virtues (*middot*), if deliberately incorporated into the school culture, would promote an environment in which violence is less likely to occur. See the section, "Related Mitzvot and Middot" on page 107.

General Perspectives

The Problem

School violence is a problem, and is on the increase, as evidenced by such high profile incidents as the attacks at Columbine High School in Littleton, Colorado in 1999. The stakes are higher with sophisticated weapons more widely available. Incidents of violence occur at every level in schools (elementary and secondary). Nonviolent crimes include physical attacks or fights without a weapon, theft or larceny, and vandalism. Violent crimes include rape or other sexual battery, robberies, and physical attacks or fights using weapons.

What or who is responsible for the increased incidence of school violence? The violence-generating "suspects" most often cited by experts follow.

Possible Biological/Psychological Factors

Genetics: Some people are born with a genetic make-up that "naturally" predisposes them to violent behavior.

Hormones: Young males (who are disproportionately involved in violent crimes) have high testosterone levels. Hormonal surges during adolescense exacerbate aggressive responses to provocative situations.

Immature brains: The pre-frontal cortex of the teenage brain is biologically immature. This part of the brain is responsible for inhibiting impulses. A teen involved in a provocative situation (with deadly weapons in reach) will not necessarily exert the same self-control as that same person will later in life.[1]

Psychiatric conditions: These aren't necessarily a direct cause of violence. Still, a "side effect" of certain conditions can be comparatively more aggressive behaviors. These conditions include mental retardation, Attention Deficit/Hyperactivity Disorder (ADHD), Reactive Detachment Disorder, serious mental illness (such as schizophrenia, mania, and recurring depressive episodes), Post-Traumatic Stress Disorder (PTSD), alcohol and drug abuse, and suicidal depression.[2]

Personality disorders: Recurring patterns of active defiance, disobedience, and open hostility toward adult authority figures characterize Oppositional Defiant Disorder, and the more extreme Conduct Disorders.

Substance abuse: Drugs and alcohol impair judgment and impede self-control. Addictions to illicit drugs may lead to criminal activity and criminal activity often entails violence.

Possible Environmental Factors

Economic environment: Poverty may lead a person to such a degraded and desperate condition that engaging in criminal activity becomes increasingly likely, perhaps just to survive. Affluence, too, can have problematic effects, including working parents who have little time for their children and families.

Inadequate schooling: An inferior school environment compromises education. Academic failure may relegate certain individuals to the permanent underclass and possibly a life of crime. Students who have trouble academically may drop out of school, join gangs, and become involved in violent street life.[3]

Discrimination: Innocent people may be victimized because of their race, ethnicity, religion, sexual preference, medical or mental disability, age, or gender. On the flip side, being the target of senseless and prejudicial hatred may arouse the victim to violent response.

Domestic violence: Abuse victims and witnesses often become filled with such rage that they become batterers and criminals themselves.

Availability of weapons: With the increasing availability of guns, when conflicts between students escalate, the results can be deadly.

The media: Violence saturates our media — TV, movies, music and video games. Strong evidence shows that watching violence increases the frequency of aggressive behavior in children.[4]

Minimal presence of responsible adults/weak leadership: Lack of adult supervision, adult listening ears, and adult mediation and counsel forces troubled students to turn elsewhere for guidance and relief. That "elsewhere" may be unhealthy and dangerous (i.e. violent web sites, gangs and other troubled teens, drugs/alcohol, suicide).

Suburban anonymity: A sense of strong community connection is difficult to nurture in suburbia. It is difficult to create the social fabric of closely knit neighborhoods among residents who are isolated from each other in increasingly bigger houses on bigger lots.

Cultural Factors

Primacy of self: A sense of personal entitlement and belief that "I always come first" may compromise feelings of responsibility toward others.

Materialism: Success becomes identified with the accumulation and consumption of material goods. Amassing wealth and prestige supercedes dedication to communal and spiritual values.

Expectations of instant gratification: Easy access to sex, drugs, pornography, and crude music undermines motivation for self-restraint. Our culture does not encourage us to curb our desires. If anything, it entices us to indulge our desires, and to indulge them now.

Lack of conflict resolution skills: Many conflicts could be kept from escalating if students and teachers had the skills to resolve problems peaceably.

Bullying, taunting, humiliating: Students who continually are subjected to this type of emotional stress may become filled with rage. They may turn feelings of powerlessness into plans for violent retaliation.

Exclusion and cliques: School cultures often revolve around groups of individuals who cluster together for all sorts of reasons. When these groups become cliques that exclude in hurtful ways, those left out may redirect painful feelings of alienation into revenge.

Gangs: Empowerment, risk taking, peer pressure, and approval are all associated with membership in gangs. Gang activities can turn lethal when violence takes center stage.

Inadequate moral education: A dearth of character education promotes a "free-for-all" atmosphere of behavioral expectations for students.

Incoherent school core values, rules, and consequences: When schools do not spend the time and effort to identify, agree upon, and commit to live by core values, rules, and consequences, serious repercussions may follow. A lack of clear expectations feeds an atmosphere of apathy or confusion. Without adequate means of disciplining with dignity, an atmosphere develops in which violent intentions can grow without notice.[5]

Conclusions about the Factors

Likely, several factors are present each time a youth turns into a killer. Though finding a means of prevention is a daunting task, promising strategies have been identified.

About Interventions

Social psychologists divide the strategies for dealing with youth violence into two categories: "Pump-Handle Interventions" and "Root Cause Interventions." The terms come from the 1854 cholera epidemic in London. Dr. John Snow, a well-known physician, traced the epidemic to a contaminated well. His first course of action was not to try to find the cause of the contamination, or to educate the people living in the area, or to persuade them not to drink the water. Rather, he simply removed the pump handle from the wellhead, and thereby stanched the epidemic. Later, Dr. Snow looked for the "root cause" of the contamination. After discovering that the source of the contamination was raw sewage, he helped instigate changes to building codes, improving the health and welfare of millions of people.[6]

This analogy applies well to school violence. "Pump-Handle Interventions" are immediate, initial steps, addressing both pressing dangers (such as easy access to weapons) and underlying causes (such as an environment that tolerates bullying). "Root Cause Interventions" address fundamental causes, the complex factors that sow the seeds of violence in the first place.

"Pump-handle" Interventions

These steps can have a direct effect on reducing violence. Possibilities include offering psychological support, decreasing access to weapons, reaching out to troubled families, confronting and educating about the problem of substance abuse, improving school security, and reducing media violence.

"Root Cause" Interventions

These efforts seek to reduce violence by addressing underlying causes. Possible strategies include "Character Education" as part of the school curriculum; learning, practicing, and implementing conflict resolution skills; identifying and living by core school values; confronting bullying; broadening learning situations that require cooperation and collaboration; teachers and administrators "practicing what they preach" (modeling the values they want their students to learn); and creating an affirmative school environment (that is warm, caring, and builds competence).

Who Is Responsible?

"Pump-handle" interventions require particular groups of specialists to take leadership roles, such as psychologists, law enforcement officials, counselors, social workers, politicians, media executives, political activists, or grass roots organizers. The challenge of "root cause" interventions is that the whole community must get involved — students, teachers, administrators, parents, and town residents. This call to the whole community is similar to the Jewish concept of *kol Yisrael aravin zeh bazeh* — all Israel is responsible for one another.

Still, initiating reform has to start with someone. Returning to the concept of the *eglah arufah*, we see that the responsibility falls on the "elders of the community." That is, adult leaders must step forward and navigate the call to change.

Summary of the Overview

The following summarizes key considerations regarding school violence.

Some Jewish insights to guide our approach to school violence include:

- The community shares responsibility for and involvement in the problems of our youth

- All people, youth included, have the potential to do good and to do wrong

- Individuals may protect themselves from others who threaten their life

- We are not to stand idly by when someone else's life is threatened

- Since everyone is created in God's image, we must treat all people respectfully

- A society's adult leaders must accept responsibility for conditions that lead to crime or tragedy. The onus is upon them to safeguard the emotional and physical well-being of the members of the community.

A combination of forces seems responsible for the increase in school violence, reflecting psychological, biological, environmental, and cultural factors.

An effective strategy for stemming school violence will use interventions that address both immediate dangers and underlying causes.

Scenarios: How Things have Changed

In today's world, we share many concerns about violence that have been discussed for centuries in Jewish sources. Moreover, we face new challenges, as environmental and cultural factors change. Adding to the complexity is our growing understanding of human biology and psychology. Below are two scenarios, intended to raise questions and spark discussion. Read each one and reflect, either individually or in group discussion, on the questions in the "For Thought and Discussion" section that follows. Then continue on to the "Text Study" section to see what Jewish and other sources have to say on the subject. Finally, you may wish to come back and answer the questions a second time, to see if your views have changed.

Scenario I: In a Jewish Community

Aryeh ("Lion") is holding a knife and chasing another youth, named Shalom ("Peace"). Shalom, seeing he is danger, stops in his tracks, buries his head in his arms, and tries to protect himself. Ezra ("Help") is standing nearby and witnesses Aryeh threatening Shalom. Ezra picks up a rock and hurls it at Aryeh's shoulder. Aryeh drops the knife. Ezra quickly grabs the weapon, and both he and Shalom tackle Aryeh. By this time, others are gathering round. Some community elders are summoned. They break up the fight. Aryeh, cradling his injured arm, is led off by the elders, along with Shalom and Ezra. The elders decide that Aryeh's actions, like that of a rodef, a "pursuer," were serious enough to deserve punishment.

Scenario II: Uncovering Additional Motivations

Let's say we see a girl we'll call "Armed," running with a knife in her hand after a girl we'll call "Unarmed." We might say "Armed" is the *rodef*, the pursuer, and "Unarmed" is the pursued (the potential victim). But what if we find out that "Armed" has been the subject of bullying and taunts for months? What if we learn that because of the hostile circumstances at her school, "Armed" has attempted suicide several times? And what if we find out that "Unarmed" spearheaded unremitting, emotionally painful, and stressful acts of humiliation toward "Armed"?

This pursuer case is not so simple. We could argue that in fact it is "Armed" who is engaged in self-defense. Before this incident, she felt her life was in danger, and the teachings of Judaism allows a person to act in self-defense when life or limb is threatened. "Armed" may consider herself the one who is pursued by a *rodef*. "Armed" — who has been "pursued" relentlessly with harmful words and intimidating acts — may claim that she is justified in chasing and threatening "Unarmed". "Armed" may proclaim that she is protecting her own threatened life.

For Thought and Discussion:

How would you judge who is at fault in each of these scenarios?

What additional information would you seek in order to understand the two conflicts?

Text Study

School violence forces us to ask difficult questions. Jewish and general textual sources provide many answers, but these answers often highlight the tension between seemingly opposing considerations. The chart below poses the questions and offers two opposing points of view. Text sources supporting each of these points of view follow.

1. **What role should schools play in the life of its students?**

    On the One Hand:

    Schools aren't rehabilitation centers. They should focus on well-behaved students who want an education. Problematic students should be expelled. Perhaps they should be put in their own schools.

    A. Wisdom is too lofty for a fool;
        He does not open his mouth in the gate.
        He who lays plans to do harm
        People call a schemer.
        The schemes of folly are sin,

    And a scoffer is an abomination to people (Proverbs 24:7-9).

    B. An intelligent son heeds instruction,
        But he who keeps company with gluttons disgraces his father (Proverbs 28:7).

    On the Other Hand:

    Schools have an obligation to try to salvage the lives of students who have gone astray. Troublemaking students should be given chances to mend their ways. Expelling them means they simply will go elsewhere (e.g. to the mall) where they may cause trouble, and where there will be no supervision. The danger will just change locations. Problematic students need to be around well-behaved kids, rather than in a situation where they will only reinforce each other's bad behavior.

    a. Rabbi Hamnuma said: Jerusalem was destroyed only because the children did not attend school . . . and loitered in the streets (*Shabbat* 119b).

    What Do You Think?

    Which text about the school's role and responsibility do you find most compelling? Why?

    Describe a possible sequence of five to ten things that might contribute to a city's demise if children weren't attending school. You might start with something like this: First kids would be bored and not know what to do with themselves. Next they would . . .

2. **To what extent should schools tolerate student misbehavior?**

    On the One Hand:

    A "zero tolerance" policy is in order for certain behaviors (such as bringing weapons to school, using drugs). Mandatory expulsions or other serious consequences would automatically apply.

    A. Rabbi Shimon ben Lakish says: "Those who are compassionate when hard-heartedness is called for will end up being hard-hearted when compassion is called for" (*Kohelet Rabbah* 7).

On the Other Hand:

We need to listen and pay attention to the unique circumstances of each individual. Not everyone should be treated equally. Rigidity of school authorities only breeds student hostility toward them.

a. I bring heaven and earth to witness that the Divine Spirit rests upon a non-Jew as well as upon a Jew, upon a woman as well as upon a man, upon a maidservant as well as a manservant. All depends on the deeds of the particular individual (*Yalkut Shimoni*, on Judges, section 42).

b. Happy is the generation whose great [leaders] listen to the small, for then it follows obviously that in such a generation, the small will listen to the great (*Rosh HaShanah* 25b).

What Do You Think?

Which group of texts, in your opinion, offers the more realistic approach? Why?

Do you see more danger in being overly compassionate or in "zero tolerance?" Explain. (Consider the story of a young girl who arrived at school with seven knives in her backpack. Since the school had "zero tolerance" for weapons, the girl was given a long-term suspension and the police were called. While waiting for the police, the girl broke down and told school officials that the night before her mother had attempted suicide. Fearing that her mother might take her life while she was at school, the girl took every knife she could find in the house with her to school that day.)

Create a "zero tolerance" scenario where the "facts" may not be as clear cut as they seem.

3. **Will improved security make a difference in safety and quality of life for schools?**

On the One Hand:

Beef up security: Install metal detectors in schools, hire more security guards, and increase monitoring of students.

A. Those who can prevent members of their household from committing a sin, but do not, are punished for the sins of their household.
    If they can prevent their fellow citizens from committing sins, but do not, they are punished for the sins of their fellow citizens.
    If they can prevent the whole world from committing sins, but do not, they are punished for the sins of the whole world (*Shabbat* 54b).

On the Other Hand:

Monitoring students more rigorously will lead to abuse of privacy. Killers intent on harm can kill outside of school grounds. Moreover, all the extra security will increase anxiety.

a. Balaam blessed the people of Israel when he saw the tribes dwelling together in tents, in such a way that everyone's privacy was respected:
    He saw each tribe dwelling by itself, not intermingled one with another; he saw that the entrances of their tents were not exactly facing each other so that one could not peer into the other's tent (Rashi on Numbers 24:2, also *Baba Batra* 60a).

What Do You Think?

These texts highlight the tension between ensuring safety and respecting privacy. Which text do you feel is more applicable in a discussion about school violence? Why?

Which do you think is the greater value — ensuring safety or respecting privacy? Explain.

Which value seems to be a higher priority at your school? At you religious school?

Forging Strategies to Deal with School Violence: Questions to Consider

The Question	On the One Hand	On the Other Hand
1. What role should a school play in the life of its students? (see page 98)	Schools aren't rehabilitation centers. They should focus on well-behaved students who want an education. Problematic students should be expelled. Perhaps they should be put in their own schools.	Schools have an obligation to try to salvage the lives of students who have gone astray. Troublemaking students should be given chances to mend their ways. Expelling them means they simply will go elsewhere (e.g. to the mall) where they may cause trouble, and where there will be no supervision. The danger will just change locations. Problematic students need to be around well-behaved kids, rather than in a situation where they will only reinforce each other's bad behavior.
2. To what extent should schools tolerate student misbehavior? (see page 98)	A "Zero Tolerance" policy is in order for certain behaviors (such as bringing weapons to school, using drugs). Mandatory expulsions or other serious consequences would automatically apply.	We need to listen and pay attention to the unique circumstances of each individual. Not everyone should be treated equally. Rigidity of school authorities only breeds student hostility toward them.
3. Will improved security make a difference in safety and quality of life for schools? (see page 99)	Beef up security: Install metal detectors in schools, hire more security guards, and increase monitoring of students.	Monitoring students more rigorously will lead to abuse of privacy. Killers intent on harm can kill outside of school grounds. Moreover, all the extra security will increase anxiety.
4. What restrictions should be placed on media regarding violent content? (see page 102)	Clamp down on violence in media.	Freedom of the press is guaranteed by the First Amendment to the United States Constitution.
5. What do we do about the proliferation of guns in our midst? (see page 102)	Ban gun ownership for private citizens.	Eliminating the threat of guns is unrealistic. While there are ways to reduce gun violence (with licensing, safety devices, education, etc.), wide access to dangerous weapons will not go away any time soon.

(continued on next page)

6. How much effort should we make in trying to help troubled individuals? (see page 103)	Some people are inherently evil. Some are naturally despicable.	Everyone has vast potential for a variety of behaviors. Labeling people or expecting bad things of them can lead to "self-fulfilling prophecies."
7. Do cliques contribute to causing school violence? (see page 103)	Cliques are a part of school culture, and there's not that much you can do about them. Large high schools, with their numerous periods a day, are impersonal places. Cliques help to close the gap. Students should be able to choose their own friends. Gangs are a type of clique that give the security of a substitute kind of family to certain kids who really need that.	Effective means for addressing exclusion must be sought. Exclusion breeds loneliness, resentment, and alienation. Those who are left out may turn to harmful behaviors as coping mechanisms. They may use violence as a means to get back at those who have hurt them.
8. How concerned should we be about bullying? (see page 104)	Let's not overreact to bullying. Some teasing helps everyone not to take themselves so seriously. Kids should learn to stick up for themselves.	Bullying can cause serious harm — the potential damage must not be underestimated. Schools must make it a priority to implement strategies aimed at eliminating bullying.
9. If we think there might be a problem, should we let someone know? (see page 105)	"Reports" of suspicious behaviors can go astray. Rumors, denials, and/or lack of parental support can make follow-through difficult. Further, the "reporters" may be shunned or endangered for revealing information to authorities.	Timely interventions and rebukes can deter more serious crime.
10. Will character education (teaching values and social skills) make a measurable difference in improving school culture? (see page 106)	How can schools be expected to shoulder the burden of so many learning agendas, such as character education, conflict resolution, empathy training, cooperative learning techniques, values clarification, etc.? Schools barely have the time to teach the basics of academics! Besides, values should be taught by parents and through students' religious education. Schools can't be expected to change a whole culture.	Character education and the teaching of social skills is as critical a part of a child's learning as anything else. When deprived of this kind of learning, the school environment — academic and social — will suffer. Learning core values intersects with the teaching of literature and history. There are (non-religious) values all segments of the school community can agree on. What happens now in schools *will* affect the culture of future generations.

4. **What restrictions should be placed on media regarding violent content?**

On the One Hand:

Clamp down on violence in media.

A. Hate evil and love good (Amos 5:15).

B. An enemy dissembles with his speech,
Inwardly he harbors deceit.
Though he be fair-spoken, do not trust him
For seven abominations are in his mind.
His hatred may be concealed by dissimulation (false pretense),
But his evil will be exposed to public view (Proverbs 26:24-26).

C. The research results are clear: In spite of the protestations of media executives, exposure to violence in films, on TV, and in video games can and does have an important impact on the behavior and feelings of children and adolescents.

But . . . it is important that we don't get carried away . . . Millions of kids watch a lot of violent stuff on TV and don't go around shooting their classmates. At the same time, it would be naive to believe that TV violence is not a contributing factor — especially if the youngsters watching all that TV are frustrated, angry, or prone to violence (Elliot Aronson, *Nobody Left to Hate*, p. 62).

On the Other Hand:

Freedom of the press is guaranteed by the First Amendment to the United States Constitution.

a. Congress shall make no law respecting an establishment of religion, or prohibiting the free exercise thereof; or abridging the freedom of speech, or of the press; or the right of the people peaceably to assemble, and to petition the government for a redress of grievances (First Amendment to the Bill of Rights of the United States Constitution).

b. What Congress can do is exert pressure on the entertainment industries to show some restraint, police themselves, and establish a useful rating system so that parents can attempt to exercise sensible vigilance over what their children watch. If broadcasters and filmmakers would succumb to this pressure, this would be a small step in the right direction (Elliot Aronson, *Nobody Left to Hate*, p. 62).

What Do You Think?

Which of the above texts do you believe has the most credibility? Why?

Freedom of the press, as we understand it today, is not a focus of emphasis in traditional Jewish texts. Rather, the emphasis is more on the dangers of *lashon ha-rah* - "evil speech" — gossip, rumors, and slander. Try to write a Jewish commentary to the First Amendment — that is, what you believe freedom of speech should and should not cover.

5. **What do we do about the proliferation of guns in our midst?**

On the One Hand:

Ban gun ownership for private citizens.

A. You shall not stand idly by when your fellow's blood is being shed (Leviticus 19:16).

B. It is forbidden to sell a heathen or a robber weapons of war which might be used in violating a mitzvah, although it is permitted to sell them defensive weapons, such as shields (*Mishneh Torah, Hilchot Rotzayach* 12:14).

On the Other Hand:

Eliminating the threat of guns is unrealistic. While there are ways to reduce gun violence (with licensing, safety devices, education, etc.), wide access to dangerous weapons will not go away any time soon.

a. [Eliminating guns would result in] a sharp reduction in multiple killings in our schools — and everywhere else, for that matter. Needless to say, this would be impossible. We would have to confiscate every gun in America. But in America, we believe in individual liberties, so it should not surprise you that an overwhelming majority of the population opposes the confiscation of guns. A less extreme and far more feasible [approach . . .] would require the licensing of guns and restricting juveniles' access to guns (Elliot Aronson, *Nobody Left to Hate*, p. 49).

What Do You Think?

Based on texts #5A and B, would you say that Jews should advocate for the complete elimination of guns?

What are Jews to do now if we want to strive "not to stand idly by," yet understand that the complete elimination of guns in America is just about impossible?

6. **How much effort should we make in trying to help troubled individuals?**

On the One Hand:

Some people are inherently evil. Some are naturally despicable.

Jewish thought does not support this point of view.

On the Other Hand:

Everyone has vast potential for a variety of behaviors. Labeling people or expecting bad things of them can lead to "self-fulfilling prophecies."

a. See, I set before you today life and good, and death and evil: in that I command you today to love the Eternal your God, to walk in God's ways and to keep God's commandments, laws, and regulations . . . Life and death I place before you, blessing and curse; now choose life, in order that you may stay alive, you and your seed, by loving the Eternal your God, by hearkening to God's voice and by cleaving to God, for God is your life and the length of your days . . . (Deuteronomy 30:15-20).

b. Ben Azzai said: Do not despise anyone. Do not underrate the importance of anything, for there is no one that does not have his/her hour, and there is no thing that does not have its place (*Pirke Avot* 4:3).

c. Ben Zoma taught: Who is mighty? Those who conquer their evil impulse. As it is written: "Those who are slow to anger are better than the mighty, and those who rule over their spirit than those who conquer a city" [Proverbs 16:32] (*Pirke Avot* 4:1).

What Do You Think?

How do you respond do the Jewish assumption that evil is a choice given to us by God?

What are the most challenging "choices" you face in your life in terms of how you treat others?

7. **Do cliques contribute to causing school violence?**

On the One Hand:

Cliques are a part of school culture, and there's not that much you can do about them. Large high schools, with their six periods a day, are impersonal places. Cliques help to close the gap. Students should be able to choose their own friends. Gangs are a type of clique that give the security of a substitute kind of family to certain kids who really need that.

This idea is foreign to traditional Jewish ways of thinking.

On the Other Hand:

Effective means for addressing exclusion must be sought. Exclusion breeds loneliness, resentment, and alienation. Those who are left out may turn to harmful behaviors as coping mechanisms. They may use violence as a means to get back at those who have hurt them.

a. Hillel taught: Do not withdraw from the community (*al tifros min ha-tzibur*) (*Pirke Avot* 2:5).

b. Belong to the persecuted rather than to be the persecutors (*Baba Kamma* 93a).

c. Rabbi Eleazar said: Since the destruction of the Temple, the gates of prayers are locked [making it harder for prayers to reach heaven].

   But even though the gates of prayers are locked, the gates of tears are not. Rabbi Hisda said: All gates are locked except the gates through which pass the cries of people who have been wronged (*Baba Metzia* 59a).

d. The rabbis hold that disgrace is worse than physical pain . . . (*Sotah* 8b).

e. Some people make vows out of hatred of their neighbor, swearing, for example, that they will not let this or that person sit at the same table with them or come under the same roof. Such people should seek the mercy of God so that they may find some cure for the diseases of their soul (Philo of Alexandria).

What Do You Think?

Imagine a dialogue between a panel of rabbis and a school committee (made of students, parents, and teachers). What would the rabbis advise concerning cliques?

What might school committee members respond?

———≫◆≪———

8. **How concerned should we be about bullying?**

On the One Hand:

Let's not overreact to bullying. Some teasing helps everyone not to take themselves so seriously. Kids should learn to stick up for themselves.

A Jewish way of thinking would argue that responding to bullying is important.

On the Other Hand:

Bullying can cause serious harm — the potential damage must not be underestimated. Schools must make it a priority to implement strategies aimed at eliminating bullying.

a. A tanna [one who memorized oral teachings] recited before Rabbi Nahman ben Isaac: "A person who publicly shames a neighbor is like someone who has shed blood." To which Rabbi Nahman answered, "You have spoken well. I have seen that when someone is shamed, the color leaves the person's face and the person becomes pale."

   Abbaye asked Rabbi Dimi "What do people in Palestine most carefully try to avoid?" He answered, "Putting others to shame" (*Baba Metzia* 58b).

b. Three categories of people are condemned to eternal hell: one who commits adultery with a married woman; one who publicly shames a neighbor; and one who calls a neighbor by a degrading nickname, even if the other is accustomed to that name . . . It would be better for one to throw oneself into a fiery furnace than publicly put a neighbor to shame (*Baba Metzia* 58b-59a).

c. If a man pulls another man's ears, plucks his hair, spits in his face, or removes his garments, or if he uncovers the head of a woman in the marketplace [married women always kept their heads covered as a sign of modesty], he must pay the other person four hundred zuz . . . (*Baba Kamma* 8:6).

What Do You Think?

Elaborate on what you think would be a generally accepted Jewish attitude toward bullying.

Do you think the rabbis get carried away in their condemnation of those who cause others shame?

9. If we think there might be a problem, should we let someone know?

On the One Hand:

"Reports" of suspicious behaviors can go astray. Rumors, denials, and/or lack of parental support can make follow-through difficult. Further, the "reporters" may be shunned or endangered for giving out revealing information to authorities.

A. You shall not deal deceitfully or falsely with one another. You shall not swear falsely by My name . . . You are not to commit corruption in justice; do not favor the poor or show deference to the rich; judge your kinsman fairly. Do not go about as a talebearer among your people (Leviticus 19:11, 15-16).

B. You are to inquire, to examine, and to investigate well, and [determine] if the claim is certain and true, the fact is established, that this abomination was indeed done in your midst . . . (Deuteronomy 13:15, referring to idol worship).

C. We must exercise the most scrupulous care, so as not to give an ill-considered and hasty decision, and so harm the innocent (*The Commandments*, vol. 1, pp. 192-193).

On the Other Hand:

Timely interventions and rebukes can deter more serious crime.

a. You are not allowed to withhold information that could help someone (*Choshen Mishpat* 426:1).

b. Those who see sin in their home and do nothing in protest are indicted as if they committed the sin (*Shabbat* 54b).

c. If a person permitted certain sins to go on without strongly objecting, that person is considered a murderer (*Moed Katan* 5a).

d. Where harm is being caused to others, the story can be told if the following seven guidelines are followed:

i. You saw the act yourself and it is not a rumor from others, unless substantiated later.

ii. You must be careful not to decide quickly if the issue is one of stealing or damage.

iii. You must reprimand the sinner first in soft language. Perhaps it will be effective and the sinner will return to the right way. If the sinner does not listen then you can tell the public of this person's willful evil.

iv. You must not make the sin out to be greater than it is.

v. Your intention must be for the [favorable] end result and not, God forbid, to enjoy the harm you are causing to your fellow or to be motivated by hatred that you harbor for your fellow.

vi. You can achieve this aim in a different way without telling *lashon harah* (i.e. talking behind someone's back), then it is totally forbidden to tell it.

vii. The telling must not cause more damage to the person than appearing in court for breaking that law would cause them.

(*Chafetz Chayim*: Laws of *Lashon Harah* 10:2)

What Do You Think?

Using the texts above as a measure, overall, do you think Judaism would fall to the side of reporting or not reporting suspicious behavior? And just how "suspicious" would the behavior have to be to merit reporting on it?

Some schools favor an anonymous tips hotline for students to call up when something seems to be amiss. Would such a hotline be acceptable from a Jewish point of view?

10. **Will character education (teaching values and social skills) make a measurable difference in improving school culture?**

On the One Hand:

How can schools be expected to shoulder the burden of so many learning agendas, such as character education, conflict resolution, empathy training, cooperative learning techniques, values clarification, etc.? Schools barely have the time to teach the basics of academics! Besides, values should be taught by parents and through students' religious education. Schools can't be expected to change a whole culture.

A. No one is poor except those who lack knowledge . . . Those who have knowledge have everything. Those who lack knowledge, what do they have? . . . (*Nedarim* 41a).

B. Rav said to Rav Samuel the son of Shilat: Before the age of six do not accept pupils; from that age you can accept them, and stuff them with Torah like an ox (*Baba Batra* 21a).

On the Other Hand:

Character education and the teaching of social skills is as critical a part of a child's learning as anything else. When deprived of this kind of learning, the school environment — academic and social — will suffer. Learning core values intersects with the teaching of literature and history. There are (non-religious) values all segments of the school community can agree on. What happens now in schools will affect the culture of future generations.

a. A heathen went to Hillel [and said to him, "Accept me as a proselyte on the condition that you teach me the whole Torah . . .]." Hillel . . . said to him, "What is hateful to you do not do to your fellow — that is the whole Torah, all the rest is commentary — now, go and learn" (*Shabbat* 31a).

b. Let people first do good deeds, and then ask God for [knowledge of] Torah. Let people first act as righteous and upright people act, and then let them ask God for wisdom. Let people first grasp the way of humility, and then ask God for understanding (*Tanna de be Eliyahu*, p. 31).

c. Rabbi Elisha ben Abuyah said that a person who has learnt much Torah and has good deeds is like a horse which has reins. The person who has the first, but not the second, is like a horse without reins — it soon throws the rider over its head (*Avot de Rabbi Natan*, verse I, xxiv, 39a).

d. Rabbi Beroka of Khuzistan often visited the market at Be Lapat. There he would meet Elijah the prophet [who, according to tradition, sometimes descended from heaven to appear to the pious on earth].

"Does anybody in this market have a share in the world to come?" Rabbi Beroka asked one day . . . While they were talking, two men came by.

Elijah said, "Those two have a share in the world to come."

Rabbi Beroka went to them and said, "What do you do?"

They said, "We are jesters. When we see a person depressed, we try to cheer that person up. And when we see two people quarreling, we work hard to make peace between them" (*Ta'anit* 22a).

What Do You Think?

In Jewish tradition learning and good deeds often are linked together. To what extent are these two values incorporated into your school? How about your synagogue school?

Do you believe the balance in these environments is the right one? If so, describe why you think this is so. If not, how could the balance be improved?

Related Middot and Mitzvot

Practicing these virtues and commandments can help diffuse the pressures that lead to school violence.

Derech Eretz (Civility): Schools that make explicit efforts to create an environment of civility reap both academic and social benefits.

Din V'Rachamim (Justice and Mercy): We must strive to find a sensitive balance between justice and mercy when dealing with troublemaking students.

Erech Apayim (Slow to Anger): Potentially violent students should be taught skills to control and channel anger appropriately.

Hachnasat Orchim (Welcoming the Stranger): Inclusion and cooperation should be stressed in the classroom and on the playground, both informally and formally (i.e. through regular use of cooperative pedagogic techniques). Special outreach should be made to newcomers who are more easily left out.

K'vod HaBriyot (Respecting Others' Dignity): School rules and consequences for breaking them must reflect fairness and the value of treating others with dignity. Otherwise, feelings of resentment and alienation will be exacerbated, possibly leading to increased hostility.

Lo Levayesh (Not embarrassing or humiliating others): An atmosphere in which embarrassing, humiliating, and bullying others is tolerated is one which "invites" acts of vengeance.

Rodef Shalom (Pursue Peace): An environment of peace is most conducive to learning.

Sayver Panim Yafot (A Pleasant Demeanor): When teachers model friendliness and warmth toward others, they set a tone that helps students see school as affirming and committed to their success.

Shmiat HaOzen (Being a Good Listener): Adults in the school community must really listen to their students in order to understand what is troubling them and how they might help them. Modeling good listening will encourage students to listen better to each other, too.

Good listening is a huge part of effective problem solving.

Tochechah (Rebuking) Troublemaking behavior (bullying, carrying weapons, threatening violence, etc.) needs to be addressed immediately with rebukes that fit the offense and that are given in a dignified manner.

Where Do I Go From Here?

When students exhibit and experience violent behavior in school, it forces school administrators to wrestle with very tough questions about the nature and purpose of education. Is there any facet of education that should fall to parents and religious communities and doesn't belong in a secular school environment, or does school violence necessitate character education delivered by the school? Where do you fit into this debate? How will the texts you've studied guide you both as an active member of your school community and as a future parent?

Following are resources that you may find helpful as you continue to explore this important and complex issue.

Books and Articles

Aronson, Elliot. *Nobody Left to Hate*. New York: Worth Publishers, 2000.

Bonilla, Denise M., ed. *School Violence*. New York: The H.W. Wilson Company, 2000.

Capozzoli, Thomas K., and R. Steve McVey. *Kids Killing Kids: Managing Violence and Gangs in Schools*. Boca Raton, FL: CRC-St. Lucie Press, 2000.

Center to Prevent Handgun Violence. *Straight Talk about Risks: A Pre-K-12 Curriculum for Preventing Gun Violence*. Washington, DC: Center to Prevent Handgun Violence, 1992.

Curwin, Richard L., and Allen N. Mendler. *As Tough as Necessary: Countering Violence, Aggression, and Hostility in Our Schools*. Alexandria, VA: Association for Supervision and Curriculum Development, 1997.

Flannery, Raymond B., Jr. *Preventing Youth Violence: A Guide for Parents, Teachers, and Counselors.* New York: The Continuum Publishing Company, 1999.

Harris, Judith Rich. *The Nurture Assumption: Why Children Turn Out the Way They Do; Parents Matter Less than You Think and Peers Matter More.* New York: The Free Press, 1998.

Kreidler, William J. *Creative Conflict Resolution: More that 200 Activities for Keeping Peace in the Classroom.* Glenview, IL: GoodYear Books, 1984.

Web Sites

The Center for Effective Collaboration and Practice: cecp.air.org/school_violence.htm
Promotes a reoriented national preparedness for dealing with children who have or are at risk of developing serious emotional disturbances. See especially "Early Warning, Timely Response — A Guide To Safe Schools")

The School Violence Watch Network: www.cyberenforcement.com/schoolviolencewatch.htm
Assists school administrators, teachers, and law enforcement officials in dealing with threats and rumors of violence, bullying, or drug abuse occurring within schools.

School Safety Report Card:
www.schoolsafetyreportcard.com
An opportunity for stakeholders in the educational system — parents, teachers, students, counselors, administrators, taxpayers, business people, law enforcement, government officials, media, and community residents — to provide input and complete a report card to grade their school district and school.

These web sites are helpful in searches for the latest stories and issues:

Education Week: www.edweek.org
The online version of Education Week magazine. Search for articles about school violence.

Yahoo: www.yahoo.com
Click "news," then search for "school violence."

The following web sites deal with character education:

Character Counts!: www.charactercounts.org
A nonprofit, nonpartisan, nonsectarian coalition of schools, communities and nonprofit organizations working to advance character education by teaching the Six Pillars of Character: trustworthiness, respect, responsibility, fairness, caring, and citizenship.

Good Character.com: www.goodcharacter.com
Character Education resources, materials, and lesson plans.

The Character Education Partnership:
www.character.org
" . . . a nonpartisan coalition of organizations and individuals dedicated to developing moral character and civic virtue in our nation's youth as one means of creating a more compassionate and responsible society."

The Character Education Network:
www.charactered.net
A place for students, teachers, schools and communities to facilitate character education. The site provides ready-to-use curriculum, activities, and resources.

The Jigsaw Classroom: www.jigsaw.org
"The jigsaw classroom is a cooperative learning technique that reduces racial conflict among school children, promotes better learning, improves student motivation, and increases enjoyment of the learning experience."

National Center for Conflict Resolution - Conflict Resolution Education, Inc.:
www.resolutioneducation.com
Promote the development of conflict resolution education programs in schools.

The Responsive Classroom:
www.responsiveclassroom.org
A practical approach for creating safe, challenging, and joyful schools.

Films

The Teen Files is an Emmy Award winning series that helps teens identify, understand, and deal with many of the issues confronting teens today. *The Teen Files Flipped* is a newer series from MTV that offers teens a fresh perspective on complex issues by "flipping" them into the shoes of young people who are coming to grips with life-changing issues. Obtain purchase information from www.aimsmultimedia.com.

The Teen Files — The Truth about Violence (2000, 57 min.)

The Teen Files Flipped — Gun Awareness (2002, 21 min.)

The Teen Files Flipped — Bullies, Loners, and Violence (2001, 21 min.)

The Teen Files Flipped — Doing Hard Time (2002, 21 min.)

The Teen Files Flipped — Tolerance (2001, 21 min.)

The following commercial films deal with issues of school violence, bullying, cliques, and alternate methods of conflict resolution in a frank and mature manner. Check with teachers or parents before viewing.

Revenge of the Nerds (1984, 89 min., rated R)
At a big college campus, a group of bullied outcasts and misfits resolve to fight back for their peace and self respect.

My Bodyguard (1980, 96 min., rated PG)
When a boy comes to a new school and gets harassed by a bully, he acquires the services of the school's most feared kid as a bodyguard.

Carrie (1976, 98 min., rated R)
A classic, somewhat campy horror flick about a shy young girl raised by a psychotic, abusive mother who is taunted ruthlessly by her classmates.

Bowling for Columbine (2002, 119 minutes, rated R)
Activist filmmaker Michael Moore explores the roots of America's predilection for gun violence. In doing so, he learns that the conventional answers of easy availability of guns, violent national history, violent entertainment and even poverty are inadequate to explain the level of violence found in American culture.

Glossary

Ben Sorer U'moreh
A stubborn and rebellious son.

Eglah Arufah
A slaughtered calf (literal meaning); the elders of a community make an offering of a calf when the murderer of an abandoned corpse cannot be found.

Ha-adam Nivra B'tzelem Elohim
All people are created in the image of God.

Lo Tachmod al Dam Rayecha
Do not stand idly while the blood of your fellow person is shed. (Leviticus 19:16)

Kol Yisrael Aravin Zeh Ba-zeh
All of Israel is responsible for one another.

Mipnay Darkay Shalom
For the sake of peace.

Rodef
A pursuer (after another person).

CHAPTER 8
ETHICS OF WAR

Overview

Introduction

"War is hell." We've all heard the expression. War is violent, destructive, brutal, and devastating. Yet, war has been a reality of human existence since humankind appeared on earth, and war doesn't seem close to disappearing. Even so, we must ask ourselves if there are ways to diminish some of war's evils.

People battle for different reasons. Some wars may qualify as worth fighting, others not. Certain nations will fight a war only to defend their very survival. Others are willing to fight to spread ideological beliefs. How do we determine a just cause for war? Who is obliged to fight? Does war have "rules"? That is, are there just means of fighting a war? How does war affect our relationship with God? How does war affect our humanity?

In this chapter we will examine difficult questions regarding the ethics of war. But we won't find easy answers. Nowhere are the stakes as high as they are in war.

Jewish Perspectives

How Do We Determine a Just Cause for War?

Killing, murder, and the intentional harming of people and other creatures are antithetical to Jewish values. Those who cause wanton damage and destruction of property and the environment are denounced, and deserve severe punishment. So how is it possible for war ever to play a legitimate role in a Jewish worldview?

Jewish law distinguishes between two types of war: *milchemet mitzvah,* an "obligatory war, and *milchemet reshut,* an "authorized or optional war."[1]

An obligatory war (*milchemet mitzvah*) fulfills specific biblical commandments, including the conquest of Canaan under Joshua and attacks against the tribe of Amalek. Maimonides includes as obligatory "a war to deliver Israel from an enemy who has attacked them" (see Text Study #1c below).

An optional war (*milchemet reshut*) is for increasing territory or "diminishing the heathens so that they shall not march against them" (see Text Study #1b below). An optional war must be initiated by a king, approved by the Sanhedrin (an ancient legislative body) and sanctioned through the *urim v'tumim* (a priestly device used for determining God's decision in certain questions and issues). Since these institutions no longer function, halachic (Jewish legal) authorities generally agree that "optional wars" are not authorized in our day.

Wars of self-defense may be permissible, and the laws of the pursuer help us define what tactics we may be able to justify (see Text Study #1a below). A difficult and timely question is whether preemptive strikes are permissible. When survival is at stake, authorities may consider preemptive strikes necessary and warranted. However, they would prohibit killings that take place in a war not based on immediate self defense. Such killings could be seen as murder.

Who Is Obliged to Fight?

As long ago as the Bible, our tradition did not compel every man who is physically able to fight to actually do so. In Deuteronomy, when the priests addressed the people as they prepared for battle, they granted exemptions from military service that included one who has built a new house but not yet lived in it; one who has planted a vineyard but not reaped its fruits; one who has betrothed but not consummated the marriage; and one who is afraid and "soft hearted" (*rach layv*) who might melt the hearts of his brothers as well (Deuteronomy 20:5-9, see Text Study #3A below).

In essence, there are two distinct categories of exemptions in the Bible. One is for those whose death would halt the completion of a life cycle event. The other is for those whose fear would have a negative influence on the morale of the troops. However, even those released from combat duty could be called to support the war through other means such as by supplying water and food or repairing roads for the army (*Sotah* 44a).

Judaism holds the path of peace in the highest esteem, yet does not support a position of unwavering pacifism. Jewish sources say war may be necessary at times. Thus, our tradition urges us to reject violence to whatever extent we possibly can and still survive.

Does War Have Rules?

The laws of the pursuer teach that use of force must not exceed the minimum necessary to repel the enemy. Force is prohibited for revenge, to punish the enemy for their aggression, or for terrorizing or humiliating the enemy. Military force is justifiable only when used for deterrence.

The Israel Defense Forces upholds the principle of *tohar ha-neshek*, "purity of arms," teaching use of weapons only to the extent necessary to subdue the enemy. Soldiers are to avoid unnecessary harm to life and property.

There can be no attacking enemies before giving them ample opportunity to make peace through nonviolent means. This principal originates in the Bible (Deuteronomy 20:10-12, see Text Study #4a below) and has been upheld by Jewish leaders over the centuries. Judaism also requires the protection of the civilian population during war, and there are specific rules for conduct during a siege. A Jewish army may surround a city only on three sides, leaving an escape route for inhabitants, and the cutting off of food and water supplies is prohibited. There are also regulations for the treatment of captives.

The Talmud prohibits waging a war that will destroy a sixth or more of the population (*Shevuot* 35b). In our day, the launching of weapons of mass destruction — nuclear, chemical, or biological — could easily escalate to the point of massive, widespread casualties, well beyond a sixth of the population. From a Jewish point of view, there is no justification for the use of such weapons.

Judaism also specifies numerous rules for protecting the environment in time of war. A prohibition against cutting down fruit trees outside a besieged city originates in the Bible (Deuteronomy 20:19, see Text Study #6c below). There are also prohibitions against wanton destruction, as well as guidelines for maintaining sanitary conditions in the war camp.

How Does War Affect Our Relationship with God?

Judaism teaches that God abhors senseless bloodshed, cruelty, violence, and wanton destruction. We become alienated from God's will when we participate in a clearly prohibited war. Our wrongful actions distance us from God and Jewish sacred teachings.

In a defensible war, as in any other challenging life situation, it seems that God wants us to be the best people we possibly can be. War forces us to face what might be the greatest challenge in terms of rising to our highest selves. The more we strive for peace, the more we come to know and understand the attribute of God that is peace.

Our great teacher Hillel said, "In a place where there are no worthy persons, strive to be a worthy person" (*Pirke Avot* 2:6). Applied to war, this teaching tells us that we must resist sinking to the inhumanity that war tends to bring out in people, and push ourselves to rise above the inclination to do evil (*yetzer hara*).

General Perspectives

What Is a Just Cause for War?

There are many reasons for war. Throughout the ages, these reasons have included:[2]

- Self defense: A nation defends its territory and safety against an aggressor.

- Rescue of hostages: A military operation seeks the safe return of citizens captured by an enemy.

- Military security/deterrence: Preemptive strikes are mounted to halt or impede an enemy's military capabilities (e.g., destruction of a weapons manufacturing plant).

- Extension of territory: Political power, influence, and riches are expected with territorial gains.

- Economic benefit: Access is sought to natural resources, treasures, trade routes, and markets.

- Ideology: A military force imposes a political system or forcibly converts others to a particular religious belief.

- Vengeance: The enemy is punished for an insult, injury, or other perceived injustice.

- Credibility of threats: A nation stages a military operation in order to prove to the enemy (and to other nations, as well) just how strong it really is and that it will back up threats with action.

- Social integration: Rival groups within a nation are united against a common enemy. Focus on a common enemy deflects attention away from a nation's own internal troubles, helping to ensure peace within that nation's own borders.

- "Feeding" the military machine: Certain political leaders, military officials, and corporate executives draw power, wealth, and prestige from continual warfare.[2]

The reasons listed above are simply descriptive. They highlight why a group might go to war, not if it should go. Figuring out if there is just cause for war is the more difficult task.

Some might argue that (1) there is just cause for declaring war on nations that ignore human rights, and (2) that attacks on such "rogue nations" are legitimate. But can we agree on what rights and values should be standard for all people? The United Nations took on the challenge, and on December 10, 1948, the General Assembly adopted without dissent the "Universal Declaration of Human Rights. Following is a synopsis of the main ideas.

- Article 1: Right to freedom and equality in dignity and rights.

- Article 2: Freedom from discrimination.

- Article 3: Right to life, liberty and security of person.

- Article 4: Freedom from slavery and servitude.

- Article 5: Freedom from torture or degrading treatment.

- Article 6: Right to recognition as a person before the law.

- Article 7: Right to equal consideration before the law.

- Article 8: Right to remedy through a competent tribunal.

- Article 9: Freedom from arbitrary arrest, detention, or exile.

- Article 10: Right to a fair trial or public hearing.

- Article 11: Right to be considered innocent until proven guilty.

- Article 12: Freedom from interference with privacy, including home, family, and correspondence.

- Article 13: Right to freedom of movement and residence in one's own country, and to leave and return at will.

- Article 14: Right to asylum.

- Article 15: Right to a nationality and freedom to change it.

- Article 16: Right to marriage and protection of family.

- Article 17: Right to own property.

- Article 18: Freedom of belief and religion.

- Article 19: Freedom of opinion and information.

- Article 20: Right to peaceful assembly and association.

- Article 21: Right to participate in government and in free elections and to equal access to public service.

- Article 22: Right to social security.

- Article 23: Right to work and fair pay for work.

- Article 24: Right to rest and leisure.

- Article 25: Right to adequate standard of living for health and well-being.

- Article 26: Right to education.

- Article 27: Right to participate in the cultural life of the community.

- Article 28: Right to social order assuring human rights.

- Article 29: Responsibilities to community are essential to free and full development of the individual.

- Article 30: Freedom from State or other interference in any of the above rights.

This Declaration is, in essence, an acknowledgement that disregard for human rights creates dangerous living conditions, and that any environment that denies basic freedoms can become so volatile that it can easily erupt into war. While the debate as to whether human rights abuses are justification for war may continue, such abuses can help explain why wars happen.

In 1941, nearly a year before the United States entered World War II, President Franklin D. Roosevelt gave a speech before the Congress of the United States in which he stated four essential freedoms, the violation of which would be just reason for going to war:

The freedoms we are fighting for, we who are free, the freedoms for which the men and women in the concentration camps and prisons and in the dark streets of the subjugated countries wait, are four in number.

The first is freedom of speech and expression — everywhere in the world.

The second is freedom of every person to worship God in his own way — everywhere in the world.

The third is freedom from want — which, translated into world terms, means economic understandings which will secure to every nation a healthy peacetime life for its inhabitants — everywhere in the world.

The fourth is freedom from fear — which, translated into world terms, means a worldwide reduction of armaments to such a point and in such a thorough fashion that no nation will be in a position to commit an act of physical aggression against any neighbor — anywhere in the world.[3]

Like the Universal Declaration of Human Rights, these "Four Freedoms" can provide important guidelines for war. Suppose we compare the principles laid out in these two documents with the straightforward reasons for war listed at the beginning of this chapter. A humanistic perspective would assert that some reasons for war are more worthy than others It would reject altogether certain rationalizations for war, for example wars waged for territorial expansion or wars of vengeance. On the other hand, it is more likely to justify war for reasons concerning defense of "life liberty, and security of person." No matter what, a humanistic perspective would demand that warring factions work as hard as possible to resolve conflicts peacefully.

Who Is Obliged to Fight?

Who can, may, or will serve in the armed forces differs from nation to nation, and from conflict to conflict. In Israel, with few exceptions, able bodied men and women must serve a term of fulltime duty in the military, and then as part of the Reserves. At times, the United States has maintained an all-volunteer army. During war or other tense periods, the country has drafted civilians into the armed forces.

In our day, there are many interesting controversies over who must fight. One has to do with "conscientious objectors": specifically, should you be exempt from a draft if you are a conscientious objector to war? What if you are a "selective conscientious objector," that is, you have moral objections to a particular war? Suppose an army is willing to exempt conscientious objectors from the draft. What should the criteria be for granting that status?

Another controversy has to do with women's role in the military. In a society that values equality of the sexes, should women serve in the military in the same capacity as men? For instance, should an army that drafts men to fight, draft women equally?

Issues of military exemptions are complex. Our aim here is not to analyze in great detail questions about who must serve. Rather, it is simply to point out that there is, in fact, a good deal of debate on the topic.

Does War Have "Rules"?

We have discussed what might be just causes for war. A related question is, are there just means of fighting wars? That is, in war, are there rules that should be followed? Civilized people can agree on certain key ideas concerning just use of force. They are outlined below.

1. The principle of discrimination: force must be directed at a military target, with damage to civilians and civilian society being incidental.
2. The principle of proportionality: force must not be greater than that needed to achieve an acceptable military result and must not be greater than the provoking cause.
3. The principle of humanity: force must not be directed against enemy personnel if they are subject to capture, wounded, or under control (as with prisoners of war).
4. The principle of necessity: force should be used only if nonviolent means to achieve military goals are unavailable.[4]

A document called The Geneva Convention, adopted by the United Nation in 1949, is a key source for international humanitarian law. Its overarching provision is that "persons taking no active part in the hostilities . . . shall in all circumstances be treated humanely" (Article 3). Following is a sampling of topics covered in this extensive document.

- No murder, mutilation, cruel treatment, or torture.
- No taking of hostages.
- No outrages upon personal dignity, in particular humiliating and degrading treatment.
- No executions without previous judgment pronounced by a regularly constituted court.
- The wounded and sick shall be collected and cared for.
- Safety and neutralized zones may be created to protect vulnerable individuals.
- No attacks on civilian hospitals, medical vehicles and aircraft, or medical workers.
- Provide care for children under fifteen who are orphaned or are separated from their families as a result of the war.
- Women shall be protected against any attack on their honor, in particular against rape, enforced prostitution, or any form of indecent assault.
- No pillaging.
- Those who want to leave the area of conflict are entitled to do so.

In addition, the Geneva Convention contains many rules concerning the conduct of occupying forces and the treatment of internees.

How Does War Affect Our Humanity?

Brutal acts are not only horrifying for the victims, but often have a devastating effect on the perpetrators. They may become paranoid, emotionally distant, rigid, indiscriminately loyal to "the cause," unable to resist immoral attitudes and pressures, and lack a sense of personal responsibility. We ended the "Jewish Perspectives" section with Hillel's teaching, "In a place where there are no worthy persons, strive to be a worthy person" (*Pirke Avot* 2:6). We said that God demands this of us. Here we can add that not only God, but all of humanity demands, and deserves, no less.

Summary of the Overview

The points below summarize key considerations regarding the ethics of war.

- We have a sacred duty to love and preserve life and to protect God's earth. We must avoid causing harm to creatures, the environment, and property.
- War has the potential to cause widespread death, suffering, and destruction, throwing into turmoil some of our most cherished values and deeply held commitments.
- Yet, when hostile forces threaten and endanger life, we must respond.
- Still, we must always seek to make peace with our enemies through nonviolent means. If that is impossible, we may use force, but limit it to demands concerning self defense.

Scenarios: How Things Have Changed

Below are two scenarios dealing with issues related to war, intended to raise questions and spark discussion. Read each scenario and reflect, either individually or in a group discussion, on the questions in the "For Thought and Discussion" section that follows. Then continue on to the "Text Study" section to see what Jewish and other sources have to say on the subject. Finally, you may wish to come back and discuss the scenarios a second time, to see if your views have changed.

Scenario I: In Biblical Days (Exodus 17:8-16)

Before the Israelites received the Torah at Sinai, they dwelt in the wilderness. While they resided in Refidim, Amalek and his men attacked. Moses instructed Joshua to prepare men for a counterattack, to make war on Amalek. Joshua did as Moses instructed him. The Israelites battled the Amalekites. Using swords, Joshua's forces overwhelmed Amalek and his people. The Israelites demonstrated perseverance, strong leadership, and faith in God's will. These elements helped them to defeat the Amalekites.

Scenario II: During World War II (1939-1945)

Many Jews lived in Europe, though they were a small minority of the population. A powerful dictator Adolph Hitler arose, leading a political movement called Nazism. Besides intending to take over Europe and other lands, Hitler was determined to annihilate the Jews. Most Jews didn't realize the extent of Hitler's intentions until it was too late. While some Jews staged resistance efforts and others tried to escape, they were in the main overwhelmed by Hitler's forces. Responding to Hitler's aggressive efforts to seize land, control territory, and impose his fanatical ideology, many nations became entangled in a war.

At the same time, for reasons that include Japan's attack on America's Pearl Harbor, many nations began to battle in the Pacific. Much of the world was at war.

After years of fighting and millions of deaths — both of soldiers and innocent civilians, including six million Jews — Hitler was defeated. In the Pacific the war ended when the United States dropped two nuclear bombs on Japan. The bombs "scorched" the earth, killing between 130,000 and 170,000 people, and injured many thousands more.

For Thought and Discussion:

Read Exodus 17:8-16 before answering the following questions about Scenario I:

Do you think the Israelites were justified in their actions against the Amalekites?

Do you think it is appropriate to carry out a war because it is God's will? Why or why not?

Are the war tactics described in Scenario II above easier or harder to justify than the biblical war described in Scenario I? Why?

Text Study

As we have seen, the ethics of war present us with many difficult questions and no easy answers. Clearly, killing, murder, and the intentional harming of people and other creatures are antithetical to Jewish values. Yet Judaism teaches that we can sanction armed conflict at times, and does recognize circumstances when fighting is mandatory. Jewish texts address these complex issues and provide us with some insight, but these guidelines often highlight the tension between seemingly opposing considerations. The chart below poses the questions and offers two opposing points of view. Text sources supporting each of these points of view follow.

1. **Is war ever justified?**

   On the One Hand:

   Killing is abhorrent. It violates the sixth commandment.

   A. You shall not kill (Exodus 20:13). (Alternate translation: "You shall not murder")

B. In the following rabbinic text, an individual is ordered by the governor of his locale to put a certain man to death. If he refuses to obey the order, he himself will be put to death. Raba is consulted, ruling that the individual must not put the innocent third party to death to save himself:

> Let him slay you rather than you commit murder. Who knows that your blood is redder? Perhaps his blood is redder? [That is, who is to say that you deserve to live more than he does?] (*Sanhedrin* 74a).

C. Whoever saves a single life, scripture regards that person as though he/she has saved the entire world, and whoever destroys a single life, scripture regards that person as though he/she has destroyed the whole world (*Sanhedrin* 4:5).

On the Other Hand:

There are just causes worth fighting for, even if need be, killing is involved.

a. If someone comes to slay you, forestall by slaying that person (*Sanhedrin* 72a).

[However,] Rabbi Jonathan ben Saul has taught: If one was pursuing his fellow to slay him, and the pursued could have saved himself by maiming a limb of the pursuer, but instead killed his pursuer, the pursued is subject to execution on that account (*Sanhedrin* 74a).

b. After reading the following passage, recall that a so-called "discretionary war" (*milchemet reshut*) requires these three conditions: the initiative of a king, approval of the Sanhedrin (legislative body), and a sanctioning of the war by the *urim v'tumim* (a priestly device used for determining God's decision in certain questions and issues). Meeting these criteria is not possible in our day.

> Said Rava: All [the Sages] agree that the wars of Joshua to conquer [the land of Canaan] were obligatory (i.e.,

milchemet mitzvah). All agree that the wars of the House of David for territorial expansion were discretionary (*milchemet reshut*). They differ with regard to [wars for the purpose of] diminishing the heathens so that they shall not march against them. [Rabbi Judah] calls it commanded and [the Sages] call it discretionary (*Sotah* 44b).

c. According to Maimonides, there are a number of reasons for which a king is obliged to wage war [*milchemet mitzvah*], including:

> [A war] to deliver Israel from an enemy who has attacked them (Maimonides, *Mishneh Torah, Hilchot Melachim* 5:1).

d. Defensive response to an attack is mandatory in order to save lives. Yet, although a preemptive strike is warranted when there is reason to anticipate danger, such preemptive action is not mandatory in the absence of overt aggression (J. David Bleich, in *Contemporary Halakhic Problems, Vol. III*, p. 284).

What Do You Think?

Many issues are presented here. Go through the texts, one by one, and in your own words, restate the main idea(s) communicated in each.

According to these passages, for what reasons might killing/war be justified? What restrictions are mentioned?

Why would approval of the Sanhedrin be a necessary criteria for launching a *milchemet reshut* (discretionary war)?

Which is more ethically justifiable, a *milchemet mitzvah* or a *milchemet reshut*? Explain.

Overall, what ideas do you definitely agree with in the texts. Why?

What ideas are you less sure about. Why?

Considerations for Making Ethical Decisions Regarding War

	The Question	On the One Hand	On the Other Hand
1.	Is war ever justified? (see page 116)	Killing is abhorrent. It violates the sixth commandment.	There are just causes worth fighting for, even, if need be, killing is involved.
2.	For what, if any reason might we knowingly risk our lives? (see page 119)	We are to avoid endangering ourselves, putting our lives at risk.	There are causes for which risking our lives may be justified.
3.	Who is obligated to participate in war? (see page 119)	Though a war may be permissible, participating in combat is not appropriate for everyone.	There are wartime circumstances for which serving in the armed forces becomes obligatory for every mentally stable, able-bodied person.
4.	How can we continue to embrace the value of peace even as we prepare for or engage in war? (see page 120)	War is a rejection of the paramount Jewish value of pursuing peace.	The enemy cannot be attacked before being given ample opportunity to make peace through nonviolent means.
5.	In war, can we adequately protect innocent bystanders from harm? (see page 121)	In war, innocent people are likely to get killed.	Efforts must be made to prevent unnecessary deaths and injuries, including giving those on the enemy side who wish to escape a conflict continual openings to do so.
6.	What might be the long term effects of war, and can some of the damage be avoided? (see page 122)	Long after a war is over, extraordinary suffering may persist for weeks, and even years as a result of environmental destruction and the lingering poisons of weapons.	While carrying out a war mission, environmental destruction and the suffering of civilians must be minimized to whatever extent possible.
7.	Do we spend too much on war? (see page 123)	The cost of war is shameful when compared with what could be purchased alternatively.	Though the cost of military preparedness is high, if our "survival" depends on it, we have to be willing to spend what is necessary.
8.	Is it possible to preserve our humanity during wartime? (see page 124)	War breeds dehumanization. Combatants are vulnerable to becoming brutal, cruel, and immune to human suffering.	Grassroots organizations, individual countries, and international alliances must be vigilant in counteracting dehumanization.
9.	How might beliefs about God shape attitudes toward war? (see page 125)	God is the Creator of all things. Since war kills and destroys, it is a desecration to God.	People may look to God for support in their efforts to achieve certain war goals.

2. **For what, if any reason, might we knowingly risk our lives?**

On the One Hand:

We are to avoid endangering ourselves, putting our lives at risk.

A. The following "watch out!" statement concerns passing through another people's territory (where the descendants of Esau reside).

> . . . Take good care of yourselves. Take heed, and guard your soul diligently . . . Take good care of your lives (Deuteronomy 2:4; 4:9, 15).

B. Rabbi Akiba said, "A person is not permitted to harm him/herself" (*Baba Kamma* 90a).

C. Throughout the ages, Jewish sages have wrestled with the ethics of giving up one life to save others. A great deal of discussion develops from these two texts:[5]

> Caravans of men are walking down a road, and they are accosted by non-Jews who say to them: "Give us one from among you that we may kill him, otherwise we shall kill you all." Though all may be killed, they may not hand over a single soul of Israel. However, if the demand is for a specified individual like Sheba son of Bichri, they should surrender him rather than all be killed (Palestinian Talmud, *Trumot* 7:20; *Genesis Rabbah* 94:9).

> Resh Lakish stated: "[He may be surrendered] only if he is deserving of death as Sheba son of Bichri." Rabbi Yochanan said: "Even if he is not deserving of death as Sheba son of Bichri" (Palestinian Talmud, *Trumot* 47a).

On the Other Hand:

There are causes for which risking our lives may be justified.

See Texts #1a-c above. Text #2C applies here as well.

What Do You Think?

To what extent is the desire not to risk one's life a valid stance to take for opposing war?

For what reasons would you be willing to risk your own life?

3. **Who is obligated to participate in war?**

On the One Hand:

Though a war may be permissible, participating in combat is not appropriate for everyone.

A. Then the officials are to speak to the people, saying: Who is the man that has built a new house and has not (yet) dedicated it? Let him go and return to his house, lest he die in the war and another man dedicate it!

> And who is the man that has planted a vineyard and has not (yet) made common use of it? Let him go and return to his house, lest he dies in the war and another man make common use of it!

> And who is the man that has betrothed a woman and has not (yet) taken her (in marriage)? Let him go and return to his house, lest he die in the war and another man take her!

> And the officers are to continue to speak to the people, they are to say: Who is the man, the one afraid and soft of heart? Let him go and return to his house, so that he does not melt the heart of his brothers, like his heart!

> And it shall be, when the officials finish speaking to the people, the commanders of the armed forces are to count by head the fighting people (Deuteronomy 20:5-9; also see *Sotah* 8:4).

On the Other Hand:

There are wartime circumstances for which serving in the armed forces becomes obligatory for every mentally stable, able-bodied person.

a. It must be noted that in some circumstances a *milchemet reshut* [discretionary war], once undertaken, may be governed by the regulations applying to a *milchemet mitzvah* [obligatory war]. As noted [in text #3A above], Deuteronomy 20:5-7 provides for the deferment of military service for certain categories of men. These exclusions apply only to a *milchemet reshut*. Hence, a king may not legitimately undertake a *milchemet reshut* unless he is confident of victory without finding it necessary to conscript such persons. However, once a war is declared and the tide of battle threatens to overwhelm the Jewish forces committed to battle, the situation is entirely different. *Chazon Ish, Orach Chayim-Mo'ed* 114:3, quite logically asserts that once a battle has been undertaken and there is danger of losing the encounter, response to such danger constitutes a *milchemet mitzvah* and, accordingly, even those persons otherwise exempt from military service are obligated to participate if their services are necessary to achieve victory. The selfsame consideration would logically apply even in the case of a war whose inception was entirely illicit. The danger of defeat creates a situation requiring the "deliverance of Israel from an enemy" which constitutes a *milchemet mitzvah* (J. David Bleich, in *Contemporary Halakhic Problems, Vol. III*, pp. 290-291).

What Do You Think?

According to Text #3A, who should be exempt from serving in military operations?

Why do you suppose those particular exemptions are permitted? According to Text #3a, what limits must be placed on exemptions? Why?

Do you think the exemptions are fair? Why or why not? What about the limits placed on exemptions?

Are there exemptions you would add or eliminate?

4. How can we continue to embrace the value of peace even as we prepare for or engage in war?

On the One Hand:

War is a rejection of the paramount Jewish value of pursuing peace.

A. Whoever desires life and is eager for years of goodness . . . avoid evil and do good. Seek peace and pursue it (Psalms 34:13,15).

B. And they shall beat their swords into plowshares, and their spears into pruning hooks; Nation shall not lift sword against nation, they shall never again know war (Isaiah 2:4).

C. In that day, there shall be a highway from Egypt to Assyria. The Assyrians shall join with the Egyptians and Egyptians with Assyrians, and then the Egyptians together with the Assyrians shall serve [the Eternal]. In that day, Israel shall be a third partner with Egypt and Assyria as a blessing on earth; for the Eternal of Hosts will bless them, saying, "Blessed be My people Egypt, My handiwork Assyria, and My very own Israel" (Isaiah 19:23-25).

D. Three days before the Messiah arrives, Elijah will come and stand upon the mountains . . . Elijah's voice will be heard from world's end to world's end. And then he will say: "Peace has come to the world" (*Pesikta Rabbati, Piska* 35).

On the Other Hand:

The enemy cannot be attacked before being given ample opportunity to make peace through non-violent means.

a. When you draw near to a town, to wage war against it, you are to call out to it terms of peace. And it shall be: if peace is what it answers you, and it opens (its gates) to you, then it shall be that all the people that are found in it shall belong to you as forced laborers, and they shall serve you. But if they do not make peace with you, and make war against you, you may besiege it . . . (Deuteronomy 20:10-12).

b. If the inhabitants [of a warring nation] make peace, accept the seven Noahide commandments, and submit to certain conditions of taxation and service, one may not kill a single person (Maimonides, Code, "Laws Concerning Kings and Wars," 6:1).

c. Joshua, before he entered the land of Israel sent three letters to its inhabitants. The first one said that those that wish to flee [the oncoming army] should flee. The second one said that those that wish to make peace should make peace. The third letter said that those that want to fight a war should prepare to fight a war (Maimonides, Code, "Laws Concerning Kings and Wars," 6:5).

What Do You Think?

According to these texts, what are the necessary conditions for peace?

What conditions for peace could a modern democratic nation reasonably demand of its enemy?

What do you believe are the most worthwhile strategies for avoiding violent conflict between nations?

5. **In war, can we adequately protect innocent bystanders from harm?**

On the One Hand:

In war, innocent people are likely to get killed.

A. Following Abram's participation in the War of the Kings, the next chapter in Genesis begins with these words: "After these things, the word of the Eternal came unto Abram in a vision, saying 'Fear not, Abram . . .'" (Genesis 15:1).

Commentators probe possible reasons for Abram's fear:[6]

> Abram was afraid, saying: "I have killed the sons of a righteous man, and now he will curse me and I shall die..."

(*Midrash Tanchuma* on *Lech Lecha* 19 ed. Buber).

Still another reason for Abraham's fear after killing the kings in battle was his sudden realization: "Perhaps I violated the Divine commandment that the Holy One Who Is Blessed commanded all people, 'You shall not shed human blood' (Genesis 9:6). Yet how many people have I killed in battle?" (*Ibid.*)

Abraham was filled with misgiving, thinking to himself: Maybe there was a righteous or God-fearing man among those troops which I slew . . . " (*Midrash Rabbah* on Genesis 44:4).

B. This passage from Josephus refers to the Roman siege of Jerusalem in 72 C.E.:

> The restraint of liberty to pass in and out of the city took from the Jews all hope of safety, and the famine now increasing consumed whole households and families; and the houses were full of dead women and infants; and the streets filled with the dead bodies of old men. And the young men, swollen like dead men's shadows, walked in the market place and fell down dead where it happened. And now the multitude of dead bodies was so great that they who were alive could not bury them; nor cared they for burying them, being now uncertain what should betide themselves. And many endeavoring to bury others fell down themselves dead upon them . . . And many being yet alive went unto their graves and there died. Yet for all this calamity was there no weeping nor lamentation, for famine overcame all affections. And they who were yet living, without tears beheld those who being dead were now at rest before them. There was no noise heard within the city . . . (Josephus, *The Wars of the Jews*, Book VI, ch. XIV, p. 721).

C. In this modern situation, the American army did not allow innocent people to escape. The repercussions were devastating.

> In August 1967, during Operation Benton, the "pacification" camps became so full that Army units were ordered not to "generate" any more refugees. The Army complied. But search and destroy operations continued. Only now the peasants were not warned before an air strike was called on their village. They were killed in their villages because there was no room for them in the swamped pacification camps (Orville and Jonathan Schell, letter to *The New York Times*, Nov. 26, 1969).

On the Other Hand:

Efforts must be made to prevent unnecessary deaths and injuries, including giving those on the enemy's side who wish to escape a conflict continual openings to do so. (For additional texts which question the morality of "sacrificing" innocent lives, see Texts #1B and #2C above.)

a. When siege is laid to a city for the purpose of capture, it may not be surrounded on all four sides but only on three sides in order to give an opportunity for escape to those who would flee to save their lives . . .

   It has been learned by tradition that this was the instruction given to Moses (Maimonides, Code, "Laws Concerning Kings and Wars," 6:7).

b. It is forbidden to sell to idolaters any weapons of war. Neither may one sharpen their weapons nor make available to them knives, chains, barbed chains, bears, lions, or anything which might cause widespread injury. One may sell to them shields or shutters which are purely defensive (Maimonides, Code, "Laws of Murder and Defense," 12:12).

   That which is prohibited for sale to idolaters is also prohibited for sale to Jews who are suspected of then selling such material to idolaters. Likewise, it is forbidden to sell

such weapons to Jewish thieves (Maimonides, Code, "Law of Idolatry," 9:8).

What Do You Think?

What precautions do these texts mention for avoiding harm to innocent people? What are some of the tactics used today to protect innocent people?

How effective are these tactics?

How should an "innocent" be defined?

⎯⎯⎯◆⎯⎯⎯

6. **What might be the long term effects of war, and can some of the damage be avoided?**

On the One Hand:

Long after a war is over, extraordinary suffering may persist for weeks, and even years as a result of environmental destruction and the lingering poisons of weapons.

The following passages are all modern, twentieth century examples of war's effects.

A. In the First World War, an entirely different category of mutilated soldiers returned from the war with these horrific wounds that were inflicted by modern ammunition. There were soldiers who returned who had suffered psychological shock. Some had been buried for hours in their dugouts and had no longer control over their extremities. These were the soldiers who had suffered and who showed, and continued to show, what suffering in the trenches had meant. They had not turned themselves into heroes. They were not even capable of functioning in the society at the end of the war. But, they were a continuous reminder of what they had gone through in the gas attack, in the bombardment, in being buried for hours under the earth, and being at the brink of psychological collapse. And, many of the population did not like to have to face these war cripples. They did not wish to be reminded continuously of what it was really like (PBS, "The Great War and the Shaping of the 20th Century," interview with Bernd Huppauf, New York University).

B. The [presumably Soviet] biplane came out of a clear sky at 9:30 one morning. It made a single run over the Laotian village of Va Houng, unleashing a stream of yellow gas that fell like rain along a one-kilometer strip and formed droplets on the ground. To the villagers, it smelled like burning peppers.

According to Gnia Pao Vang, a subdistrict chief in Vientiane Province, the gas killed 83 of the 473 residents of Va Houng, as well as all village animals, the chickens succumbing first.

The people died in pain, usually after two or three days of intense diarrhea and vomiting. Like other survivors, Mr. Gnia suffered for weeks from headaches and dizziness, impaired vision, a running nose, painful breathing and a swollen throat. For days he spit phlegm and blood (Barry Wain, "The Chemical Warfare in Southeast Asia." *Wall Street Journal*, September 21, 1981).

C. Long after peace returned to Mozambique, the number of war casualties continued to grow. Civilians, especially women and children, were the main victims of land mines that had been buried throughout the country. They were usually planted off main roads on bush paths, at water sites, or in people's fields. These have claimed over 10,000 lives and wounded many more. With these hidden dangers, it is very difficult for people to feel secure in peace (Report by Oxfam: "Mozambique — The Effects of War").

On the Other Hand:

While carrying out a war mission, environmental destruction and the suffering of civilians must be minimized to whatever extent possible.

a. When you besiege a town for many days, waging war against it, to seize it: you are not to bring ruin on its trees, by swinging away (with) an ax against them, for from them you eat, them you are not to cut down — for are the trees of the field human beings, (able) to come against you in siege? Only those trees of which you know that they are not trees for eating, them you may bring to ruin and cut down, that you may build siege works against the town that is making war against you (Deuteronomy 20:19-20).

b. It is forbidden to cut down fruit-bearing trees outside a (besieged) city, nor may a water channel be deflected from them so that they wither, as it is said: "You are not to bring ruin on the trees . . . " (Deuteronomy 20:19) (Maimonides, Code, "Laws Concerning Kings and Wars," 6:8).

c. Not only one who cuts down (fruit-producing) trees, but also one who smashes household goods, tears clothes, demolishes a building, stops up a spring, or destroys articles of food with destructive intent, transgresses the command: "You shall not destroy" (Maimonides, Code, "Laws Concerning Kings and Wars," 6:10).

What Do You Think?

What destructive effects of war might outlast the conflict itself? Can some of these be eliminated? How?

If destructive repercussions of war cannot be eliminated entirely, how might lasting damage be minimized?

⸺⧓⸺

7. **Do we spend too much on war?**

On the One Hand:

The cost of war is shameful when compared with what could be purchased alternatively.

Contemporary concerns confront this issue more directly than do traditional Jewish sources:

A. Every gun that is made, every warship

launched, every rocket fired signifies, in the final sense, a theft from those who hunger and are not fed, those who are cold and are not clothed. This world in arms is not spending money alone. It is spending the sweat of its laborers, the genius of its scientists, the hopes of its children (Dwight D. Eisenhower, quoted in *Peace Prayers* by Carrie Leadingham, et al, p. 23).

B. Think of what a world we could build if the power unleashed in war were applied to constructive tasks! One-tenth of the energy that the various belligerents spent in the war, a fraction of the money they exploded in hand grenades and poison gas, would suffice to raise the standard of living in every country and avert the economic catastrophe of worldwide unemployment. We must be prepared to make the same heroic sacrifices [for peace that we make] for the cause of war. There is no task that is more important or closer to my heart (Albert Einstein, quoted in *Peace Prayers,* by Carrie Leadingham, et al, p. 35).

On the Other Hand:

Though the cost of military preparedness is high, if our survival depends on it, we have to be willing to spend what is necessary.

a. Like other nations, the United States finds itself boxed in. While military expenditures are costly in terms of benefits foregone, failing to make them may well open us to attack. In light of [the majority of humankind's] bellicose history . . . , such an assumption, unfortunately, appears well-founded. Only in the event of a miracle by which all nations become pacifists and all danger of attack ceases will lack of military preparedness make sense. And there is no indication of any such miracle in the offing (James M. Henslin, *Social Problems,* p. 589).

What Do You Think?

What are some of the "costs" of war besides the loss of human lives? What might be the long-term effects of spending such high sums on military preparedness?

Is there an alternative to this kind of spending and use of resources?

Is it possible to preserve our humanity during wartime?

8. **Is it possible to preserve our humanity during wartime?**

On the One Hand:

War breeds dehumanization. Combatants are vulnerable to becoming brutal, cruel, and immune to human suffering.

The following texts warn against dehumanizing the enemy. Clearly, the assumption is that such a tendency is a hazard during times of conflict.

A. Do not rejoice when your enemy falls, And do not let your heart be glad when [your enemy] stumbles. If your enemy is hungry, give bread to eat, and if [your enemy] is thirsty, give water to drink. Happy are those who always have a sense of fear, but those who harden their hearts (or consciences) will fall into evil (Proverbs 24:17, 25:21, 28:14).

B.   In that hour when the Israelites crossed the Red Sea, the ministering angels wanted to sing a song of praise before God. But God said to them: "My handiwork [the Egyptians] is drowning in the sea, yet you want to sing a song before me!?" (*Sanhedrin* 39b).

On the Other Hand:

Grassroots organizations, individual countries, and international alliances must be vigilant in counteracting dehumanization.

a. A medieval Jewish source movingly tells us that one hundred shofar sounds at our New Year services correspond to the one hundred groans by the mother of Sisera (Judges 5:28) when she saw [that] her son

[was] killed in his battle against the Israelites:

> Sisera was a brutal tyrant, wreaking terror on our people. His death was our salvation. Yet, he had a mother, and to this day we hear her cries and recall her grief over the death of her child.
>
> Even terrorists have mothers, and we must not be indifferent to their anguish. This is but one of the remarkable features of Judaism in an effort to ensure that even war does not harden us to the point of not caring for the loss and suffering of our enemies (Sir Immanuel Jacobovitz, "The Morality of Warfare," in *L'EYLAH,* vol. 2, no. 4, 1983).

b. No one shall be subjected to torture or to cruel, inhuman or degrading treatment or punishment (From "The Universal Declaration of Human Rights," Article 5, adopted by the United Nations, December 10, 1948).

What Do You Think?

Are the views expressed above realistic? Why or why not?

Do you believe there are ever times when it is necessary to dehumanize the enemy in order to effectively fight for a particular cause? Explain your answer.

What are some effective ways to minimize dehumanization of the enemy?

In modern Israel, one aspect of military policy is tohar haneshek — "purity of arms." This principle states that Israeli soldiers are to use their firearms only to defend themselves, never to oppress or loot an enemy. Is this policy realistic? enforceable?

How might beliefs about God shape attitudes toward war?

⎯⎯◆⎯

9. **How might beliefs about God shape attitudes toward war?**

On the One Hand:

God is the Creator of all things. Since war kills and destroys, it is a desecration to God.

A. After the flood, God addresses Noah regarding murder:

> Whoever now sheds human blood, for that human shall his/her blood be shed, for in God's image did God make humankind (Genesis 9:6).

B. If one sheds blood, it is as if that person had diminished God's image (*Mechilta* to Exodus 20:13).

C. David said to Solomon, "My son, as for me, it was in my heart to build a house unto the name of the Eternal my God [the First Temple]. But the work of the Eternal came to me, saying, 'You have shed blood abundantly and have made great wars; you shall not build a house unto My name, because you have shed much blood upon the earth in my sight'" (I Chronicles 22:7-8).

On the Other Hand:

People may look to God for support in their efforts to achieve certain war goals.

a. For the Eternal your God is the one who goes with you, to wage war for you against your enemies, to deliver you! (Deuteronomy 20:4).

b. David replied to the Philistine, "You come against me with sword and spear and javelin; but I come against you in the name of the Eternal of Hosts, the God of the ranks of Israel, whom you have defied . . . And this whole assembly shall know that the Eternal can give victory without sword or spear. For the battle is the Eternal's, and God will deliver you into our hands" (I Samuel 17:45, 47).

What Do You Think?

Do the passages in the "On The One Hand"

section above make a strong enough argument against war to convince you that it is always a desecration before God? Why or why not?

What dangers might there be in "bringing God" into war?

When, if ever, is it appropriate to suggest that God plays a particular role in a war? Explain.

Related Middot and Mitzvot

These virtues and commandments can help infuse war decisions with Jewish values:

Anavah (Humility): Any decisions about use of force should come from a place of humility. The mastery of anavah is probably the best "guarantee" against the abuse of power.

Bal Tashchit (Protecting the Environment/Not Destroying) War efforts must avoid causing any more harm to the environment than is absolutely necessary.

Din (Law and Justice): Jewish law establishes grounds for fighting wars — only for a just cause and in a just manner. International law can help promote justice in war on a world level.

Lo Tignov (Not Stealing): Looting and pillaging are equivalent to stealing, and are forbidden.

Lo Tikom (Not Taking Revenge) Using force to punish or take vengeance on the enemy is forbidden.

Lo Tirtzach (Not Murdering): Killing enemies in war, for reasons unrelated to self-defense, is murder.

Nedarim (Keeping Promises): Treaties are promises among nations and other autonomous groups. When treaties are honored, there is a better chance that peace will prevail.

Ometz Lev (Courage of Heart): Beyond physical might and bravery, this middah encompasses the will to act morally and responsibly.

Rachamim (Compassion): We must have com- passion, even on our enemies.

Rodef Shalom (Pursuing Peace): Solving conflict through nonviolent means is the ideal. We must be relentless in our pursuit of peaceful alternatives to war.

Where Do I Go From Here?

War is a complicated issue from both a secular and a religious perspective. It touches the lives of most people in very tangible ways. At any given time in history, there have always been war- ring countries or tribes somewhere in the world. As globalization occurs, these conflicts affect larger populations. When do these conflicts deserve your support? How do you identify the "good guys" and the "bad guys?" When is a war really the necessary course of action? Continue to ask yourself these tough questions as you make judgments about wars, drawing on Jewish tradi- tion to guide you.

Following is a list of resources that you may find helpful as you continue your exploration of this complex and timely issue.

Books and Articles

Artson, Bradley Shavit. *It's a Mitzvah! Step-by-Step To Jewish Living*. West Orange, NJ: Behrman House and New York: The Rabbinical Assembly, 1995.

Bleich, J. David. "Preemptive War in Jewish Law." In *Contemporary Halakhic Problems, Vol. III*, pp. 251-292. New York, NY: KTAV Publishing House, Inc., and Yeshiva University Press, 1989.

Broyde, Michael J. "Fighting the War and the Peace: Battlefield Ethics, Peace Talks, Treaties, and Pacifism in the Jewish Tradition." In *Jewish Law Articles: Examining Halacha, Jewish Issues and Secular Law*, www.jlaw.com, copyright by Ira Kasden, 1997-2001.

Falk, Richard. "Ends and Means: Defining a Just War." In *The Nation*, October 29, 2001.

Freeman, Susan. *Teaching Jewish Virtues: Sacred Sources and Arts Activities*. Denver, CO: A.R.E. Publishing, Inc., 1999.

Gendler, Everett E. "War and the Jewish Tradition." In *Contemporary Jewish Ethics,* edited by Menachem Marc Kellner. New York: Sanhedrin Press, 1978.

Henslin, James M. "War, Terrorism, and the Balance of Power." In *Social Problems.* Englewood Cliffs, NJ: Prentice Hall, 1990.

Josephus. *The Jewish War.* Middlesex, England: Penguin, 1984. (Or see the Loeb Classic Library Edition, Cambridge, MA: Harvard University Press, 1978).

Kadden, Barbara Binder, and Bruce Kadden. *Teaching Mitzvot: Concepts, Values, and Activities.* Rev. ed. Denver, CO: A.R.E. Publishing, Inc., 2003.

Lackey, Douglas P. *The Ethics of War and Peace.* Englewood, NJ: Prentice Hall, 1989.

Leadingham, Carrie, et al., eds. *Peace Prayers: Meditations, Affirmations, Invocations, Poems, and Prayers for Peace.* San Francisco, CA: Harper San Francisco, 1992.

Sokolow, Moshe. *The Pursuit of Peace.* New York: CAJE, 1993.

Walzer, Michael. *Just and Unjust Wars: A Moral Argument with Historical Illustrations.* New York: Basic Books, 1977.

Web Sites

American Jewish World Service: www.ajws.org
Helping to alleviate poverty, hunger, and disease among the people of the world regardless of race, religion, or nationality.

CARE: www.care.org
A humanitarian organization fighting global poverty

Human Rights Watch: www.hrw.org
Dedicated to protecting the human rights of people around the world.

Oxfam America: www.oxfamamerica.org
Committed to creating lasting solutions to poverty, hunger, and social injustice.

Physicians for Human Rights: www.phrusa.org
Promotes health by protecting human rights.

Physicians for Global Survival (Canada): www.pgs.ca
A physician-led organization committed to the abolition of nuclear weapons, the prevention of war, the promotion of non-violent means of conflict resolution and social justice in a sustainable world.

Refugees International: www.refintl.org
An organization that advocates for refugees of war and victims of humanitarian crisis around the world.

Save the Children USA: www.savethechildren.org
A nonprofit child-assistance organization to make lasting positive change in the lives of children in need.

The following two organizations have at times taken actions and promoted ideas that have been controversial in the Jewish community:

Amnesty International: www.amnesty.org
A worldwide campaigning movement that works to promote internationally recognized human rights.

Doctors without Borders: www.doctorswithoutborders.org
Delivers emergency aid to victims of armed conflict, epidemics, and natural and man-made disasters, and to others who lack health care due to social or geographical isolation.

Films

The following commercial films deal with war in an often intense and graphic manner. Check with parents or teachers before viewing.

Apocalypse Now (1979, 153 minutes, rated R)
Based on Joseph Conrad's Heart of Darkness. The story of an army Captain in Vietnam who is sent on a mission to "terminate with extreme prejudice" a renegade Green Beret Colonel who has succumbed to madness and set himself up as God among a remote jungle tribe.

Band of Brothers (2001, 10 episodes at 60 minutes each, not rated)
The HBO miniseries that tells the story of Easy Company of the U.S. Army Airborne Paratrooper division and their mission in

France during World War II.

Casualties of War (1989, 113 minutes, rated R)
During the Vietnam war, a girl is taken from her village by five American soldiers. Four of the soldiers rape her, but the fifth refuses. The young girl is killed, and the fifth soldier is determined to see justice done.

Full Metal Jacket (1987, 116 minutes, rated R)
A group of soldiers develop dehumanized personalities in their training and it shows in their tour of duty in Vietnam.

Platoon (1986, 120 minutes, rated R)
A young recruit in Vietnam faces a moral crisis when a sergeant orders the massacre of villagers.

Saving Private Ryan (1998, 170 minutes, rated R)
A World War II drama about a platoon of men sent behind enemy lines to find and send home a soldier whose three brothers have been killed in the war.

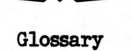

Glossary

Milchemet Chovah:

A compulsory war, sometimes distinguished from a milchemet mitzvah.

Milchemet Mitzvah:

An obligatory or commanded war.

Milchemet Reshut:

An authorized or optional war.

PART
III

Citizens of the Planet

**Animal
Experimentation**

**Consumerism:
How Much is Too Much?**

CHAPTER 9
ANIMAL EXPERIMENTATION

Overview

Is it ethical to use animal lives in the hopes of obtaining information that may improve the quality of human life? Many ethicists and activists challenge the morality of using millions of animals each year in medical experiments, as part of cosmetic and household product research, and in classroom instruction (for dissection).

For our study of animal experimentation, we will examine beliefs about animal welfare and animal rights — what is the basis for these concepts and how far do we go with them. In addition, we will look at the objectives of experiments. Perhaps not all experiments are of equal merit. For instance, is testing mascara as worthy a research goal as investigating a possible cure for cancer? If animals are living, sentient creatures and not disposable objects, do they deserve compassion and do they have the right to be protected from abuse? Just how far can we go in justifying the use of animals' lives for human benefit?

The Jewish Perspective

Judaism most definitely expresses concern for animal welfare. Several *mitzvot* dealing with the treatment of animals come under the category of *Tza'ar Ba'alay Chayim*, literally "the pain of living creatures." From the Bible, we learn that animals are God's creatures, deserving of respectful regard. Cruelty toward animals is forbidden, and numerous laws protect them from harm and compel humans to behave mercifully toward them. Animals deserve rest on Shabbat, and share in sabbatical year privileges. Hunting for sport is expressly prohibited. Jewish dietary laws also reflect concern for animals, and provide strict guidelines for slaughtering animals in ways that minimize pain and suffering. Some rabbis, in fact, question whether eating meat is permissible at all, and many prominent Jewish leaders have embraced vegetarianism as the ideal Jewish diet.

The Challenge of Animal Rights

This clear concern for the welfare of animals leads us to question the morality of using animals for any human benefit we can imagine. There are three significant Jewish views of the relationship between human beings and the rest of the created world:

(1) humans are part of a "web" of creation in which everything has a place and purpose,

(2) humans have dominion over the created world, and

(3) humans are earth's caretakers.

These three roles exist in tension with one another. Human dominion over the creatures of the earth often conflicts with our other roles as "members of a web" and caretakers. If we are to embrace all our various roles, we must reject unrestrained use of animals and recognize that not all reasons for human use of animals are equally valid.

Judaism teaches us that there are instances when animal rights take priority over human needs, and even over Jewish law. There are circumstances under which Shabbat and holiday restrictions can be lifted for the sake of animals; in fact, we are obliged to put aside the human benefit of Shabbat rest to care for animal needs. For example, if an animal falls into a ditch on Shabbat and is unable to remove itself, we are to relieve its suffering and provide for its sustenance until Shabbat ends and the animal can be moved. The extensive dietary laws of *kashrut* also reflect a concern for the welfare of animals, and impose restrictions that force us to restrain our cravings for meat (that is, use of animals for our dining pleasure).

Jewish Views of Animal Feelings

Jewish sources recognize that animals can feel fear and experience emotional pain, and that mother animals feel love and tenderness for their young. In Leviticus 22:28 we learn that "it is forbidden to slaughter an animal and its young on the same day." Certain texts even grant animals moral responsibility for their actions — as if animals choose to do right or wrong.

Why such concern for the feelings of animals? Cruelty leads to callousness, and callousness toward animals increases the risk that we will become callous to human suffering, as well. Maimonides puts it this way: "If the Torah provides that such grief should not be caused to animals or to birds, how much more careful must we be that we should not cause grief to humans" (*Guide of the Perplexed* 3:48).

Guidelines: Using Animals to Benefit Humans

Though we may understand Judaism's concern for animal welfare, it still is challenging to know how to approach the question of animal experimentation. Jewish sources offer some practical guidelines in evaluating the use of animals for human benefit.

The sixteenth century sage Moses Isserles gave one fairly lenient opinion: that anything necessary for medical or other useful purposes is excluded from the prohibition of cruelty to animals. He adds that there are still behaviors that we refrain from, despite their permissibility, because they are cruel. For example, he writes that we are permitted to pluck feathers from living geese in order to obtain quills for writing, but we refrain from this because it is cruel. We may have "dominion" in the world, but we exercise our role as "caretakers." In this way, Isserles resolves the tension between the various roles humans play in the world.

In the nineteenth century, Jacob Ettlinger proposed limits on Isserles' view that animals could be used for medical and other useful purposes. He said that we may use animals for medical purposes, but not for financial gain (Responsa *Binyan Zion*, no. 108). Another nineteenth century sage, Joseph Saul Nathanson, was even more restrictive. Nathanson wrote that we only may disregard the prohibition against *tza'ar ba'alay chayim* — causing pain to living animals — if the human benefit gained is proportionate to the pain inflicted on the animal. Should the potential gain for human beings be of a lesser magnitude than the pain inflicted on the animal, Jewish law would forbid it.[1]

Contemporary Jewish Opinions

Contemporary scholars continue to debate the issues surrounding the use of animals for medical experimentation. A current majority Jewish opinion probably would allow animal experimentation for medical benefits. However, if the desired benefit can be gained in another way, then the research would not be permitted. This stipulation would apply to both medical research and dissection (for the training of medical personnel). Most Jewish authorities would agree that it is unacceptable to use animals for experiments testing cosmetics or household products.

General Perspectives

Animal Organizations, Laws, and Studies

In the secular world, there are a number of organizations dedicated to the protection of animals. They focus on various issues and use different tactics, ranging from education and advocacy to activism, which sometimes includes illegal means such as vandalism or violence.

American law requires research institutions to establish an Institutional Animal Care and Use Committee (IACUC) to monitor and regulate acceptable use of animals. In addition, the Animal Welfare Act (AWA), in place since 1966, sets standards for the housing, handling, feeding, and transportation of animals to be used in experiments.

Zoologists and other animal behavior researchers have published numerous findings that would support and extend the Jewish notion of animal rights. Advocates seek to publicize these studies, which recognize such factors as levels of consciousness in animals, genetic similarity of animals to humans (reportedly humans are 99.5% similar to chimpanzees[2]), the ability of animals to "think," socialization, communication, logic, math, counting abilities, use of tools, self-awareness, imitation, ability to teach, intentional deception, and empathy.[3]

If we accept that animals have some rights, it is difficult to know how far those rights extend. What's to stop us from admitting them rights equal to humans? If we are reluctant to grant animals such liberal rights, what is the rationale? How do we justify elevating human benefits above animal needs? These philosophical questions can be unsettling, and can lead to strong opinions on both sides of the issue.

Using Animals for Research and Education: Points of Contention

Animal researchers and animal advocates disagree on a number of important points. Each side has its own stance on such questions as:

- To what extent should we seek alternatives to animal experimentation?
- To what extent should we require testing of experimental drugs on animals?
- By what means should we question the scientific merit of certain experiments?
- Do animal experimentation and dissection desensitize individuals to animals' pain?
- To what degree should we rely on alternatives to using animals in experiments, involving use of cells, tissue cultures, computer models, and chemical tests?
- Are educational institutions using alternatives to animal dissection as much as possible?
- How much cost should the public shoulder for intended benefits of animal experimentation?
- To what extent should we shift some of our research abilities and financial resources toward public health measures and preventive medicine?

Moderate Suggestions and Guidelines

The scholars Hugh LaFollette and Niall Shanks propose useful guidelines for dealing with these volatile and unsettling questions. They offer proposals in three areas:

A. Scientific proposals
   1. We must more accurately define what we mean by "success" when we apply that goal to animal research.
   2. We need to improve the methods by which we judge whether or not a practice is "successful."
   3. We must determine the worthiness of the contribution of experiment results to human well-being.

B. Moral proposals
   1. We must increase our understanding of the nature of non-human animals.

   2. We must think more carefully about how to make moral judgments when comparing the worth of different creatures.
   3. We must learn how to measure and evaluate animal pain more accurately.

C. Derivative proposals:
   1. We need stronger public health measures to reduce chronic illness caused by environmental factors.
   2. Universities should reconsider the criteria for granting tenure to animal researchers.
   3. There should be increased support for developing alternatives to animal research.
   4. We should be open to consider and assess evidence offered by theorists on all sides of the debate.[4]

Summary of the Overview

Ethicists and activists question the morality of using millions of animals each year in medical experiments, as part of cosmetic and household product research, and in classroom instruction (for dissection).

1. Through experiments involving animals, we attain helpful information for improving the quality of human life.

2. Animals are living, sentient creatures, not disposable objects. They deserve compassion and have the right to be protected from abuse.

3. All experiments are not necessarily equally legitimate. Some reasons for conducting animal experiments include: for medical information that may save human lives (cancer or AIDS research), for medical reasons that may improve certain health conditions (treatment of acne or mosquito bite itching), for cosmetic purposes (testing mascara for irritability to eyes), for household products (toxicity of floor wax), for psychological information (determining the stress of infant animals raised in isolation from mothers and others), or for general educational purposes (dissection of animals in school science classes).

4. Our challenge is to come up with guidelines that evaluate the legitimacy of human needs and desires, plus take into account animal welfare and animal rights.

Scenarios: How Things Have Changed

The question of the morality of using millions of animals each year in medical experiments, as part of product research, and for dissection is certainly not new. Human beings have always struggled with the issue of proper treatment of animals, and from the beginning of our written history Jewish texts have commented on the subject. Below are two imaginary scenarios, intended to raise questions and spark discussion. Read each one and reflect, either individually or in group discussion, on the questions in the "For Thought and Discussion" section that follows. Then continue on to the "Text Study" section to see what our Jewish sources have to say on the subject. Finally, you may wish to come back and answer the questions a second time, to see if your views have changed.

Scenario I: In Ancient Days

Chaya lives with her family on a small farm outside a Jewish village. She has only lived there for a few years. Every summer, Chaya has noticed that certain bushes produce plump pink berries. But Chaya knows that the berries could be poisonous even though they look tantalizing, and doesn't dare eat the berries. Last summer, Chaya questioned local villagers to see if the berries were safe to eat. The villagers were non-committal in their opinions. This summer, Chaya has decided to conduct her own berry experiment. It happens that she has a sheep that has become lame and seems to be in increasing amounts of pain. Chaya feels that at some point over the summer, she will have to put the animal to sleep. This is her idea: Why not mix some of the mashed berries into the sheep's food one day and see what happens? If the sheep becomes sick or dies, she will know that the berries could also be poisonous to people. And since the sheep is going to need to be put to sleep anyway, she isn't doing anything overly cruel to

the animal. If nothing unusual happens to the sheep as a result of ingesting the berries, Chaya would feel that she could safely eat small quantities of the berry until she herself becomes more certain that just as the berries didn't hurt the sheep, neither would they be detrimental to humans.

After completing her "experiment" (in which nothing happens to the sheep), Chaya tells her friend about what she did and what she learned. The friend scolds Chaya, "Didn't God provide enough good fruits and plants for you to eat without having to subject your poor sheep to berries which could have made that sick animal suffer even more?!"

Scenario II: Contemporary Times

Eve is a researcher for a pharmaceutical company. She has been doing research on drugs that would be safe for pregnant women to take (safe for mother and developing fetus). Some pregnant women experience nausea, even to an incapacitating level, particularly in the early stages of their pregnancies. Recently, Eve read a report about a tribe in the Amazon jungle that uses a certain berry to treat nausea. Though within the Amazon tribe, the berry isn't used by pregnant women per se, perhaps there are good prospects for the purposes which interest Eve.

A preliminary experiment is devised using rats and mice. Eve is scrupulous in following Federal regulations concerning care for animals during experiments. After a long wait, the IACUC (Institutional Animal Care and Use Committee) at the University where Eve works approves her proposal. The berry is given to the animals. The rats show no reaction to the berry, whereas mice given very high quantities of the berry show signs of dizziness. More animal experiments are planned, with the goal being to refine the conclusions. The next phase of experiments will involve giving animals a nausea-producing substance prior to giving them the berry. This way the effects of the drug can be observed in animals that are suffering from nausea to begin with. Though Eve feels conflicted by the decision to begin her next series of experiments by deliberately making animals feel sick, she believes the potential benefit to humans (in this case, pregnant women) is worth the suffering the animals will go through.

For Thought and Discussion:

In Scenario I, who do you think was right, Chaya or her friend? Why?

How is Eve's experiment in Scenario II fundamentally different from Chaya's?

Do you feel that the first phase of Eve's experiment is justified? Why or why not?

Is the second phase of Eve's experiment justified? Why or why not?

Text Study

There are many difficult questions to consider concerning animal welfare, animal rights, and the ethics of animal experimentation. Jewish textual sources provide many answers, but these answers often highlight the tension between seemingly opposing considerations. The chart on the next page poses the questions and offers two opposing points of view. Text sources supporting each of these points of view follow.

1. **What is the relationship between human beings and the rest of the created world?**

On the One Hand:

Humans have dominion over the earth.

A. God blessed them and God said to them, "Be fertile and increase, fill the earth and subdue it! Have dominion over the fish of the sea, the birds of the sky, and all the living things that crawl about the earth" (Genesis 1:28).

B. [God said to Adam], "The fear and the dread of you shall be upon all the beasts of the earth and upon all the birds of the sky — everything with which the earth is astir — and upon all the fish of the sea; they are given into your hand. Every creature that lives shall be yours to eat; as with the green grasses, I give you all of these (Genesis 9:2-3).

On the Other Hand:

Humans are part of nature's "web," plus play a role as earth's caretakers.

a. And God saw all that God had made, and found it very good (Genesis 1:31).

The following is a commentary on Genesis 1:31:

> Each created thing is "good" in itself; but when combined and united, the totality is proclaimed "very good." Everything in the universe was as the Creator willed it — nothing superfluous, nothing lacking — a harmony. "This harmony bears witness to the unity of God who planned this unity of Nature" (Luzzato) (J.H. Hertz, *The Pentateuch and Haftorahs,* London: Soncino Press, 1979, p. 5).

b. The Eternal God took the man and placed him in the garden of Eden, to till it and tend it (Genesis 2:15).

c. In the hour when the Holy One Who Is Blessed created the first human being, God took him and let him pass before all the trees of the Garden of Eden and said to him: "See my works, how fine and excellent they are? Now all that I have created, for you have I created them. Think upon this and do not corrupt and desolate My world. For if you corrupt it, there is no one to set it right after you" (*Ecclesiastes Rabbah* 7:28).

What Do You Think?

How does Genesis express humans' relationship with the world?

Which human role is most pronounced in our day — master and ruler of nature; harmonious member of nature's unity or "web;" or earth's caretaker and protector? Explain.

What do humans need to work on most in their relationship with nature?

Making an Ethical Decision about Animal Experimentation: Questions to Consider

The Question	On the One Hand	On the Other Hand
1. What is the relationship between human beings and the rest of the created world? (see page 135)	Human beings have dominion over the earth.	Human beings are part of nature's "web," plus play a role as earth's caretakers.
2. What is the status of human vs. non human animals in the "eyes of God?" (see this page)	The special role of human beings in the world is God-given.	All creatures are under God's care.
3. What human uses of animals are acceptable? (see this page)	Human beings are allowed to use animals in ways that benefit them.	There are significant restrictions on the use of animals.
4. How much pain is it permissible to cause animals? (see page 137)	Causing pain to an animal is permitted if it leads to the benefit of human beings.	We try to avoid causing pain to animals — physical or emotional — whenever possible.
5. Which deserves higher priority, human needs or animal rights? (see page 138)	Taking care of human needs should be our first priority.	Animals have rights that sometimes supersede those of human beings.

2. What is the status of human vs. non human animals in the "eyes of God?"

On the One Hand:

Humans' special role in the world is God-given.

A. When I look at Your heavens, the work of Your hands, the moon and work which you have established, what are humans that You are mindful of them, and the children of humans that You care for them? Yet You have made them little less than God, and do crown them with glory and honor. You have given them dominion over the works of Your hands, You have put all things under their feet . . . (Psalms 8:4-7).

On the Other Hand:

All creatures are under God's care.

a. The Eternal is good to all, and God's mercy is upon all God's works" (Psalms 145:9).

b. The eyes of all look to You expectantly, and You give them their food when it is due. You give it openhandedly, feeding every creature to its heart's content (Psalms 145:15-16).

What Do You Think?

What is unique about our human role in the world? Why might humans have a role different from other creatures?

What expectations does God have of us that God doesn't have of other creatures?

3. What human uses of animals are acceptable?

On the One Hand:

Humans are allowed to use animals in ways that serve them.

A. It was taught: Rabbi Simeon ben Eleazar said, "In my whole lifetime I have not seen a deer engaged in gathering fruit, a lion carrying burdens, or a fox as a shop-keeper, yet they are sustained without trouble, though they were created only to serve me, whereas I was created to serve my Maker . . . " (*Kiddushin* 82b).

On the Other Hand:

We are constrained by laws reflecting concern for animals.

a. When you see the ass of your enemy lying under its burden and would refrain from raising it, you must nevertheless raise it with him (Exodus 23:5).

b. Six days you shall do your work, but on the seventh day you shall cease from labor, in order that your ox and your ass may rest and that your bondsman and the stranger may be refreshed (Exodus 23:12).

c. No animal from the herd or from the flock shall be slaughtered on the same day with its young (Leviticus 22:28).

d. I will also provide grass in the fields for your cattle — and thus you shall eat your fill (Deuteronomy 11:15).

The Talmud comments:

> Thus said Rabbi Judah in the name of Rav: It is forbidden for people to taste anything until they have given food to their animal, as it says [first], "I will also provide grass in the fields for your cattle," and then [second], "and thus you shall eat your fill" (*Gittin* 62a).

e. Make sure that you do not partake of the blood; for the blood is the life, and you must not consume the life with the flesh (Deuteronomy 12:23).

The commentator Rambam adds:

> The oral tradition has taught that the biblical verse, "and you must not con-sume the life with the flesh" is a refer-ence to the prohibition against eating a limb severed from a living animal (Rambam, *Hilchot Ma'achalot Assurot* 5:1).

f. You shall not plow with an ox and an ass together (Deuteronomy 22:10).

g. You shall not muzzle an ox while it is threshing (Deuteronomy 25:4).

What Do You Think?

How would you describe the relationship between humans and animals as outlined in these pas-sages?

Do you agree that the animal world was created for the purpose of serving human beings?

Suppose you wanted to add new laws that would address current threats to the welfare of animals. What are a few that you would include?

⟫◆⟪

4. **Is it permissible to cause animals pain?**

On the One Hand:

Causing pain to an animal is permitted if it leads to the benefit of humans.

A. Regarding anything that is needed for healing or for any purpose whatsoever — the prohibition against *tza'ar ba'alay chayim* (causing pain to animals) does not apply. For example, it is permitted to pluck down feathers from live geese. In such a case, you need not be concerned about *tza'ar ba'alay chayim* (Joseph Karo, *Shulchan Aruch, Even ha-Ezer* 5:14).

B. It appears that the prohibition against *tza'ar ba'alay chayim* (causing pain to ani-mals) does not apply if one is using [the animals] for the benefit of humankind, since all creatures were created to serve humankind" (Israel Isserlein, *Terumat ha-Deshen, Pesakim u-Ketavim* 105, 15th c. Germany).

On the Other Hand:

We try to avoid causing pain to animals — physical or emotional — whenever possible.

a. This is the crucial gloss to Joseph Karo's comment (see #4A above):

Nevertheless, people hold back from doing it [plucking down feathers from live geese], since it is indeed cruel. [The practice is technically permitted, but it is to be avoided if possible.] (Moshe Isserles, gloss to Joseph Karo's *Shulchan Aruch, Even ha-Ezer* 5:14, 1572).

b. [The 19th century scholar] Rabbi Joseph Saul Nathanson says that one may disregard the prohibition against *tza'ar ba'alay chayim* — causing pain to living animals — only if the human benefit gained is proportionate to the pain inflicted on the animal. Should the potential gain for human beings, however, be of a lesser magnitude than the pain inflicted on the animal, he claims that Jewish law would forbid it (As quoted in *Who Renews Creation* by Earl Schwartz and Barry D. Cytron, p. 78).

c. The reason for the prohibitions [against cruelty to animals] is to teach us the trait of compassion and that we should not be cruel, for cruelty expands in the human soul (Nachmanides, Commentary on Deuteronomy 22:6).

d. Maimonides instructs us to avoid not only an animal's physical pain, but its emotional pain, as well:

> [We] avoid slaughtering the young animal in front of its mother. For in these cases, animals feel very great pain, there being no difference regarding this pain between humankind and the other animals. For the love and the tenderness of a mother for her child is not consequent upon reason, but upon the activity of the imaginative faculty, which is found in most animals just as it is found in humans (Maimonides, *Guide for the Perplexed*, 3:48).

We are to shoo a mother away before taking her fledglings or eggs from the nest (Deuteronomy 22:6-7) out of sensitivity for a mother animal's emotional pain:

> "If then the mother is let go and escapes of her own accord, she will not be pained by seeing that the young are taken away." (Maimonides, *Guide for the Perplexed*, 3:48).

What Do You Think?

How does the opinion is passage #4c depart from the opinions expressed in the other texts?

Do you agree that causing pain to an animal is acceptable if it leads to the benefit of humans? Are there "benefits" not worthy of the pain that would be caused to animals in order to gain them?

Would it be acceptable to you to use a medicine that involved research painful to animals?

Would it be acceptable to you to use a cosmetic that involved research painful to animals? How about a household product (such as floor wax)?

5. **Which deserves higher priority, human needs or animal rights?**

On the One Hand:

Taking care of human needs should be our first priority.

See Texts #4A and #4B above.

On the Other Hand:

Animals have rights that sometimes supersede those of humans.

a. We are allowed to handle pillows and mattresses in ways normally prohibited on Shabbat for the purpose of tending to an animal that has fallen into a water-filled canal (*Shabbat* 128b).

b. If we return from a journey on Friday night with an animal carrying a heavy load, we must relieve it of its burden, even if Shabbat has begun. Under no circumstances may we leave the load on the animal since that would cause the animal to suffer (Maimonides, *Mishneh Torah, Hilchot Shabbat* 21:9-10).

c. We are forbidden to eat prior to feeding our animals (*Brachot* 40a and *Gittin* 62a).

d. Perhaps the ideal for compassion is that it be boundless, whether directed toward human or non-human animals:

> A concern for animal suffering hardly excludes concern for human suffering. There is no limit to human moral concern (Richard H. Schwartz, *Judaism and Vegetarianism*, p. 111).

What Do You Think?

What would you say is the main thrust behind the tradition's concern about animals, based on the texts above?

How would you define animal rights?

Do you think animals deserve rights? Explain.

Would you say that concern for animals distracts from more pressing human problems? Or, do you believe that increased compassion for animals can only add to the sum benefit of more compassion for all of God's creatures — human and non-human animals alike?

Related Middot and Mitzvot

Practicing these virtues and commandments will help enhance ethical treatment of animals.

Anavah (Humility): Usually we talk about humble individuals, but not about humble species. Perhaps we need to examine how human animals collectively see themselves — as better than non-human animals — and strive for more communal anavah.

Bal Tashchit (Preserving the Earth, not destroying): Animals are part of God's precious domain. We have a responsibility to ensure that animals are not unnecessarily "wasted" or destroyed.

Histapkut (Contentedness): We must be vigilant about asking what our real needs are. For example, if we were more content with the types and varieties of products available to us, perhaps fewer animals would need to give their lives for the purpose of testing products for us.

Kashrut (Dietary laws): Limiting (or eliminating) meat in our diets, plus requiring humane slaughter, can be ways of increasing sensitivity to animals.

K'vod et Ha-Briyot (Honoring created things): Besides refraining from wasteful or destructive environmental practices (bal tashchit) and recognizing the pain of animals (tza'ar ba'alay chayim), we can go one step further. We can cultivate a sense of honor and respect for all created things.

Tochechah (Rebuking): Abuse or intentional cruelty to animals is as deserving of rebuke as other sinful actions.

Tza'ar Ba'alay Chayim (Compassion for animals): This literally means concern for the "pain of living creatures."

Yirah (Awe and Reverence): To be in awe of God includes striving for an attitude of reverence toward all of God's creatures.

Where Do I Go From Here?

Hopefully, you've seen from this chapter that the issue of animal rights affects many of the decisions you make in daily life. What role do animals play in the clothing we buy, the food we eat, the cosmetics we wear, or the medications we take? You will have to decide how much the human benefits of animal experimentation outweigh the suffering an animal may experience. Jewish tradition offers several approaches, and it's important to become familiar with all of them in order to make up your own mind.

Following are resources that you may find helpful as you continue to explore this important and complex issue.

Books and Articles

The Animal Rights Handbook. Los Angeles, CA: Living Planet Press, 1990.

Bernstein, Ellen and Dan Fink. *Let the Earth Teach You Torah.* Wyncote, PA: Shomrei Adamah, 1992, pp. 165-169.

Bleich, J. David. "Judaism and Animal Experimentation." In *Animal Sacrifices: Religious Perspectives on the Use of Animals in Science,* edited by Tom Regan. Philadelphia, PA: Temple University Press, 1986.

Bleich, J. David. "Vegetarianism and Judaism." In *Contemporary Halakhic Problems, vol. III.* Hoboken, NJ: KTAV Publishing House, Inc. and New York: Yeshiva University Press, 1989.

Borowitz, Eugene B., and Frances Weinman Schwartz. *The Jewish Moral Virtues.* Philadelphia, PA: Jewish Publication Society, 1999.

Dresner, Samuel H.; Seymour Siegel; and David M. Pollock. *The Jewish Dietary Laws.* New York: The Rabbinical Seminary of America, 1982.

Freeman, Susan. *Teaching Jewish Virtues: Sacred Sources and Arts Activities.* Denver, CO: A.R.E. Publishing, Inc., 1999.

Kadden, Barbara Binder, and Bruce Kadden. *Teaching Mitzvot: Concepts, Values, and Activities.* Rev. ed. Denver, CO: A.R.E. Publishing, Inc., 2003.

Rosner, Fred. "Animal Experimentation." In *Modern Medicine and Jewish Ethics.* Hoboken, NJ: KTAV Publishing House, Inc. and New York: Yeshiva University Press, 1991.

Kalechovsky, Roberta. *Vegetarian Judaism: A Guide for Everyone.* Marblehead, MA: Micah Publications, Inc., 1998.

LaFollette, Hugh, and Niall Shanks. *Brute Science: Dilemmas of Animal Experimentation.* London: Routledge, 1996.

Shochet, Elijah Judah. *Animal Life in Jewish Tradition: Attitudes and Relationships.* New York: KTAV Publishing House, Inc., 1984.

Schwartz, Earl, and Barry D. Cytron. *Who Renews Creation.* New York: United Synagogue of Conservative Judaism, Department of Youth Activities, 1995.

Schwartz, Richard H. *Judaism and Vegetarianism.* New York: Lantern Books, 2001.

Toperoff, Shlomo Pesach. *The Animal Kingdom in Jewish Thought.* Northvale, NJ: Jason Aronson, 1995.

Wise, Steven M. *Rattling the Cage: Toward Legal Rights for Animals.* Cambridge, MA: Perseus Books, 2000.

Web Sites

Many of these web sites have clear positions to promote and publicize. Some are supportive of animal research, others are adamantly opposed to it. By surfing through several of the sites, one can get a sense of the range of perspectives, plus a feeling for some of the emotion behind the words.

American Anti-Vivisection Society: www.aavs.org
A non-profit animal advocacy and educational organization dedicated to ending experimentation on animals in research, testing, and education.

CHAI (Concern for Helping Animals in Israel): www.chaionline.org
Assists the Israeli animal protection community in their efforts to improve the condition and treatment of Israel's animals.

Foundation for Bio-Medical Research: www.fbresearch.org
Dedicated to improving human and animal health by promoting public understanding and support for the humane and responsible use of animals in medical and scientific research.

Judaism 101— Treatment of Animals: www.jewfaq.org/animals.htm
An overview of the Jewish view of animal treatment.

Physicians Committee for Responsible Medicine: www.pcrm.org
Promotes preventive medicine, conducts clinical research, and encourages higher standards for ethics and effectiveness in research.

The Schwartz Collection on Judaism, Vegetarianism, and Animal Rights: schwartz.enviroweb.org
A large collection of articles, FAQs, divrei Torah, and book reviews relating to Judaism and vegetarianism.

Films

The following films contain specific sections that are valuable for illustrating certain aspects of the topic of animal experimentation. Check with parents or teachers before viewing.

Chicken Run (2000, 84 minutes, rated G)
A claymation adventure about chickens attempting to escape from the cruelty of a sinister chicken farm. Available from video stores.

Project X (1987, 107 minutes, rated PG)
A young inductee into the military is given the task of looking after chimpanzees used in the mysterious "Project X" experiment. Soon he begins to suspect that there is more to the secret project than he is being told. Available from video stores.

The Secret of Nimh (1998, 149 minutes, rated G)
An animated film in which the characters include rats who were freed from a National Institute of Mental Health testing lab, but only after being subjected to mind altering experiments. Available from video stores.

Tools for Research: Questions about Animal Rights (1983, 37 minutes, unrated)
A classic animal rights documentary that raises important questions about the use of animals in laboratories. Available from Bullfrog Films, www.bullfrogfilms.com.

CHAPTER 10

CONSUMERISM: HOW MUCH IS TOO MUCH?

Overview

Consumerism presents diverse and troubling ethical quandaries. Arguably, consumerism affects more vast and critical realms than other topics we deal with in this book. In exploring the issues, the urgency of the challenges becomes clear. Specifically, our planet — along with our very humanity — is at stake with the consumption choices we make. Consumerism confronts us with spiritual questions, as well. This chapter offers us opportunities to scrutinize our priorities and evaluate what really is important in the end. A particular wrinkle to this topic is this: If we benefit personally from the consumer practices of our culture; if our standard of living is high compared to the rest of the world, consumption offenses may be the easiest ethical breaches to ignore.

Jewish Perspectives

Regarding Wealth

Judaism is not a religion of denial. We do not applaud poverty. Having the financial means to sustain ourselves is desirable. But just as Judaism rejects denial and poverty, it scorns indulgence and wastefulness. Moderation and modesty characterize the ideal way of life. "Who is rich?" asks Ben Zoma. "One who is happy with what one has" (*Pirke Avot* 4:1).

In thinking about the challenges to Jewish ethical living that consumer excesses raise, we must evaluate our attitudes toward wealth. We can separate further examination of our topic into these categories: the environment, social justice, quality of life concerns, and spiritual values.

Environment

Human consumption habits, particularly in Western countries, are a terrible strain on our planet. Two Jewish ideas in particular will help us flesh out an ethical approach to protecting the environment.

First is the challenge of balancing human dominion on earth with our role as the planet's caretakers. Early in the Bible, God gives us the tasks of "mastering the earth" (Genesis 1:28), and also "tilling and tending" it (Genesis 2:15). A tension exists between dominating the earth, using it however we see fit, and preserving and protecting it. Dominating the earth to the point of devastation violates the balanced relationship to the planet that Judaism requires of us.

Second is the Jewish value of *Bal Tashchit*, not wasting or destroying. Throughout the ages, Jewish sages have expressed concern about environmental devastation. As God warns in a Midrash, "make sure you don't ruin or devastate My world. For if you do, there will be no one after you to fix it" (*Ecclesiastes Rabbah* 7:28).

Judaism is also sensitive to how individual acts affect the common good of the community. One person's or community's use of the world's resources can have widespread repercussions. Rabbi Shimon ben Yochai offers the following parable:

> A group of people sat in a boat. One of them took a drill and began making a hole beneath his seat. His companions said to him, "What are you doing?" He replied, "What do you care? Aren't I drilling beneath my own seat?" They answered, "But the waters will rise and drown all of us!" (*Vayikra Rabbah* 4:6)

One person's actions can have widespread repercussions, perhaps very serious ones. How one community uses the planet's resources can harm other communities. Judaism frowns on wasting, destroying, and polluting. While human survival and basic comforts may require drawing on natural resources, Judaism implores us to minimize environmental damage and consume only what is truly necessary.

Social Justice

Global distribution of wealth is vastly unequal. Impoverished workers toil in often oppressive conditions as they produce goods for consumers in wealthier nations. What might Judaism say about these concerns?

Tzedakah or charity (literally, "righteousness") and other forms of aid may help alleviate some suffering. Avoiding purchases from companies that take advantage of their workers is another worthy effort. Still, these actions, while consistent with good Jewish values, won't make the problems of inequality go away.

True, perfect equality around the globe may seem unrealistic. Even so, we must be aware that individuals do not live in isolation, and that our actions affect one another. When large populations across the globe live in poverty while small minorities enjoy immense wealth, the impoverished may become filled with a sense of humiliation. The commandment to love one's fellow person as one's self (*V'ahavta L'rayacha Kamocha*) requires us to conduct our lives so as to preserve, as much as possible, the dignity of others around the globe. We must share space and resources so that others have more opportunity, better health, living wages, and a cleaner, safer environment. Doing so will require us to curb our consumer appetites.

Quality of Life Concerns

With excessive consumerism, pursuit of wealth and material goods can displace other important individual, familial, and societal values. On the one hand, our sages point out that "Where there is no bread, there is no Torah" (*Pirke Avot* 3:21). That is, without basic sustenance, we will be unable to embrace other important values. On the other hand, the sages do not suggest that "Where there is no caviar, there is no Torah." Insisting on caviar — that is, a life filled with luxuries — leaves little time or energy for much else.

Judaism recognizes the importance of work and earning a living: "The Eternal will bless you in all the works of your hands" (Deuteronomy 2:7) . . . "No blessing rests on persons except by the work of their hands" (*Tosefta Brachot* 7, 8). But even as we direct energy toward meeting basic needs, we must strive for balance in our lives. We must leave time for Torah, make time for study and personal growth, for family and friends, and for community events and concerns.

Spiritual Values/Wealth Belongs to God

A spiritually centered lifestyle embraces the values of modesty, moderation, and contentedness. Greed, envy, indulgence, and excessiveness corrupt spiritual well being. It is all too easy to ignore God's role in the world, to lose the sense that something exists beyond ourselves, beyond our needs and desires. Commonly, people believe that if they work for something, they deserve what they gain. This sense of "entitlement" is a foreign notion to Judaism. Rather, we say that awareness of God leads to the understanding that all wealth belongs to God.

General Perspectives

Regarding Wealth

We may not be wholly conscious of all the factors influencing our relationship with money. Following is an example of how one individual might describe his/her views on wealth:

> "It is important to me that I can support myself and my family. I want to have enough to live on, plus some extra for special items, emergencies, travel, and charity. I also want to be able to save money for my children's college education and for retirement. I want to be comfortable, but I don't want money to control my life."

Such a philosophy doesn't seem unusual for a person living in America or Canada today. Yet, let's consider the rational limits of this individual's desires, ambitions, and possessions. Someone in our culture who lives modestly or lavishly might make the following statements:

- I want some extra [money] for special items.
- I want to be comfortable.
- I don't want money to control my life.

We can see how these three statements can mean vastly different things. For instance, is the "special item" a wool blanket for extra warmth on winter nights, or is it a $60,000 luxury car? Does "being comfortable" require a 1500 square foot home for a family, or a 3500 square foot home? Does resistance to "money controlling my life" mean I will leave a good paying job in which I often feel miserable and take a serious pay cut for a new, less stressful job? That is, would I make a change that would still allow me to make ends meet, but would force me to live much more frugally?

Attitudes toward money may reflect more than philosophy or moral intentions. Other factors influence our striving for achievement and accumulation: cultural conditioning (including media, advertising, and social expectations), competitiveness (i.e., concern about relative position in the social hierarchy); and even human biology — in males the hormones seratonin and testosterone become elevated with certain successes, facilitating behaviors that help achieve and maintain high status.

Judaism warns of the dangers associated with excessive wealth, including such traits as envy, jealousy, greed, anxiety, selfishness, and stinginess. Clearly, avoiding excessiveness requires us to examine our values and strive for moral self-discipline. However, to create a responsible and healthy relationship to money, we must also be aware of forces that exist under the surface. To control money, rather than have it control us, communities must address the influences of cultural conditioning and increase understanding of human nature.

Environment

The aspiration to become more virtuous may or may not convince typical consumers to change their consumption habits. In contrast, the impact of consumer wealth on the environment raises urgent and concrete concerns, difficult to ignore. The rate at which human beings are depleting the world's natural resources is alarming. Pollution and other environmental destruction are endangering the health of our planet and its creatures. Scholars, researchers, ecologists, politicians, and grassroots activists warn that current trends in consumption are leading us in the direction of collapse. Avoiding catastrophe will require a combination of strategies including limiting material production, limiting population, developing tech-

nologies for increasing the efficiency of resource use, decreasing pollution, controlling erosion, and increasing land yields.[1]

Social Justice

In "Jewish Perspectives: Social Justice" above, we touched on the troublesome challenges of the inequality of global distribution of wealth, and oppressive work conditions for impoverished laborers. How bad, really, are these injustices? Some of the "Text Study" pieces below illustrate the situation. In essence, the citizens of wealthy industrial nations (such as the U.S.A.) consume huge quantities of resources and are responsible for disproportionate amounts of pollution in comparison to other citizens around the globe. Low wages and inadequate and unhealthful working conditions plague workers in many poorer countries, and the wage gap between First World and Third World citizens is enormous. Escalating resentment between the "haves" and the "have-nots" has the potential to ignite dangerous conflicts and crises around the world. With declining global stability, insecurity, both on a national and personal level, increases.

As for our moral responsibility to address economic injustices, a spectrum of responses exists. On one side of the responsibility spectrum is Libertarianism, which emphasizes the rights of individuals to make decisions for themselves, including about how they spend money. Also on this side of the spectrum would be what we can call the "Philosophy of Entitlement," which essentially suggests that, "If I earned this money (or inherited it) I have a right to spend it the way I want. I'm entitled to what I own and what I may choose to buy (or consume)." Neither of these philosophies is consistent with cherished Jewish values.

On the other side of the responsibility spectrum are individuals who seek to replace what they view as reckless consumerist trends with more responsible alternatives. These might include:

- Green Consumerism, which encourages the consumption of items that are less damaging to the ecosystem and planetary resources;

- Ethical Consumerism, an approach that judges manufacturers on a wider variety of concerns than just ecological credentials. Such issues as worker conditions, involvement in the arms trade, or support of oppressive regimes are monitored to encourage trade to be as responsible as possible;

- Anticonsumerism, which challenges many assumptions about what we need in contemporary society and advocates different ways of living, trading, and working. The goal is to "live more lightly" on the earth and be less dependent on buying things to feel good about ourselves.[2]

Quality of Life Concerns

An emphasis on consumerism raises quality of life issues. Critics of consumer culture claim that when the pursuit of material things becomes a priority, other values may suffer. Jeremy Brecher and Tim Costello, authors of *Global Village or Global Pillage* argue: When public policy and social practice seek solely to maximize private profit in the market, they slight other values of great significance."[3] Some of these values may include democratic decision making, environmental protection, social caring, equality, human solidarity, community stability, individual and family security, long-term public and private planning and investment, dignity in the work process, goods and services consumed collectively, and cultural diversity.[4]

We pay a heavy price for consumption excesses. Consumer debt bankruptcy claims continue to rise. The quality of our work environments diminishes — for example, workers have fewer days off (resulting in more stress), and workers often must deal with frustrating commuter challenges such as traveling long distances, traffic congestion, and less time with family and friends.[5]

Sacrifices take place in the public sphere as well. When we priortize resources for conspicuous consumption, we have less available to direct toward such things as clean drinking water, air quality standards, safe agricultural regulations, better pay for public school teachers, bridge and highway maintenance, and drug treatment and prevention programs.[6]

Shifting Values

Positive change begins with each individual. However, individual action, by itself, is not enough to alter runaway consumer trends. Any proposed agenda for change must seek to improve the lives of the great majority of the world's people over the long run. Besides our personal efforts, science and technology play a crucial role. We urgently need global policies that will promote responsible economic development throughout the world, help stabilize world population, integrate the interests of people in all parts of the world, provide handles for action at a variety of levels, and make it easier, not harder, to protect the environment and preserve natural resources.[7]

Summary of the Overview

The following statements summarize the main points about consumerism as discussed in the Overview:

1. Well-being for individuals and society does not depend on increasing levels of consumption.

2. Current consumption trends are causing environmental devastation.

3. Current consumption trends are causing alarming rates of natural resource depletion.

4. Consumer patterns around the globe reveal deep disparities of wealth and consumption in richer versus poorer populations.

5. The consumer demands of richer populations contribute to economic injustices and instances of worker exploitation in impoverished societies.

6. A focus on money distorts personal and communal priorities.

7. A focus on money distorts spiritual values. A Jewish view would suggest that God is the source of wealth, and everything belongs to God.

Scenarios: Comparing Types of Consumers

How do we compare the consumer choices people make? Should we pronounce judgments, or should we refrain from doing so? Do we suggest that certain lifestyles are modest and ethical, whereas others are excessively consumerist and overly indulgent? Undoubtedly, a complex combination of factors influences consumer decisions.

Below are two imaginary scenarios, set in two different communities, illustrating the challenging ethical questions that have concerned Jews and non-Jews through the ages. They are intended to raise questions and spark discussion. Read each scenario and reflect, either individually or in a group discussion, on the questions in the "For Thought and Discussion" section that follows. Then continue on to the "Text Study" section to see what Jewish and other sources have to say on the subject of consumerism. Finally, you may wish to come back and discuss the questions a second time, to see if your views have changed.

Scenario I: Long Ago and/or Far Away (from Wealthy Suburban America)

Members of the BenDor household include a father and mother, four sons, and a grandmother and her sister — eight people altogether. Originally, the BenDor home had two bedrooms — one for the parents and one for the sons, a bathroom, and a kitchen/dining area. When the grandmother and her sister moved in, the family built on another small bedroom for the two women to share. The home, at 1400 square feet, is now one of the largest in the village. Walking is the family's main mode of transportation. In addition, the father helps his brother maintain two work horses, and thus can borrow them and a wagon now and then.

The family barely makes ends meet. There are days when there doesn't seem to be enough to eat. While everyone in the BenDor family contributes however they can toward the family income, they wish they had a little more. With a bigger financial cushion, they would have enough stocks of food, wood for the stove, animals of their own, and money to pay for the education of their sons.

Scenario II: In a Wealthy American Suburban Community

The Bender household includes a father and mother, two sons, and two golden retrievers — four people and two dogs altogether. Originally, their 1700 square foot ranch home had three bedrooms — one for the parents and one for each son, two bathrooms, an eat-in kitchen, a formal dining room, and a living room.

Since the family had been doing well financially and since the home was beginning to feel a bit cramped, the family decided to remodel. A second and third story to their home added two more bedrooms, two offices, a recreation room, a media entertainment center, and three more bathrooms. The Benders also remodeled the master bedroom and kitchen, and landscaped the backyard anew, adding a swimming pool and large hot tub. The home is now 3600 square feet. Before the remodeling, their home was one of the smaller ones in the neighborhood. Now, it is at least as large as, if not larger than, most of the homes.

For transportation the family has three cars (though the boys do not drive yet) — a van, a sedan, and a sports car. In addition, the family owns four mountain bikes and two motorized scooters.

The Bender parents work hard and have very little leisure time. With all the pressures they are under, they can barely get involved in their sons' activities, much less in community events and issues at large.

While the parents' salaries are decent, expenses are high. Both sons currently attend private schools, and the family needs to save for their college educations. Black-tie affairs for each boy's bar mitzvah required enormous outlays of cash. Besides these expenses, the family will make significant purchases in the next few years. The family has acquired lakefront property two hours away. Currently, bulldozers are clearing trees and shrubbery from the land, to make way for the four-bedroom vacation cottage the Bender's plan to build. The family also intends to buy a motor boat and a couple of kayaks.

For Thought and Discussion:

How do we compare the BenDors and the Benders? Do we judge them?

Does one family's lifestyle seem more ethical than the other? Explain your answer.

Text Study

Consumerism raises many difficult questions regarding our attitudes toward wealth, the environment, social justice, and quality of life concerns. Jewish and other textual sources provide many answers, but these answers often highlight tensions between seemingly opposing considerations. The chart below poses the questions and offers two opposing points of view. Text sources supporting each of these points of view follow.

1. **To what extent are human beings entitled to use of the world's resources?**

    On the One Hand:

    The world has abundant riches for humans to use and enjoy.

    A. God blessed them and God said to them, "Be fertile and increase, fill the earth and subdue it! Have dominion over the fish of the sea, the birds of the sky, and all the living things that crawl about the earth" (Genesis 1:28).

    B. You have given [humans] dominion over the works of Your hands; You have put all things under their feet . . . (Psalms 8:7).

    C. If destruction is necessary for a higher and more worthy aim, then it ceases to be destruction and itself becomes wise creating. [For example] cutting down a fruit tree which is doing harm to other more valuable plants, [and] burning a vessel when there is a scarcity of wood in order to protect one's weakened self from catching cold . . . (Samson Raphael Hirsch, *Horeb: A Philosophy of Jewish Laws and Observance*, p. 281).

On the Other Hand:

Our consumption practices are contributing to alarming rates of depletion of the earth's resources.

a. "And have dominion over the fish of the ocean" (Genesis 1:28). Rabbi Chanina said: "Humanity will rule over if they deserve to; if they do not deserve to, then they will go under" (Genesis *Rabbah* 8:12).

b. Do not believe that all things exist for the sake of humanity. On the contrary, one must believe that . . . everything exists for its own sake and not for anything or anyone else (Maimonides, *Guide of the Perplexed* 3:14).

c. Global demand for many key materials is growing at an unsustainable rate . . . Population increase accounts for only part of the explosion in demand; of equal importance is the spread of industrialization to more and more areas of the globe and the steady worldwide increase in personal wealth, producing an insatiable appetite for energy, private automobiles, building materials, household appliances, and other resource-intensive commodities . . . (Michael T. Klare, *Resource Wars*, p. 15).

d. While the earth is blessed with vast quantities of most vital materials — water, arable land, minerals, timber, and fossil fuels — there are practical limits to what can be extracted from the global environment. According to one recent study, the earth lost nearly one-third of its available natural wealth between 1970 and 1995 as a result of human activity, more than in any other period in history. This study, released by the World Wildlife Fund (WWF) in 1998, revealed a significant decline in the availability or quality of many critical resources, including forest cover, marine fisheries, freshwater systems, and fossil fuels . . . (Michael T. Klare, *Resource Wars*, p. 18).

What Do You Think?

What guidance can we glean from these texts regarding ethical use of the world's natural resources?

What restrictions should Jews impose upon themselves regarding use of earth's resources?

———❖———

2. **Must we take personal responsibility for the environmental repercussions of consumer choices?**

On the One Hand:

We must live for today. Let politicians, scientists, and technology experts worry about clean and efficient production.

Jewish sources would not advocate this position. We must reach to find any published opinion favoring such a view.

A. "I have affixed to me the dirt and dust of countless ages. Who am I to disturb history?" (Bob Herbert, quoting Pig-Pen, the filthy and proud-of-it character from the "Peanuts" cartoon, in "Fouling Our Own Nest" Op-Ed, *The New York Times*, July 4, 2002, p. A).

B. We've been trashing, soiling, even destroying the wonders of nature for countless ages . . . Oh, the skies may once have been clear and the waters sparkling and clean. But you can't have that and progress, too. Can you? (Bob Herbert, making a sarcastic remark, in "Fouling Our Own Nest" Op-Ed, *The New York Times*, July 4, 2002, p. A).

On the Other Hand:

Our level of production and consumption exacerbates, often to dangerous degrees, pollution and other environmental damage.

a. See the Overview, page 143, for Rabbi Shimon ben Yochai's parable on how individual actions make an impact on the community.

b. Upon creating the first human being, God

took him around the Garden of Eden . . . saying: Look at my creations! See how beautiful and perfect they are? I created everything for you. Make sure you don't ruin or devastate My world. For if you do, there will be no one after you to fix it" (*Ecclesiastes Rabbah* 7:28).

c. Destruction [includes] making use of more things and more valuable things when fewer and less valuable ones would suffice; or if this aim is not really worth the means expended for its attainment. [For example] kindling something which is still fit for other purposes for the sake of light; . . . wearing down something more than is necessary . . . consuming more than is necessary . . . (Samson Raphael Hirsch, *Horeb: A Philosophy of Jewish Laws and Observance*, p. 281).

d. The use of property for the creation of wealth, in ways which disturb or damage the property, health or aesthetic pleasure of others, creates ethical and economical problems. This is true even where legal possession is undisputed and the actions are performed solely within the confines of the private domain of the user (Meir Tamari, *In the Marketplace: Jewish Business Ethics*, p. 129, drawing on Mishnah, *Baba Batra* 2:7 and 2:9).

e. Unrestrained resource consumption for energy production and other uses, especially if the developing world strives to achieve living standards based on the same levels of consumption as the developed world, could lead to catastrophic outcomes for the global environment . . . Some of the environmental changes may produce irreversible damage to the earth's capacity to sustain life. Many species have already disappeared, and many more are destined to do so ("Population Growth, Resource Consumption, and a Sustainable World," statement by the Royal Society and the National Academy of Sciences, 1992).

f. If the majority of the world's citizens are also to achieve a consumerist standard of

Consumerism: How Much Is Too Much? Questions to Consider

	The Question	On the One Hand	On the Other Hand
1.	To what extent are human beings entitled to use of the world's resources? (see page 148)	The world has abundant riches for humans to use and enjoy.	Our consumption practices are contributing to alarming rates of depletion of the earth's resources.
2.	Must we take personal responsibility for the environmental repercussions of consumer choices? (see page 149)	We must live for today. Let politicians, scientists, and technology experts worry about clean and efficient production.	Our level of production and consumption exacerbates — often to dangerous degrees — pollution and other environmental damage.
3.	How should we respond to global inequalities in wealth? (see page 151)	If I work hard (or legitimately inherit what my loved ones worked hard for), I am entitled to my wealth.	Regardless of how hard a particular individual works, global distribution of wealth is indefensibly unequal.
4.	What are our responsibilities to workers around the globe? (see page 152)	In capitalist democracies (like America) everyone has opportunities to prosper. Don't deny me, and I won't deny you.	In feeding consumption appetites, wealthy industrialized nations are responsible for exploiting poor workers across the globe.
5.	What economic benefits do individuals and societies derive from consumption? (see page 153)	Our consumption creates needed jobs for poor people.	Serving the consumption of wealthy nations is not always the best way for developing nations to improve their lot.
6.	How might money factor into my personal happiness and well-being? (see page 154)	Spending money and acquiring possessions give me pleasure.	Beyond a moderate level, more consumption does not make for increased well-being.
7.	What value should I attach to wealth? (see page 155)	Wealth and owning certain things will make me feel good about myself.	Dedication to materialism and financial competitiveness divert attention away from more important values, both individual and societal.
8.	How much is reasonable for us to consume? (see page 155)	Judaism is not a religion of denial.	Materialism and indulgent consumption alienate us from essential Jewish/spiritual qualities.

living . . . , then all of the present levels of global pollution and waste are going to more than quadruple . . . No amount of technology would be capable of bringing environmental damage under control if all of the world's citizens were to achieve a standard of living even remotely comparable to that of the consumer class ("Enough: Anticonsumerism Campaign," www.enough.org.uk).

What Do You Think?

What are the problems with the "On the One Hand" position? What are our responsibilities to the environment according to the "On the Other Hand" texts?

Do your personal consumption habits reflect the "On the One Hand" or the "On the Other Hand" position?

⊷◆⊶

3. **How should we respond to global inequalities in wealth?**

On the One Hand:

If I work hard (or legitimately inherit what my loved ones worked hard for), I am entitled to my wealth.

The following two passages illustrate this Libertarian position.

A. The libertarian objects that Tom's unhappiness about Bill's increased consumption simply does not constitute legitimate grounds for curbing Bill's consumption. Tom may be unhappy, but it is nonetheless Tom's responsibility to simply mind his own business. The libertarian argues that to restrict Bill's consumption because it makes Tom unhappy is essentially no different from telling Bill he can't wear a purple shirt because Tom doesn't like the color purple. Tough luck, Tom! Bill has a right to wear a purple shirt, and those who don't like it had just better get used to it (Robert H. Frank, *Luxury Fever*, p. 195-196).

B. I have no right to decide how you should spend your time or your money. I can make that decision for myself but not for you, my neighbor. I may deplore your choice of lifestyle, and I may talk with you about it provided you are willing to listen to me. But I have no right to use force to change it . . . Where do my rights end? Where yours begin. I may do anything I wish with my own life, liberty and property without your consent, but I may do nothing with your life, liberty and property without your consent. If we recognize the principle of [human's] rights, it follows that the individual is sovereign of the domain of [his/her] own life and property, and is sovereign of no other domain (John Hospers, "What Libertarianism Is" in *The Libertarian Alternative*, edited by Tibor R. Machan. Chicago, IL: Nelson-Hall company, 1974, p. 6).

On the Other Hand:

Regardless of how hard a particular individual works, global distribution of wealth is indefensibly unequal.

a. There are factors in the world over and above the right to property and the creation of economic wealth . . . Morally, economic growth of the individual and of society should be limited to the provision of necessities alone, however these may be defined (Meir Tamari, *In the Marketplace: Jewish Business Ethics*, p. 130).

b. The U.S.A. alone, with only six percent of the world's population, consumes 30 percent of its resources . . . What causes global hunger is not a shortage of resources, but the unequal distribution of those resources in favour of the rich . . . . 20 percent of the world's population, (in other words its wealthy consumer class), is responsible for over 50 percent of its "greenhouse effect" atmospheric pollutants, 90 percent of its ozone-depleting CFC gases, 96 percent of its radioactive waste . . . and so on ("Enough: Anticonsumerism Campaign," http://enough.org.uk).

c. If you are a member of an average American college-grad household, you are richer than 99.9 percent of the human beings who have ever lived. You are stinking rich (David Brooks, *The New York Times Magazine*, June 9, 2002, p. 91).

What Do You Think?

What would Meir Tamari (Text #3a) say about libertarianism?

Would Judaism support a libertarian attitude? Explain.

Do you agree that "global distribution of wealth is indefensibly unequal?" Explain.

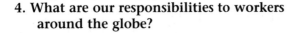

4. What are our responsibilities to workers around the globe?

On the One Hand:

In capitalist democracies (like America) everyone has opportunities to prosper. Don't deny me, and I won't deny you.

Also see the Libertarian position presented in "Text Study" #3B above.

A. The environment of abundance accounts for the energy, creativity and dynamism that marks national life. The lure of plenty, pervading the landscape, encourages risk and adventure (David Brooks, "Why the U.S. Will Always Be Rich," *The New York Times Magazine*, June 9, 2002, p. 91).

On the Other Hand:

In feeding consumption appetites, wealthy industrialized nations are responsible for exploiting poor workers across the globe.

a. Jewish law recognizes that the community, whether seen as neighbors in a courtyard, citizens in a town, or a people in a larger community, has rights which have to be protected against injury from the action of individuals. These express themselves in the communal right to taxation — which,

in effect, takes property from individuals to finance communal needs — but also in the right to limit activities of individuals which damage the environment or detract from the community's scenic beauty. These rights are the basis of Jewish zoning laws and of communal action to protect even a non-physical aspect of property rights (Meir Tamari, *In the Marketplace: Jewish Business Ethics*, p. 130).

b. Today young, mostly female workers in Bangladesh, a Muslim country that is the fourth-largest garment producer for the United States market, are paid an average of 1.6 cents for each baseball cap with a Harvard logo that they sew. The caps retail at the Harvard bookstore for $17, which means the garment workers, who often are younger than the Harvard students, are being paid a tenth of 1 percent of the cap's price in the market. Also in Bangladesh, women receive 5 cents for each $17.99 Disney shirt they sew. Wages like these are not enough to climb the ladder with (Tom Hayden and Charles Kernaghan, "Pennies an Hour, and No Way Up," *The New York Times*, Op-Ed, July 6, 2002, p. A27).

c. If we choose to continue consuming more than our share of the world's resources, we are placing ourselves in danger. Those who are left without are unlikely to passively tolerate the situation. Conflicts will arise, producing a more policed, more governed, more insecure world. Some argue that this has already begun, and yet few commentators point to correcting these disparities as a solution ("Enough: Anticonsumerism Campaign," http://enough.org.uk).

What Do You Think?

What would a Jewish response be to Text #4A above? Explain.

Though some may argue otherwise, let's assume that wealthy nations' consumptive habits compromise the living conditions and environment of poor workers across the globe.

To what extent would Judaism suggest we restrict individual freedom for the sake of the well-being of others?

━━◆━━

5. **What economic benefits do individuals and societies derive from consumption?**

On the One Hand:

Our consumption creates needed jobs for poor people.

A. The value of preventing damage or promoting the ecological welfare of society has to be gauged against the potential benefits to be earned from economic activity. The individual corporation has to consider the ecological costs suffered by the community, or by individuals, as part of its production of goods or services. Given the jobs created, the goods or services provided and even the tax payments paid by the corporation, society must weigh these against the cost of, for example, pollution to air, or a lower quality of life (Meir Tamari, *In the Marketplace: Jewish Business Ethics*, p. 130).

B. Some economists argue that even the most exploited and impoverished workers are better off than those who are unemployed or trapped in slave labor (Tom Hayden and Charles Kernaghan, "Pennies an Hour, and No Way Up," *The New York Times*, Op-Ed, July 6, 2002, p. A27).

On the Other Hand:

Serving the consumption of wealthy nations is not always the best way for developing nations to improve their lot.

a. The Eternal is good to all, and God's mercy is upon all God's works" (Psalms 145:9).

b. About 2.8 billion people of the world's 6 billion people live on less than $2 [American] a day. More than 60 countries have lower per capita incomes now than they did in 1990 (Barbara Crossette, "U.N. Report Says New Democracies Falter," *The New York Times*, July 24, 2002, p. A8).

c. Women in Bangladesh say they could care for their children if their wages rose to 34 cents an hour, two-tenths of 1 percent of the retail price of the Harvard hat (Tom Hayden and Charles Kernaghan, "Pennies an Hour, and No Way Up," *The New York Times*, Op-Ed, July 6, 2002, p. A27).

d. The distribution of [economic] competitiveness is now uneven . . . This pattern raises the disturbing prospect of a "globalization gap" between the winners and the losers . . . Leaders of the losers often blame outsiders or unpopular insiders for economic hardship. Some foment crises to distract domestic attention from joblessness and hunger (Institute for National Security Studies, 1999, quoted by Michael T. Klare, *Resource Wars*, p. 24).

e. Refer to Text #5B above. That comment seems open to the claim that consumption in wealthy countries creates needed jobs. However, the commentators immediately add:

> But that argument is not about offering anyone a ladder up, but about which ring of Dante's inferno people in developing nations are consigned to (Tom Hayden and Charles Kernaghan, "Pennies an Hour, and No Way Up," *The New York Times*, Op-Ed, July 6, 2002, p. A27).

What Do You Think?

Does Tamari make a valid point in passage #5A above? Why or why not?

Jews believe the Eternal is good to all, and that God's mercy is upon all God's works. We also believe we are to strive to be like God (*halachta bidrachav*). That is, we must try to be "good to all." What should "being good to all" require of us regarding our responsibilities toward workers around the world?

━━◆━━

6. **How might money factor into my personal happiness and well-being?**

On the One Hand:

Spending money and acquiring possessions give me pleasure.

A. The noblest, most creative and fullest life is not to be found by the backwaters of Walden Pond but in the rushing mainstream of life, in the office parks and the malls and the Times Squares twinkling with lights, screens and money (David Brooks, "Why the U.S. Will Always Be Rich," *The New York Times Magazine*, June 9, 2002, p. 124).

B. The culture [is] no longer concerned with how to work and achieve, but with how to spend and enjoy (Daniel Bell in a 1970 study called "The Cultural Contradictions of Capitalism," quoted by Patricia Cohen, *The New York Times*, July 7, 2002, section 9, p. 2).

On the Other Hand:

Beyond a moderate level, more consumption does not make for increased well-being.

a. Those who love money never have their fill of money, nor do those who love wealth have their fill of income (Ecclesiastes 5:9).

b. It is characteristic of wealth, that when one has little, one desires more, and when one attains more, one desires double of what already has been acquired, and so ad infinitum. Thus, a midrash teaches, "No person leaves this world with even half of his or her desires attained. If one has one hundred, one desires two hundred . . . " (*Ecclesiastes Rabbah* 1:13). Wealth is like a fire: the more wood one adds, the more the flame increases and the fire blazes (Bahya ben Asher, as quoted in *Creating an Ethical Jewish Life*, p. 127).

c. Once one passionately seeks wealth, one discovers that it entails immense efforts of thought and exertion, keeping one awake at night and plagued by responsibilities by day so that even when one has acquired what one desires, one can't sleep properly . . . When people make money the object of all their strivings and devote themselves to it with mad ambition and avidity . . . then the love of money becomes for them like a consuming fire, like a wilderness, like death or barrenness that are never sated (Saadiah Gaon, *The Book of Beliefs and Opinions*, Book 10, Chapter 8).

d. When we subordinate other desires to money, we lose our ability to recognize "enough." Those goals and desires that are capable of satisfaction have been co-opted by money, and the desire for money has no natural limit. Since it cannot in itself satisfy anything, we can never have enough. A number of rich men have acknowledged that they could satisfy all their material needs — and even whims — with a fraction of what they hold, yet are unable to stop trying to make more. Once money is given priority there is no longer any basis for deciding when and where to stop accumulating (Philip Slater, *Wealth Addiction*, p. 43).

e. Behavioral scientists find that once a threshold level of affluence is reached, the average level of human well-being in a country is almost completely independent of its stock of material consumption goods (Robert H. Frank, *Luxury Fever*, p. 65).

What Do You Think?

From a Jewish perspective, what would make the viewpoints expressed in Texts #6A and #6B problematic?

Does wealth contribute to well-being? Explain. When does spending become excessive?

7. What value should I attach to wealth?

On the One Hand:

Wealth and owning certain things will make me feel good about myself.

A. Consumer culture in one sense is "democracy's highest achievement, giving meaning and dignity to people when workplace participation, ethnic solidarity and even representative democracy have failed" (Patricia Cohen, quoting Gary Cross in "In Defense of Our Wicked, Wicked Ways," *The New York Times*, July 7, 2002, section 9, p. 2).

B. A house may be large or small; as long as the surrounding houses are equally small, it satisfies all social demands for a dwelling. But if a palace rises beside the little house, the little house shrinks into a hut" (Karl Marx as quoted by Robert H. Frank in *Luxury Fever*, p. 137).

C. Compelling evidence [exists] that concern about relative position is a deep-rooted and ineradicable element of human nature (Robert H. Frank, *Luxury Fever*, p. 145).

On the Other Hand:

Dedication to materialism and financial competitiveness divert attention away from more important values, both individual and societal.

a. Don't exhaust yourself trying to make money. You see it and then it's gone. It grows wings and flies away (Proverbs 23:4-5).

b. When told of a man who had acquired great wealth, a sage replied, "Has he also acquired the days in which to spend it?" (Ibn Gabirol, "Choice of Pearls," in Leo Rosten's *Treasury of Jewish Quotations*, p. 536).

c. An across-the-board reduction in the rate of growth in conspicuous consumption would, in time, free up literally trillions of dollars worth of resources annually . . . These resources could be used to support more time with family and friends, more

freedom from congestion and pollution, greater autonomy and flexibility in the workplace, and increases in a variety of other forms of inconspicuous consumption that would enhance the quality of our lives (Robert H. Frank, *Luxury Fever*, p. 194).

What Do You Think?

What is the relationship between competitiveness and excessive consumption? What benefits might come from shifting our spending away from conspicuous consumption, and toward other values?

What values do you think suffer most in our society from an overemphasis on consumption?

How would your own life be different if you focused less on accumulating material possessions?

8. How much is reasonable for us to consume?

On the One Hand:

Judaism is not a religion of denial.

A. Wealth which comes to us with justice, trust, and uprightness is one of the desirable eminences . . . For when we have wealth we can sustain ourselves without suffering, without great effort, and without great deliberation in the areas of livelihood, economy and welfare (Yechiel ben Yekutiel, *Sefer Ma'alot Ha-middot*, pp. 248-249).

B. In passing from this world and then confronting ultimate judgment, one will be obliged to explain, among other penetrating questions, why one abstained from enjoying the pleasures and delights of this world (Jerusalem Talmud, *Kiddushin* 4:12, as explained by Reuven Bulka in *Judaism on Pleasure*, p. 4).

C. [O]n balance, it can be safely stated that Judaism rejects the notion of denial for denial's sake, even as it recognizes special situations calling for denial. And those special situations do not negate the general affirmation of the obligation to taste the appealing things of this world (Reuven Bulka, *Judaism on Pleasure*, p. 4).

On the Other Hand:

Materialism and indulgent consumption alienate us from essential Jewish/spiritual qualities.

a. Give me neither poverty nor riches, but provide me with my daily bread, lest being sated, I renounce, saying "Who is the Eternal?" Or, being impoverished, I take to theft and profane the name of my God (Proverbs 30:8-9).

b. Why do you spend money for what is not bread, your earnings for what does not satisfy? (Isaiah 55:2).

c. Ben Zoma said: Who is rich? One who is happy with what one has (*Pirke Avot* 4:1).

d. Envy, lust, and pursuit of honor will ruin a person's life (*Pirke Avot* 4:30).

e. [We condemn] the deterioration in the character of the bar mitzvah "affair." The extravagant consumption, the conspicuous waste, and the crudity of many of these affairs are rapidly becoming a public Jewish scandal. The lowering of standards as reflected in many bar mitzvah celebrations is in direct violation of the teaching of the Torah. The trend toward the abandonment of aesthetic standards can lead to the abandonment of ethical standards as well (The Central Conference of Reform Rabbis, 1964).

f. In a certain community, Orthodox rabbinical authorities created guidelines to curtail extravagant spending on weddings. One of the authorities, Rabbi Shafran, explained:

> The rationale for the guidelines . . . is not only social and economic but also religious. The concept of modesty, not only in dress but in behavior and expression is central to the Torah . . . Limiting excess, whether in general lifestyle or celebrations, is an inherently Jewish ideal" (Francine Parnes, "A Big Wedding with a Smaller Bill,"

The New York Times, May 25, 2002, p. A13).

What Do You Think?

Compose a Jewish response to this question, using the texts above as your guide: Is rejecting extravagance equivalent to denial?

Should communities (Jewish and general) impose spending restrictions on members/citizens?

Do you feel materialism and indulgent consumption alienate us from essential values? Explain.

Related Middot and Mitzvot

Practicing these virtues and commandments enhances efforts to keep consumer habits in check.

Bal Tashchit (Not Destroying, Protecting the Environment): Rampant consumerism takes an enormous toll on the environment. Minimizing consumption to meet only essential needs will help preserve the earth and its resources.

Emet (Truth): Luxurious lifestyles and material abundance have hidden costs. Corporations, merchants, advertisers, and some politicians have an interest in shielding consumers from certain uncomfortable truths regarding environmental destruction and worker exploitation.

Lo Tachmod (Not Coveting): Jealousy, envy, wanting what others have — these sentiments intensify consumer appetites.

Lo Titeyn Michshol (Not Placing a Stumbling Block): Production of many goods today involves worker exploitation or results in devastating environmental damage. Merchants who sell such goods might be accused of placing a stumbling block before the blind. That is, they might be accused of involving unsuspecting consumers in unethical business practices.

Ometz Lev (Courage): It takes a special kind of

strength and discipline to live simply in the face of pressures to achieve wealth and accumulate. One needs resolve to resist social expectations and media assaults that extol materialism.

Samayach Be'Chelko (Contentment with Your Lot): Habituating yourself to satisfaction with what you have helps you avoid succumbing to materialistic excesses.

Simchah (Joy and Happiness): Beyond a modest standard of living, having more wealth and owning more things do not bestow greater happiness.

Tochechah (Rebuking): Speaking out against consumer excesses presents especially delicate challenges. Our culture generally sees wealth as a private matter. If you criticize others' consumer habits, they may accuse you of being judgmental, jealous, self-righteous, and simply out-of-line (i.e., "my spending habits are none of your business!").

Tzeniyut (Modesty): A modest lifestyle discourages indulgence and extravagance.

V'ahavta L'rayacha Kamocha (Loving One's Fellow Person as Oneself): If we love others as ourselves, we do not exploit them for our gain. Rather, we live in ways in which it is possible for all people to enjoy living wages, safe work conditions, and a healthy environment.

Where Do I Go From Here?

Your own spending decisions and habits are much more meaningful than you may have thought before you studied this Hot Topic. Your Judaism should not only help you come to terms with the role consumerism will play in your own physical and emotional well being, but also with the global effect your consumerism will have.

Following is a list of resources that you may find helpful as you continue your exploration of this timely and challenging topic.

Books and Articles

Bernstein, Ellen, and Dan Fink. *Let the Earth Teach You Torah*. Wyncote, PA: Shomrei Adamah, 1992.

Borowitz, Eugene B., and Frances Weidman Schwartz. *The Jewish Moral Virtues*. Philadelphia, PA: The Jewish Publication Society, 1999.

Brecher, Jeremy, and Tim Costello. *Global Village or Global Pillage: Economic Reconstruction from the Bottom Up*. Boston, MA: South End Press, 1994.

Brooks, David. *Bobos* in Paradise: The New Upper Class and How They Got There*. New York: Simon and Schuster, 2000. (* = Bourgeois Bohemians)

Brooks, David. "Why the U.S. Will Always Be Rich," *The New York Times Magazine*, June 9, 2002, p. 124.

Bulka, Reuben P. *Judaism on Pleasure*. Northvale, NJ: Jason Aronson Inc., 1995.

Cross, Gary. *An All-Consuming Century: Why Commercialism Won in Modern America*. New York: Columbia University Press, 2000.

Frank, Robert H. *Luxury Fever: Why Money Fails to Satisfy in an Era of Excess*. New York: The Free Press, 1999.

Freeman, Susan. *Teaching Jewish Virtues: Sacred Sources and Arts Activities*. Denver, CO: A.R.E. Publishing, Inc., 1999.

Gaon, Saadiah, *The Book of Beliefs and Opinions*. Samuel Rosenblatt, trans. New Haven, CT: Yale University Press, 1948.

Henslin, James M. "Economic Justice." In *Social Problems*, Englewood Cliffs, NJ: Prentice Hall, 1990.

Hirsch, Samson Raphael Hirsch. *Horeb: A Philosophy of Jewish Laws and Observances*, I. Grunfeld, trans. New York: Soncino Press, 1981.

Kadden, Barbara Binder, and Bruce Kadden. *Teaching Mitzvot: Concepts, Values, and Activities*. Rev. ed. Denver, CO: A.R.E. Publishing, Inc., 2003.

Klare, Michael T. *Resource Wars: The New Landscape of Global Conflict*. New York: Metropolitan Books, Henry Holt and Company, LLC, 2001.

Nathanson, Stephen. *Economic Justice*. Upper Saddle River, NJ: Prentice Hall, 1998.

Salkin, Jeffrey K. *Putting God on the Guest List: How to Reclaim the Spiritual Meaning of Your Child's Bar or Bat Mitzvah*. Woodstock, VT: Jewish Lights Publishing, 1996.

Sherwin, Byron L., and Seymour J. Cohen. *Creating an Ethical Jewish Life: A Practical Introduction To Classic Teachings on How to Be a Jew*. Woodstock, VT: Jewish Lights Publishing, 2001.

Siegel, Seymour. "A Jewish View of Economic Justice." In *Contemporary Jewish Ethics and Morality*, ed. by Elliot N. Dorff and Louis E. Newman. New York: Oxford University Press, 1995.

Slater, Philip. *Wealth Addiction*. New York: E.P. Dutton, 1980.

Tamari, Meir. *In the Marketplace: Jewish Business Ethics*. Southfield, MI: Targum Press, Inc., 1991.

Yekutiel of Rome, Yechiel ben. *Sefer Ma'alot Ha-middot*. Jerusalem: Eshkol, 1978. (This thirteenth century Italian author's ideas were first published in Istanbul in 1512.)

Twitchell, James B. *Living It Up: Our Love Affair with Luxury*. New York: Columbia University Press, 2002.

Web Sites

Earthscan . . . delivering sustainability: www.earthscan.co.uk
> *Earthscan describes itself as the "world's leading publisher on environmentally sustainable development."*

Enough: Anticonsumerism Campaign: http://enough.org.uk
> *This "critical look at consumerism, poverty, and the planet" presents powerful information and arguments.*

Envirolink — The Online Environmental Community: www.envirolink.org
> *Clearinghouse for environmental information on the Internet.*

Global Exchange: www.globalexchange.org
> *An international human rights organization dedicated to promoting political, social, and environmental justice globally.*

The Center for a New American Dream: www.newdream.org
> *An organization with the mission of "helping Americans consume responsibly to protect the environment, enhance quality of life, and promote social justice."*

The New Road Map Foundation: www.newroadmap.org
> *Claims to provide "people with practical tools and innovative approaches for managing and mastering basic life challenges," including personal finances, how we relate to money, and how to live more simply. "People need new ways to navigate the road of life — ways based on a vision of a cooperative human community in a diverse yet interconnected world."*

The Northwest Earth Institute: www.nwei.org
> *Offers discussion courses on "sustainability, deep ecology, living in place, and the practice of simplicity."*

Films

The Cost of Cool: Youth, Consumerism, and the Environment (2001, 26 minutes, grades 6-12).
> Looks at everyday items, from t-shirts to sneakers, and tracks the effect of their manufacture on the world's resources and environments. Teenagers examine their learned buying patterns, recognizing that much of the stuff they acquire is not needed. (Available from The Video Project, 1-800-4PLANET/ 1-800-475-2638 or www. videoproject.net)

Erasable You (1998, 85 minutes, unrated).
> A dark comedy about a woman, hooked on incontrollable consumerism, who plots to rob her ex-husband and his nice new wife of all their earnings. Available from video stores or from amazon.com (www.amazon.com).

PART IV

Sexuality

The Foundations of
Sexual Ethics

Masturbation

Birth Control

Homosexuality

Sex Outside of Marriage

CHAPTER 11
THE FOUNDATIONS OF SEXUAL ETHICS

Overview

Jewish Perspectives

We are part of God's creation. In Judaism we believe in the goodness of God and the purposefulness of God's work. Whereas some belief systems and the language of "the streets" may attach shamefulness and crudity to the sex organs, Judaism stresses that we must treat our whole selves with honor and gratitude.

Appreciating Our Bodies

Jews serve God by living according to the values and teachings of our tradition. Our bodies and our sexuality can be vehicles for holiness while serving very tangible purposes, as well. These include procreation — "to be fruitful and multiply" — (Genesis 1:28), companionship, and pleasure. Not all these purposes are as straightforward as they may at first seem.

Procreation

Judaism considers it a mitzvah to have children, unless there are physical reasons why a person is unable do so. Children are a source of joy. Through children, we pass along traditions and values. Raising children can help us to better people — less self-focused, more generous, patient, and caring. Children teach us about love. A specific Jewish concern is sustaining our small population, especially in the face of the losses we suffered through the Holocaust and the more recent strains of assimilation.

Having children may be a prevailing value in Judaism. However, for a variety of reasons some choose not to raise children. While some might say these adults are neglecting their responsibilities, others might say it is wrong to judge the personal choices others make or to be insensitive to their life circumstances.

Another challenge to our value of having children is the worry about overpopulation in the world. Many Jewish leaders acknowledge the concern, but feel that because of Jewish demographics today, we can't afford to see our population diminish any more than it has in the last 100 years or so.

Companionship

The value of an intimate partnership first appears in Genesis: "It is not good for the human to be alone. I will make a fitting companion (*ezer k'negdo*) for him" (Genesis 2:18). Together, partners can complement each other and create a greater "whole." Consistent with this biblical notion, in the Jewish wedding ceremony, we call the two companions, the bride and groom, "*ray-eem ahoov-eem*" or "loving friends."

Pleasure

"Loving friends" want to please each other. This includes giving each other sexual pleasure. Many explicit Jewish sources describe ways in which sex should be pleasurable.

"Black and White" and "Gray" Areas of Sexuality

Judaism widely accepts certain "black and white" views of sexual relationships. For instance, Judaism clearly upholds marriage as the ideal adult partnership. Married couples may have children, enjoy loving companionship, and share sexual pleasure. Other sexual relationships, such as incestuous or adulterous ones, are explicitly prohibited. Beyond these clear-cut guidelines, however, sexuality issues get more challenging. Masturbation, homosexuality, and sex outside of marriage are three subjects fraught with complicated feelings and mixed attitudes.

Overwhelmingly, Orthodox Jewish authorities would denounce these practices. Outside of Orthodoxy, however, many Jews place these sexual experiences within what we might call the "gray areas" of sexuality. Liberal Jews are more likely to reconsider traditional views of masturbation, homosexuality, and sex outside of marriage, taking into account modern sources of information and life experiences.

Not everyone will agree on what belongs in the "gray areas." Societal pressures direct us to try to find ways to address sexuality that doesn't fit into clear-cut categories. A few decades ago, innovative Jewish thinkers suggested a "sliding scale of sexual values" — with marriage at the uppermost point. (For a more detailed explanation of this idea, see "Sex Outside of Marriage," Text Study #1a, p. 200.)

Holiness

Judaism sees the sexual relationship within marriage as a vehicle for holiness. But what is holiness? One possible explanation is this: To make something holy is to transform a mundane, everyday kind of experience into something special. For example, we can seize upon a plate of food and gobble it up, or we can transform it into something special, which recognizes God's role in the experience. That is, we can wash and bless before eating, and offer gratitude following the meal.

Similarly, we can have a casual sexual encounter with a near-stranger. A euphemism for this kind of intercourse is "hopping into bed" — something that brings to mind rabbits rather than human beings. Unlike rabbits (or other animals), human beings can express love and enduring commitment, enjoy companionship, and care about each other's pleasure during sex. These elements help transform a physical urge into something special or holy.

To sanctify an act requires discipline — we cannot always have exactly what we want, when we want it. Instant gratification is devoid of meaning. To gain anything meaningful requires discipline. Disciplining ourselves to pursue deep, caring relationships will be more fulfilling in the end.

The Hebrew word for the marriage ceremony is "kiddushin," related to the word "kedusha," meaning "holiness." When something is "kadosh," it is set apart. A bride and groom "separate" each other from all others. The exclusivity of the relationship contributes to its holiness.

Holiness in sexual intimacy implies a deep "knowing" of the other, an experience of union and oneness. Rabbis throughout the ages suggest that when two married people unite sexually, so too does a deeper bonding with God take place (see Text Study #7A – F below).

Modesty / Tzeniyut

From a Jewish perspective, holiness in sexuality begins with modesty or tzeniyut. Tzeniyut has to do with privacy and concealment. To be modest means you are respectful and humble, that you don't show off. When you casually reveal your body and allow easy access to it by others, you are like an object, not a "vehicle for holiness." Modesty stands in contrast to the "overexposure" associated with pornography, Internet sex, and elaborate body decoration (such as tattoos). Without modesty, people become "used" rather than "loved." God created us for higher purposes.

Revealing Ourselves

Judaism refers to illicit sexual liaisons as *gilui arayot*, or uncovering nakedness. Essentially, *gilui arayot* are improper revelations of self, and Judaism sees such "self exposure" as destructive and painful. In contrast, we refer to trusting, loving revelations of self as "knowing" another. Being modest helps us consistently to nurture holiness in our sexual behavior. Revealing ourselves only with great care and in an appropriate relationship allows us to remain on the path of holiness.

General Perspectives

We who live in open societies are influenced by the "norms" of the sexual behaviors around us. Many ideas from the secular world can complement Jewish strategies for ethical behavior. One straightforward guideline in determining moral behavior is the "values formula" directing individuals to help and not to hurt. For instance, we should ask "how and who is helped by being careful about sex, and how and who is hurt when people are not careful about sex."[1]

A Planned Parenthood brochure suggests that a healthy relationship must have seven basic qualities: respect, honesty, equality, good communication, trust, fairness, and responsibility.[2]

The same brochure offers "Guidelines for Sex Partners." These include having each other's consent, never using pressure to get consent, being honest with each other, treating each other as equals, being attentive to each other's pleasure, protecting each other against physical and emotional harm, guarding against unintended pregnancy and sexually transmitted infection, being clear with each other about what you want to do and don't want to do, respecting each other's limits, and accepting responsibility for your actions.[3]

Judaism certainly encompasses many of these values. Our tradition teaches us to love one another ("love your neighbor as yourself"[4]), to honor and respect each other, to be truthful and fair, and to take responsibility for our actions. We are to strive to be kind and helpful in our relationships. As the contemporary Rabbi Michael Gold puts it, "Human beings are created in God's image, and anything that hurts or diminishes the dignity of a human being is an affront to God."[5]

Summary of the Overview

- God created our bodies and our sexuality for good.

- Important values in a sexual relationship include procreation (when it is physically possible), loving and enduring companionship, and pleasure.

- Values, such as the above, can help transform a physical act into an experience of holiness.

Scenarios: How Things Have Changed

Love and sex have always been complicated — touching on our deepest hopes, desires, and vulnerabilities. From the beginning of our written history, Jewish texts have commented on the subject. Below are two imaginary scenarios, one set in an earlier era, and one set in contemporary times. These scenarios are intended to raise questions and spark discussion. Read each scenario and reflect, either individually or in group discussion, on the questions in the "For Thought and Discussion" section that follows. Then continue on to the "Text Study" section to see what Jewish

and other resources have to say about the foundations of sexual ethics. Finally, you may wish to come back and discuss these scenarios a second time, to see if your views have changed.

Scenario I: A "Simpler Time and Place" (If It Ever Really Existed):

Moshe and Leah's parents introduced them a few months ago. Moshe is 18 years old, and Leah is 16. They have visited together several times at Leah's home. Moshe has joined the family for dinner on occasion. Leah's parents have asked her if she would like to marry Moshe. Leah sees Moshe as a kind, considerate person who takes an interest in her. She agrees to the marriage. A wedding ceremony is arranged to take place in a few months.

On their wedding night, the bride and groom spend time embracing and touching each other. They tentatively begin to explore each other's bodies. Leah feels nervous about sexual intercourse. Moshe, knowing that it is wrong to force his wife to have sex, suggests they take their time in getting to know each other's bodies. When they both feel ready, they will engage in sexual intercourse. In the meantime, in the privacy of their bedroom, they continue to be physically loving with one another. After a few weeks, they feel trusting enough to reveal themselves fully to one another in their lovemaking. Over the years, the pleasure of their sexual relationship grows as they learn more about what pleases the other, and as they feel love and friendship deepen between them.

Scenario II: Nowadays:

Marc and Liana meet for the first time at a high school basketball game. Liana is playing in the game, and Marc is there watching. He is dating a student on the opposing team. It turns out Marc's girlfriend is someone Liana knows from her elementary school, but hasn't seen for years. After the game, they all decide to go out and get a bite to eat. At the restaurant, the "chemistry" shifts. Marc is charmed by Liana, and Liana is quite intrigued with Marc. They are pleased to find that each other is Jewish, as well. Marc calls Liana the next day, and they begin exclusively dating each other. Marc is 18 years old and Liana is 16.

Though they are young, they are physically mature. After a few months of dating, they feel they want to spend the rest of their lives together.

For Thought and Discussion:

What are some of the positive aspects of Moshe and Leah's relationship?

What challenges might Moshe and Leah face in their relationship?

What are some of the positive aspects of Marc and Liana's relationship? What do you think about their plans to marry?

(Note: For a continuation of Marc and Liana's scenario, see Chapter 15, "Sex Outside of Marriage, page 200.)

Text Study

In many ways, the Jewish path of love and marriage as framed hundreds of years ago sets the stage for the ideal sexual relationship. However, our present culture and lifestyles have introduced new questions and complexities into love, sex, and marriage. Jewish textual sources provide many important guidelines, but these guidelines often highlight the tension between seemingly opposing considerations. The chart on the next page poses the questions and offers two different responses. Text sources supporting each of these points of view follow below.

1. **How do our physical bodies and our sexuality fit into the framework of Creation?**

   On the One Hand:

   God created everything for good — including all our body parts and our sexuality.

   A. God saw everything God had made and behold it was very good (Genesis 1:31).

   B. A comment on the above verse states:

      Nothing in the human organs are created flawed or ugly. Everything is created with divine wisdom and is therefore complete, exalted, good, and

pleasant (*The Holy Letter*, attributed to Nachmanides, p. 45, 48).

C. For in the image of God, did God make humankind (Genesis 9:6).

On the Other Hand:

We must do our part in protecting and honoring God's creation.

a. . . . Take good care of yourselves (Deuteronomy 2:4).

b. A blessing we are to include in daily worship:

   Blessed is our Eternal God, Sovereign of the Universe, who has made our bodies with wisdom, combining openings and closings — arteries, glands, and organs — into a finely balanced network . . .

c. I praise You, for I am awesomely, wondrously made. Your work is wonderful; I know it very well (Psalms 139:14).

d. Judaism does not despise the carnal. It does not urge us to desert the flesh but to control and to counsel it; to please the natural needs of the flesh so that the spirit should not be molested by unnatural frustrations . . . Judaism teaches us how even the gratification of animal needs can be an act of sanctification (Abraham Joshua Heschel, *Man Is Not Alone: A Philosophy of Religion*, New York: Farrar, Straus and Giroux, 1972, p. 263).

What Do You Think?

What would a Jewish response be to comments such as, "I hate the way I look" or "I can't stand my body"?

Would you describe sexuality as a "gift"? Explain your answer.

What might "taking good care of yourself" mean in regard to one's sexuality? Should a person offer a prayer of thanks prior to or following sexual relations?

The Foundations of Sexual Ethics: Questions to Consider

The Question	On the One Hand	On the Other Hand
1. How do our physical bodies and our sexuality fit into the framework of Creation? (see page 164)	God created everything for good — including all our body parts and our sexuality.	We must do our part in protecting and honoring God's creation.
2. Is procreation a necessary function of sexuality? (see this page)	One purpose of sexuality is procreation.	Not everyone is able to procreate; some choose not to.
3. What does sexuality contribute to our emotional lives? (see page 167)	A key facet of sexuality is companionship and the expression of love.	Opportunities for anonymous sex, casual sex, sex that provides physical release, variety, and/or excitement are readily available in secular culture.
4. To what extent should pursuit of pleasure be a contributing factor to a healthy sexual relationship? (see page 168)	There are duties and responsibilities regarding sex.	Sex should be a source of pleasure.
5. Is the context of the relationship important in evaluating the validity of engaging in sex? (see page 169)	Judaism consistently affirms and approves of sex in certain contexts.	Judaism consistently disapproves of sex in other contexts.
6. Should we embrace modesty as a worthy value in our day? (see page 170)	Modesty (*tzeniyut*) is a value for all Jews.	While all Jews should embrace modesty, not everyone accepts the same "code" of behavior.
7. What role might sexuality play in our spiritual lives? (see page 172)	Sexual intimacy can be an expression of holiness.	Misusing our sexuality can lead to alienation from what God ultimately wants for us (i.e., love, companionship, pleasure).

2. Is procreation a necessary function of sexuality?

On the One Hand:

One purpose of sexuality is procreation.

Note: Texts in Chapter 13, "Birth Control," (page 181) have relevance here, too.

A. God blessed them and said to them, "Be fruitful and multiply, fill the earth and master it; and rule over the fish of the sea, and the birds of the sky, and every living thing that moves on the earth (Genesis 1:28).

B. A man may not refrain from fulfilling the commandment "Be fruitful and multiply" unless he already has children. The School of Shammai ruled he must have two sons. The School of Hillel ruled: a son and a daughter, for it is written, "Male and female God created them" (Genesis 5:2) (*Mishnah, Yevamot* 6:6).

C. Ben Azzai said: those who do not engage in propagation of the race act as though they shed blood and diminish the divine image in the world . . . " (*Yevamot* 63b).

D. We Jews numbered approximately 18 million before the Holocaust, and we lost a third of our numbers during those terrible years. Even if we forget about replenishing the numbers we lost, we are not replacing ourselves as we are now . . . [Statistics show] we are endangering ourselves demographically as a people. The world's overpopulation problem is real, but Jews are only 0.2% of the world's population, and so even if the reproductive rate of Jews increased to the replacement rate, the impact upon the world's population problem would be minimal. That would still be true even if the Jewish people increased to replenish the six million lost in the Holocaust. Sacrificing the existence of the Jewish people is neither an effective solution nor a warranted one to reduce the world's problems of overpopulation and limited resources. These important concerns are better addressed by increasing the availability and usage of contraception worldwide and by fostering the responsible use of resources. The contemporary, demographic problem of the Jewish people, then, must also be a factor which figures into the thinking of Jews using contraception (Rabbi Elliot N. Dorff, *This Is My Beloved, This Is My Friend: A Rabbinic Letter on Intimate Relations*, p. 27-28).

E. Reform Judaism approves birth control, but we also recognize our obligation to maintain a viable and stable Jewish population. Therefore, couples are encouraged to have at least two or three children (Resolution by the Central Conference of American Rabbis, 1978).

On the Other Hand:

Not everyone is able to procreate; some choose not to.

a. In the discussion that continues from Text #2C above, the bachelor Ben Azzai is called to account for his failure to have children.

They said to Ben Azzai: Some preach well and act well, others act well but do not preach well; you, however, preach well but do not act well!

Ben Azzai replied: But what shall I do, seeing that my soul is in love with the Torah? The world can be carried on by others (*Yevamot 63b*).

b. Intercourse with a woman incapable at all of childbearing is permissible, and the prohibition of *hash-hatat zera* [improper emission of seed] is not involved so long as the intercourse is in the manner of procreation; for the rabbis have in every case permitted marriage with women too young or too old for childbearing. No prohibition is involved with a barren or sterile woman, except that the mitzvah of procreation is not thus being fulfilled (*Nimmukei Yosef*, early 15th c., commentary to Rabbi Isaac Al Fasi's Code to *Yevamot*, chapter 5).

c. It is not amiss that the reason why women are exempt from the obligation of procreation is grounded in the reasonableness of the judgments of the Eternal and the Eternal's ways. The Torah did not impose upon Israel burdens too difficult for a person to bear . . . Women, whose lives are jeopardized by conception and birth, were not enjoined (*Meshekh Chochmah* to Genesis 9:7, quoted by David S. Shapiro in Jewish Bioethics, p. 65).

What Do You Think?

Why do you think the Torah instructs human beings to "be fruitful and multiply"? What is Ben Azzai's dilemma concerning this commandment (as described in Text #2a)? Is Ben Azzai's explanation for not fulfilling the commandment legitimate?

What are good reasons to have children in our time? What might be good reasons not to have children?

Are we obligated to have children? Should guidelines for procreation be different for Jews as opposed to non-Jews?

3. **What does sexuality contribute to our emotional lives?**

On the One Hand:

A key facet of sexuality is companionship and the expression of love.

A. It is not good for the human to be alone. I will make a fitting companion (*ezer k'neg-do*) for him (Genesis 2:18).

B. Therefore a man leaves his father and mother and clings to his wife, so that they become one flesh (Genesis 2:24).

C. Oh, give me of the kisses of your mouth,
For your love is sweeter than wine . . .
My beloved is mine
And I am his . . .
You have captured my heart,
My own, my bride,
You have captured my heart . . .
I am my beloved's,
And his desire is for me . . .
Let me be a seal upon your heart,
Like the seal upon your hand.
For love is fierce as death,
Passion is mighty as Sheol;
Its darts are darts of fire,
A blazing flame.
Vast floods cannot quench love,
Nor rivers drown it . . .
(Song of Songs 1:2; 2:16; 4:9; 7:11; 8:6-7).

D. This blessing chanted during the wedding ritual refers to the bride and groom as "*ray-eem ahuveem*" or "loving companions":

> We praise You, Eternal God, who causes bride and groom to rejoice. May these loving companions rejoice as have Your creatures since the days of creation.

E. In a right and perfect union, the love of a man and a woman is, and should be, inseparable from sexual experience. The emotion of love which is spiritual expresses itself in sexual acts which are physical, so as to create total human par-ticipation. The sex-love relationship is not complete unless it is accompanied by a feeling of permanence. It is not an act of deception or even honest hyperbole that impels lovers to swear that their love will endure forever. What is deep and all-inclusive will not be satisfied without the conviction that it will endure.

The love of a man and a woman expresses itself not only in a physical desire for each other but also by a sense of concern for one another, a desire to make the partner happy at any cost, even a major sacrifice (Robert Gordis, *Love and Sex: A Modern Jewish Perspective*, p. 105).

F. Before sex he should speak sweet words to her, according to his ability . . . and he should soothe her and make her happy, so that they will feel love for each other (*Sefer Kedushah v'Tzniyut*, p. 26b, #22).

On the Other Hand:

Opportunities for anonymous sex, casual sex, sex that provides physical release, variety, and/or excitement are readily available in secular culture.

a. It is part of human nature for a people to emulate the conduct of their immediate society (Maimonides, *Mishneh Torah, Hilchot De'ot* 6:1).

b. David G. Myers, a professor of psychology, explains what can happen as a result of succumbing too readily to sexual opportunities :

> Early promiscuity helps predict an individual's statistical risk of sexually transmitted disease, sexual coercion and rape, extramarital sex, nonmarital pregnancy, cohabitation — and, for some of these reasons, the risk of future marital unhappiness and divorce (*An American Paradox*, p. 18).

c. This comment was made by the feminist Sally Cline. She refers to the sexual revolution, in retrospect, as the "Genital Appropriation Era":

What the Genital Appropriation Era actually permitted was more access to women's bodies by more men; what it actually achieved was not a great deal of liberation for women but a great deal of legitimacy for male promiscuity; what it actually passed on to women was the male fragmentation of emotion from body, and the easily internalized schism between genital sex and responsible loving (Cline, 1993 as quoted in *A Return to Modesty: Discovering the Lost Virtue*, p. 192).

What Do You Think?

God makes a fitting companion or *"ezer k'neg-do"* for Adam (Text #3A). In the Hebrew *"ezer k'neg-do"* literally means "a helper opposite or against him." What do you think this means — that is, what is the significance of choosing such a phrase for characterizing an appropriate mate?

In Text #3D, the wedding blessing speaks of ray-eem ahuveem or loving companions. Elaborate on what specifically this might mean (e.g., sharing thoughts and feelings, spending time together pursuing common interests, traveling together, etc.).

Text #3E says an important aspect of an intimate, loving relationship is that it is enduring, that the partners are committed to it lasting a lifetime. Song of Songs gives the same impression (Text #3C). Do you believe intimate companionship should include the feeling that the relationship will be permanent?

What would be Jewish objections to anonymous or casual sex?

———◆———

4. **To what extent should pursuit of pleasure be a contributing factor to a healthy sexual relationship?**

On the One Hand:

There are duties and responsibilities regarding sex.

A. The times for conjugal duty prescribed in the Torah are: for men of independent means, every day; for laborers, twice a week; for donkey drivers [who travel about during the week], once a week; for camel drivers [who travel for long periods], once in thirty days; for sailors [who may travel for months], once in six months (Ketubot 61b).

. . . Suppose a man wants to change occupations from a donkey-driver to camel-driver [which pays more but keeps him from home for longer periods]? The answer: a woman prefers less money with enjoyment to more money with abstinence . . . (*Ketubot* 62b).

B. A man is forbidden to compel his wife to have marital relations . . . Rabbi Joshua ben Levi similarly stated: One who compels his wife to have marital relations will have unworthy children (*Eruvin* 100b).

C. Rabbi Joshua ben Levi said: One who knows his wife to be a God-fearing woman and does not duly visit her is called a sinner (*Yevamot* 62b).

D. The husband and the wife are equal partners in marriage, and they are likewise equal partners in the sexual union. It is true that biologically the sexual act seems to incline toward the man as the initiator and the woman as cooperator with the initiating male. This is true merely in biological fact, but not to the extent of designating the man as the active partner and the woman as the passive partner. Talmudic tradition is very clear about the fact that the woman is not merely a passive partner, and, in many instances, her active role is even greater than that of the man (Rabbi Reuven P. Bulka, *Judaism on Pleasure*, p. 145).

On the Other Hand:

Sex should be a source of pleasure.

a. His left hand was under my head,
His right hand caressed me.
I adjure you, O maidens of Jerusalem:
Do not wake or rouse
Love until it please!
(Song of Songs 8:3-4).

b. People will have to render an account [to God] for all the good things which their eyes beheld but which they refused to enjoy (*Talmud Yerushalmi, Kiddushin* 2:65).

c. Sensual pleasure is unlike other pleasures in two main respects. First . . . for sensual pleasure to approach ultimate bliss, it takes the cooperation of the two involved . . . Second, the sensual experience, if improperly approached, can be very painful, physically and emotionally, for either or both of the individuals. There is thus an implicit challenge in the sensual experience, to each of the partners, to approach the situation properly and to thus assure that it is a pleasurable rather than a painful event (Rabbi Reuven P. Bulka, *Judaism on Pleasure*, p. 132).

d. This text and the one that follows simultaneously address both responsibility and pleasure:

> There must be close bodily contact during sex . . . Rav Huna ruled that a husband who says, "I will not perform my marital duties unless she wears her clothes and I mine," must divorce her and give her also her *ketubah* (marriage contract) settlement (*Ketubot* 48a).

e. . . . When you are ready for sexual union, see that your wife's intentions combine with yours. Do not hurry to arouse her until she is receptive. Be calm, and as you enter the path of love and will, let her insemination (i.e., orgasm) come first . . . (*The Holy Letter*, attributed to Nachmanides).

What Do You Think?

What responsibilities do lovers have according to these texts? What additional responsibilities do other texts you've studied address?

In Text #3c, Rabbi Reuven Bulka says that sensual pleasure can turn painful. What could this mean? In an intimate relationship, what are the most important things for people to work on to avoid causing pain to each other?

5. **Is the context of the relationship important in evaluating the validity of engaging in sex?**

On the One Hand:

Judaism consistently affirms and approves of sex in certain contexts.

A. Betrothal (*Erusin*) used to take place a year before the actual wedding ceremony (*Kiddushin*) under the canopy (*chupah*). Today, a couple undergoes *Erusin* and *Kiddushin* in one ceremony. This *Erusin* blessing introduces the first step in the formal Jewish sanctioning of sexual relations.

> Praised are You, Eternal our God, Ruler of the Universe, who has sanctified us with Your commandments and commanded us regarding forbidden relations, forbidding sexual relations with our betrothed, permitting marital relations following *chupah* and *Kiddushin*. Praised are You, who sanctifies Your people Israel by *chupah* and *Kiddushin*.

B. Maimonides includes exceptions to the following "rule." Nevertheless, the fundamental principle is quite openminded. Note that Maimonides' permissive attitude toward a man's sexual behavior with his wife presupposes her interest and willingness to receive his advances.

> A man's wife is permitted to him. Therefore a man may do whatever he wishes with his wife. He may have intercourse with her at any time he wishes and kiss her on whatever limb of her body he wants. He may have natural or unnatural sex, as long as he does not bring forth seed in vain (Maimonides, *Mishneh Torah, Hilchot Isuray Bi-ah* 21:10).

On the Other Hand:

Judaism consistently disapproves of sex in other contexts.

a. You shall not commit adultery (Exodus 20:13).

b. If a man is found lying with another man's wife, both of them — the man and the woman with whom he lay — shall die. Thus you will sweep away evil from Israel (Deuteronomy 22:22).

c. The Bible specifies forbidden sexual relations for a man (a comparable list would apply for a woman):

> His mother (Leviticus 18:7).
> His stepmother (Leviticus 18:7).
> His sister, including his half-sister (Leviticus 18:9).
> His daughter (Leviticus 18:10 refers to granddaughter; but daughter is inferred, too).
> His biological aunt (Leviticus 18:12, 13).
> His uncle's wife (Leviticus 18:14).
> His son's wife (Leviticus 18:15).
> His brother's wife (Leviticus 18:16).
> His stepdaughter or mother-in-law (Leviticus 18:17).
> Two sisters (Leviticus 18:18. He may marry a second sister after the first dies).

d. For all transgressions in the Torah, if a person is told "transgress and do not die," he should transgress and not die. (For example, better to break Shabbat than be killed or eat non-kosher food than be killed, etc.) The exceptions are for idolatry, incest-adultery, and murder. For example, if someone says, "Have sex with that man's wife or I'll kill you" or "Have sex with your father or I'll kill you," you still should not do it (Sanhedrin 74a).

e. "I will clear you of those who rebel and transgress against Me" (Ezekiel 20:38). Rabbi Levi said: These [rebels and transgressors] are the offspring which result from nine types [of objectionable sexual relations] (Nedarim 20b):

> Children of a man who makes his wife afraid and forces her to have intercourse;
> Or who dislikes his wife and thinks of another woman during relations;

> Or who is forbidden to have sexual relations by rabbinic decree;
> Or who was not sure which of his wives was with him;
> Or who had intercourse when angry at his wife after a quarrel;
> Or who was drunk;
> Or who had already made up his mind to divorce his wife;
> Or children of a woman who had intercourse promiscuously with many men;
> Or a woman who demands sexual relations with her husband in an immodest way.

What Do You Think?

The above texts draw out "black and white" areas of permitted and forbidden sexual relationships. From ancient days through our day, Judaism consistently approves of sexual intercourse within marriage. On the other hand, incest and adultery have always been considered wrong. Can you think of other types of objectionable sexual relations besides the ones Rabbi Levi mentions in Text #5e?

(Note: For texts that deal more with the "gray areas" in sexual relationships, see the "Text Study" section in Chapter 15, "Sex Outside of Marriage," page 197.)

6. **Should we embrace modesty as a worthy value in our day?**

On the One Hand:

Modesty (*tzeniyut*) is a value for all Jews.

A. It has been told to you what is good, and what the Eternal requires of you; only to do justly, to love mercy, and to walk modestly (*hatzne'a*) with your God (Micah 6:8).

B. Standing around naked inevitably decreases a person's dignity (*Tosefta, Brachot* 2:14).

C. The rabbis asked why Balaam, sent to curse the Jews, blessed them instead. They answered:

Each tent was arranged so that no doorway faced another doorway. No one could ever easily look into another's tent. Balaam was so impressed that Israel valued privacy and modesty that he changed his curse into a blessing (Rashi on Numbers 24:5).

D. Marital intercourse should be modest and holy, carried on in a spirit of restraint and delicacy, in reverence and silence (Eliezer b. Samuel of Mainz, *Hebrew Ethical Wills*, as quoted in *The Jewish Moral Virtues*, p. 155).

On the Other Hand:

While all Jews should embrace modesty, not everyone accepts the same "code" of behavior.

a. The text below and others like it has led the most traditional Jewish communities to embrace restrictive codes of dress and behavior. Not every Orthodox community interprets the standards in the same way. However, at their strictest, the standards may include: requiring women to keep most of their bodies and all their hair covered, disallowing women to sing in front of men who are not close relatives, and not permitting men to listen to women on radio, television, or recordings, nor attend opera or theater.

Rav Hisda said: A woman's leg is *ervah* (sexually suggestive) . . . Shmuel said: A woman's voice is *ervah* . . . Rav Sheshet said: A woman's hair is suggestive (*Brachot* 24a).

b. Elliot Dorff, a Conservative rabbi, offers his take on modesty for our times:

The privacy that Judaism requires of sex requires (in Hebrew, *tzniut*, modesty) affects our clothing, our speech, and our public activities. We may dress in accord with the styles of the times, but never should our apparel accentuate the sexually arousing parts of our bodies. Thus sexually suggestive or revealing clothes for either men or women are not in keeping with Jewish law or sensibilities.

Similarly, our speech patterns should manifest respect for our bodies as creations of God, and this includes the generative parts of our bodies. Sexual language which is crass or violent bespeaks discomfort with one's body and disrespect for its divine value. It also cheapens the level of discourse, thereby diminishing the stature of everyone concerned, including especially the speaker.

Judaism's expectations of modesty also affect our behavior in public. Sexual activity should be reserved for private quarters. This is not to demean sex as something sordid which one must hide; quite the contrary, it is to sanctify it as the intense, intimate, mutual expression of love that it should be. Such love is understood within Jewish sources to be a great good, but a private one (*This Is My Beloved, This Is My Friend: A Rabbinic Letter on Intimate Relations*, p. 9-10).

c. A Reform statement on modesty:

The classic *Iggeret Ha-Kodesh*, "The Holy Letter," sets forth the Jewish view that the Holy One did not create anything that is not beautiful and potentially good. The human body in itself is never to be considered an object of shame or embarrassment. Instead, ". . . it is the manner and context in which it is utilized, the ends to which it is used, which determine condemnation or praise." Our behavior should never reduce the human body to an object. Dress, language and behavior should reflect a sensitivity to the Jewish respect for modesty and privacy. As Jews we acknowledge and celebrate the differences between public, private and holy places as well as the differences between public, private and holy time (Ad Hoc Committee On Human

Sexuality, Report to the CCAR
Convention, June 1998).

What Do You Think?

What is the connection between "walking modestly with God" (Text # 6A) and being a modest person in dress and behavior? What does a person gain by being modest? What does a person lose by being immodest?

Do you feel there should be a higher standard of modesty in our culture? Explain.

Should there be a higher standard of modesty in your own social group? Explain.

—————◆—————

7. **What role might sexuality play in our spiritual lives?**

On the One Hand:

Sexual intimacy can be an expression of holiness.

A. You shall be holy, for I, the Eternal your God, am holy (Leviticus 19:2).

B. What is that small verse on which hangs all the critical principles of the Torah? "In all your ways, know God" (Proverbs 3:6) (*Brachot* 63a).

C. [A man and woman] should have the same intentions in sex, and when they are thus united, the two are one in body and soul. In soul — for they cleave to one another with one will and desire, and in body — for a person who is unmarried is only half a body. When male and female unite sexually they become one body. So there is then one soul and one body, and together they are called "one person," and the Holy One, Who Is Blessed comes to rest on that one (*Reshit Chochmah, Sh'ar ha-Kedushah*, chapter 16, #3, quoted in *Sefer Kedushah v'Tzniyut*, and by Yitzhak Buxbaum, *Jewish Spiritual Practices*, p. 593).

D. "From my flesh, I shall see God . . . " The sexual organ is the seat of one's greatest physical pleasure. This pleasure comes

about when man and woman unite, and it thus results from unification. From the physical, we perceive the spiritual (Baal Shem Tov, quoted by Jacob Joseph of Polnoye, *Toledot Yaakov Yosef*, Jerusalem, 1960, volume 1, p. 57).

E. There is no sexual intercourse without embracing and kissing preceding it. And there are two kinds of kissing: the first is before sexual intercourse, where the purpose of kissing is that the man soothe the woman and arouse the love between them; the other kind is during intercourse itself, where the purpose is to accomplish the two kinds of union, the lower one and the supernal one together (*Siddur Yabetz* quoted in *Sefer Kedushah v'Tzniyut* p. 29, # 28, and by Yitzhak Buxbaum, *Jewish Spiritual Practices*, p. 604).

F. Physically, one sexual relationship looks pretty much like another. Biologically the process is the same, whether the relationship is a casual pickup at a bar, an adulterous liaison at a hotel, a couple in love but not ready for the commitment of marriage, or a married couple sharing a bed as they build a home together. Yet in Judaism only the last relationship is called *kiddushin*, marriage — literally, holiness . . .

Our task as Jews is to connect ourselves to the realm of the holy by making *kedushah* part of our lives . . .

Holiness is achieved by walking a middle road between asceticism and hedonism. It comes through discipline, through the understanding that pleasure comes through observing the commandments, and through making an act special and set apart. Judaism claims that sex attains this level of holiness only within the context of marriage . . . (Rabbi Michael Gold, *Does God Belong in the Bedroom?*, p. 20-21, 25).

On the Other Hand:

Misusing our sexuality can lead to alienation from what God ultimately wants for us (i.e., love, companionship, pleasure).

a. Sin diminishes the Image of God (*Yevamot* 63b).

b. "God saw everything God had made and behold it was very good" (Genesis 1:31).

   . . . Nothing in the human organs are created flawed or ugly. Everything is created with divine wisdom and is therefore complete, exalted, good, and pleasant. But when one sins, ugliness becomes attached to these matters (Attributed to Nachmanides, *The Holy Letter*, p. 45, 48).

c. Sex, as understood in the Jewish tradition, can distance one from God if one violates some of Judaism's norms relevant to it, but sex can also bring human lives closer to God as one fulfills the divine purposes of companionship and procreation (Rabbi Elliot N. Dorff, *This Is My Beloved, This Is My Friend*, p. 13).

What Do You Think?

Using the above passages as your guide, can you discern makes a relationship holy?

Why is holiness important in a sexual relationship?

How will you or do you conduct yourself so that you pursue holiness in an intimate relationship?

Related Middot and Mitzvot

These virtues and commandments help infuse decisions about sex with Jewish values:

Emet (Truthfulness): Lovers must be able to trust one another (see above). Being truthful is a necessary element of building trust.

Emunah (Trustworthiness): In sexual relationships, partners make themselves vulnerable as they reveal themselves to each other. This requires the individuals to deeply trust each other.

Lo Levayesh (Not Embarrassing): A person's body and sexuality are private. What happens between two people as part of their intimate life is private as well. It is wrong to tease or embarrass others about personal matters.

Ma'akeh (Preventing Accidents): Unwanted pregnancies and sexually transmitted diseases can occur when people do not take the necessary precautions. Those who engage in sex must be responsible for preventing "accidents."

Mechabayd Zeh et Zeh (Honoring Others): Honor and care about others' dignity. Do not treat people as objects (i.e., physical machines), but respect them as full, complex human beings.

Ohev Zeh et Zeh (Loving Others): At some time in our lives, we may have a special love for one person. Along the way, as we encounter potential partners, love for our fellow human beings requires us not cause hurt.

Shmirat HaGuf (Taking Care of Your Body): In terms of sexuality, this includes: getting regular physical check-ups, being responsible about birth control, keeping clean, avoiding circumstances that might lead to getting or giving a sexually transmitted disease, and getting help when a relationship feels dangerous or has become violent.

Simchah (Joy and Happiness): We celebrate the pleasures of sexual relationship.

Tzeniyut (Modesty): This includes being respectful and humble, not showing off. Casually revealing your body and allowing easy access to it by others, makes you more like an object than a "vehicle for holiness."

Where Do I Go From Here?

From this chapter, you have learned that sex is not an issue Judaism takes lightly. It is a physical manifestation that represents many facets of a loving relationship. Hopefully you will consider Jewish tradition, including the texts you have studied in this chapter, when you enter into romantic relationships. Your conduct in these relationships should be determined by more than just your gut feelings — it should be determined by your understanding of the sexual ethics that Judaism provides.

Following is a list of resources that you may find helpful as you continue to explore the Jewish view of sexuality.

Note: The sources listed here are relevant for all five chapters dealing with issues of sexuality found in Part IV of Hot Topics: A Student Companion.

Jewish Sources

Balka, Christine, and Andy Rose. *Twice Blessed: On Being Lesbian, Gay, and Jewish*. Boston, MA: Beacon Press, 1989.

Borowitz, Eugene B. *Choosing a Sex Ethic: A Jewish Inquiry*. New York: Schocken Books for B'nai B'rith Hillel Foundation, 1969.

Borowitz, Eugene B., and Francine Weinman Schwartz. Chapters on *Tzeniyut* (Modesty) and *Emunah* (Trustworthiness). In *The Jewish Moral Virtues*. Philadelphia, PA: The Jewish Publication Society, 1999.

Bulka, Reuven P. *Judaism on Pleasure*. Northvale, NJ: Jason Aronson Inc., 1995.

Buxbaum, Yitzhak. *Jewish Spiritual Practices*. Northvale, NJ: Jason Aronson Inc., 1990.

Cohen, J. Seymour, trans. *The Holy Letter*. New York: KTAV Publishing House, Inc., 1996. (Traditionally attributed to Nachmanides, but actual authorship unknown. First published in Rome in 1546.)

Dorff, Elliot N. *Matters of Life and Death: A Jewish Approach To Modern Medical Ethics*. Philadelphia, PA and Jerusalem: The Jewish Publication Society, 1998.

———. *"This Is My Beloved, This Is My Friend" (Song of Songs 5:16): A Rabbinic Letter on Intimate Relations*. New York: The Rabbinical Assembly, 1996.

Eisen, Efraim, and Rosalie Eisen. *To Meet Your Soul Mate, You Must Meet Your Soul*. (Part of the "LifeLights" series) Woodstock, VT: Jewish Lights Publishing, 2002.

Feldman, David M. *Marital Relations, Birth Control, and Abortion in Jewish Law*. New York: New York University Press, 1968. Republished by New York: Schocken Books, 1974.

Freeman, Susan. *Teaching Jewish Virtues: Sacred Sources and Arts Activities*. Denver, CO: A.R.E. Publishing, Inc., 1999.

Gittelsohn, Roland B. *Love in Your Life*. New York: UAHC Press, 1991.

Gold, Michael. *Does God Belong in the Bedroom?* Philadelphia, PA: The Jewish Publication Society, 1992.

Gordis, Robert. *Love & Sex: A Modern Jewish Perspective*. New York: Farrar, Straus and Giroux, 1978.

Jacob, Walter, ed. *American Reform Responsa*. New York: Central Conference of American Rabbis, 1983.

Kadden, Barbara Binder, and Bruce Kadden. *Teaching Mitzvot: Concepts, Values, and Activities*. Rev. ed. Denver, CO: A.R.E. Publishing, Inc., 2003.

Lamm, Maurice. *The Jewish Way in Love and Marriage*. San Francisco, CA: Harper & Row, 1980.

Lamm, Norman. "Judaism and the Modern Attitude toward Homosexuality," *Encyclopaedia Judaica Yearbook*. Jerusalem: Keter Publishing House, 1974.

Levine, Judith. "Thinking about Sex." In *Tikkun, an Anthology*, ed. by Michael Lerner. Oakland, CA and Jerusalem: Tikkun Books, 1992.

Marder, Janet. "Jewish and Gay." In *Keeping Posted* 32, 2; November 1986.

Olitzky, Kerry M., and Joel Lurie Grishaver. *Body Ethics: Modesty* (Instant Lesson). Los Angeles, CA: Torah Aura Productions.

Orenstein, Debra. *Life Cycles: Volume 1: Jewish Women on Life Passages and Personal Milestones*. Woodstock, VT: Jewish Lights Publishing, 1994.

Parent Education for Parents of Adolescents: Teacher's Manual. New York: United Synagogue Commission on Jewish Education, Family Education Committee, 1981.

Polish, Daniel F., Daniel B. Syme, and Bernard M. Zlotowitz. *Drugs, Sex, and Integrity*. New York: The UAHC Press, 1991.

Prevention Is a Mitzvah (Instant Lesson). Los Angeles, CA: Torah Aura Productions, 1992.

Rosner, Fred, and J. David Bleich. *Jewish Bioethics*. New York: Sanhedrin Press, 1979.

Sherwin, Byron L., and Seymour J. Cohen. *Creating an Ethical Jewish Life: A Practical Introduction To Classic Teachings on How to Be a Jew*. Woodstock, VT: Jewish Lights Publishing, 2001.

Strassfeld, Sharon, and Michael Strassfeld, eds. *The Second Jewish Catalogue*. Philadelphia, PA and Jerusalem: The Jewish Publication Society, 1976, Ch. 1, pp. 10-150.

Tendler, Moshe. *Pardes Rimonim*. New York: The Judaica Press, 1979.

Waskow, Arthur. *Down-To-Earth Judaism: Food, Money, Sex, and the Rest of Life*. New York: William Morrow & Co., 1995.

Yedwab, Paul. *Sex in the Texts*. New York: The UAHC Press, 2001.

General Sources:

Calderone, Mary, and Eric Johnson. *The Family Book about Sexuality*. New York: Harper and Row, 1989.

Eyre, Linda and Richard. *Teaching Your Children Values*. New York: Simon and Schuster, 1993.

Gordon, Sol and Judith. *Raising a Child Conservatively in a Sexually Permissive World*. New York: Simon and Schuster, 1983.

Gravelle, Karen. *What's Going on Down There? Answers To Questions Boys Find Hard to Ask*. New York: Walker and Company, 1998.

Maguire, Daniel C. *Sacred Choices: The Right To Contraception and Abortion in Ten World Religions*. Minneapolis, MN: Fortress Press, 2001.

McCoy, Kathy, and Charles Wibbelsman, M.D. *Growing and Changing: A Handbook for Preteens*. New York: The Berkley Publishing Group, 1986.

Madaras, Lynda. *The What's Happening To My Body? Book for Boys*. New York: Newmarket Press, 1988.

———. *The What's Happening To My Body? Book for Girls*. New York: Newmarket Press, 1988.

Mayle, Peter. *What's Happening To Me?* Secaucus, NJ: Lyle Stuart Inc., 1975.

Myers, David G. *The American Paradox: Spiritual Hunger in an Age of Plenty*. New Haven, CT and London: Yale University Press, 2000.

Palardy, Debra J. *Sweetie, Here's the Best Reason on the Planet to Say No To Your Boyfriend: Even If You've Already Said Yes*. Pittsburgh, PA: Dorrance Publishing Co., Inc., 2000.

Pollack, Rachel, and Cheryl Schwartz. *The Journey Out: A Guide for and about Lesbian, Gay, and Bisexual Teens*. New York: Puffin Books, 1995.

Shalit, Wendy. *A Return To Modesty: Discovering the Lost Virtue*. New York: Touchstone, 1999.

Web Sites

Human Rights Campaign Fund: www.hrc.org
Advocates for lesbian, gay, bisexual, and transgender equal rights. Also, click on "Links" to see numerous links to other relevant organizations.

Parents, Families and Friends of Lesbians and Gays (PFLAG): www.pflag.org
Promotes the health and well-being of gay, lesbian, bisexual and transgendered persons, their families and friends through support, education, and advocacy.

Planned Parenthood: www.plannedparenthood.org
Advocates for the fundamental right of each individual, throughout the world, to reproductive self-determination.

Population Connection (formerly Zero Population Growth): www.populationconnection.org
A national grassroots population organization that educates young people and advocates progressive action to stabilize world population at a level that can be sustained by Earth's resources.

Religious Coalition for Reproductive Choice: www.rcrc.org
Works to ensure reproductive choice through the moral power of religious communities.

Spiritual Youth for Reproductive Freedom: www.syrf.org

Pro-choice, pro-faith education and advocacy.

United Nations Population Fund: www.unfpa.org

The world's largest international source of funding for population and reproductive health programs.

World Congress of Gay, Lesbian, Bisexual, and Transgender Jews (*Keshet Ga'avah*): www.wcgljo.org

Representing the interests of lesbian, gay, and bisexual Jews around the world.

CHAPTER 12

MASTURBATION

Overview

Jewish Perspectives

Often, Judaism expresses a range of views on a topic — that is, in any given era of discussion, some scholars will give restrictive opinions and others more lenient ones. This exchange of ideas has not been part of the masturbation discussion, however. Traditional Jewish sources denounced masturbation, often in strong language. The focus historically has been on male masturbation; female masturbation was not considered a serious concern. In recent decades, views of masturbation have opened up considerably, though less so in Orthodox Judaism.

There are several reasons why Jews today might reconsider masturbation in a more lenient light. One is that medical experts have discounted the detrimental physical concerns associated with male masturbation. Traditional Jewish texts express concern regarding "wasting the seed," as if men are endowed with a limited, irreplaceable supply. We know that men continually produce sperm throughout their lives, and that the "extra" ejaculations (of typical masturbation) will not damage a man's fertility.

Some express concerns that masturbation turns a sexual experience into a selfish one, rather than one shared with a partner. In contrast, others say that to enjoy one's own body does not cancel out a person's ability to enjoy sex with a partner. Masturbation helps relieve a physical urge — an ethically neutral event.

Some may suggest that masturbation is "indecent" or "immodest." Others might respond that if masturbation remains private, modesty is not compromised.

Our culture places new demands on sexual ethics in many ways. A central one is that, though young men and women are fully physically mature and have sexual urges by their mid-teens, they often do not marry for another ten to twenty years. Forbidding sexual release for that amount of time is difficult to expect of people. Since masturbation does not have the potential consequences of sex with a partner (i.e., pregnancy or sexually transmitted diseases) liberal Jewish authorities tend to agree that masturbation can be an appropriate and helpful way to deal with sexual urges.

General Perspectives

While masturbation can be an embarrassing topic, sex educators generally try to remove the stigma from it. They see masturbation as a normal activity, something most people experience at some point or even continually throughout their lives. They may point out positive benefits of masturbation, such as getting to know your body better and learning what gives you pleasure. As stated above, medical experts overwhelmingly dismiss any physical danger as a consequence of masturbation. As long as thoughts and experiences of masturbation don't infringe on living a healthy life, there is no (general) reason to worry if it is something you enjoy doing.

Summary of the Overview

- While traditional Jewish sources denounce masturbation, lenient Jewish attitudes have become more prevalent.

- Key elements influencing opinions on masturbation include: traditional Jewish views, modern medical expertise, modesty and privacy, questions of the validity of pleasing oneself, and the need to respond to young people's lifestyles today.

- Sex researchers generally see masturbation as normal, not something to be ashamed about, having some practical benefits, as well.

Scenarios: How Things have Changed

Jewish thinkers are reevaluating traditional attitudes toward masturbation. The two scenarios below reflect the trends of Jewish opinion about masturbation. These scenarios, one set in ancient days and one in contemporary times. are intended to raise questions and spark discussion. Read each scenario and reflect, either individually or in a group discussion, on the questions in the "For Thought and Discussion" section that follows. Then continue on to the "Text Study" section to see what Jewish and other sources have to say on the subject. Finally, you may wish to come back and answer the questions a second time, to see if your views have changed.

Scenario I: In the Days of the Talmud

Shimon and Reuven are sixteen years old. Both feel tremendous sexual tension, thinking about sex all the time, imagining themselves having intercourse, and often unexpectedly having erections. They, of course, have never spoken about this private matter. Both boys know that Judaism teaches that they shouldn't masturbate. Shimon resists the urge, though it is uncomfortable, even painful to do so. Reuven does masturbate and enjoys great relief and pleasure in this activity. However, he feels guilty about his actions, and often feels depressed because he worries that he is a sinner.

Scenario II: Nowadays

Simon and Richard are sixteen years old. Both feel tremendous sexual tension, thinking about sex all the time, imagining themselves having intercourse, and often unexpectedly having erections. Each has masturbated privately for a couple of years. They have never spoken about this personal matter with anybody but each other. It helps to have at least one person to confide in. In their sex education class and from their reading, the boys feel assured that masturbation is a normal and acceptable way to relieve sexual tension. When they begin to study recent Jewish teachings on the matter, they remain comfortable with their choice to masturbate. They enjoy great relief and pleasure from this activity. They feel they are not ready for intercourse with their girlfriends. Masturbation has helped them resist pressuring their girlfriends to have sex.

For Thought and Discussion:

Did Shimon and Reuven deal with their sexual feelings appropriately? Did Simon and Richard?

Text Study

Though historically Judaism has taken an unequivocal stance on the question of masturbation, in modern times that attitude has begun to change. Jewish texts and other sources express varying viewpoints that highlight the tension between seemingly opposing considerations. The chart on the following page highlights the key Jewish question about masturbation. Text sources supporting the two opposing points of view follow.

1. **What is Jewish opinion on masturbation?**

    On the One Hand:

    Historically, Judaism has frowned on masturbation.

    A. Although it is difficult to isolate a biblical sanction against masturbation, David M. Feldman summarizes some of the negativity expressed in various rabbinic texts:

        > With or without literal biblical sanctions, the sin, in the rabbinic view, is serious enough. He who destroys his generative seed commits murder, acts like a beast which takes no heed what it does, cannot receive the Sh'khinah [Presence of God], stands "under the ban" [akin to excommunication], and is guilty of autoerotic indecency. (*Marital Relations, Birth Control, and Abortion in Jewish Law*, p. 114)

    B. Though not referring to masturbation, Maimonides (lived 1135 – 1204) offers his opinion about medical consequences of ejaculation:

Masturbation: A Question to Consider

The Question	On the One Hand	On the Other Hand
1. What is Jewish opinion on masturbation? (see page 178)	Historically, Judaism has frowned on masturbation.	Modern liberal attitudes tend to be more accepting of masturbation.

Semen constitutes the strength of the body, its life, and the light of the eyes. Its emission to excess causes physical decay, debility, and diminished vitality . . . Whoever indulges in sexual dissipation becomes prematurely aged; his strength fails; his eyes become dim; a foul odor proceeds from his mouth and armpits; the hair of his head, eyebrows, and eyelashes drop out; the hair of his beard, armpits, and legs grow abnormally; his teeth fall out; and besides these, he becomes subject to numerous other diseases . . .
(Maimonides, *Mishneh Torah, Laws of Ethics* 4:19)

On the Other Hand:

Modern liberal attitudes tend to be more accepting of masturbation.

Note: Text Study 1a in Chapter 13, "Birth Control" (page 181) concisely explains historical attitudes regarding "wasting the seed" — an issue relevant to masturbation, as well.

a. In modern times, many Orthodox Jews retain [restrictive] beliefs and prohibitions [concerning masturbation], but Conservative, Reform, and unaffiliated Jews largely do not. The grounds for this change are largely medical: neither physicians nor laypeople believe that masturbation has the medical consequences described by Maimonides. Moreover, few believe the mystical tradition's depiction of the dire results of masturbation. To date, none of the three movements has taken an official position validating masturbation, but in practice the tradition's abhorrence of masturbation is largely ignored. (Rabbi Elliot N. Dorff, *Matters of Life and Death*, p. 119)

b. While, in Rabbinic and especially post-Rabbinic literature . . . there is editorial comment denouncing the practice, no punishment is set down. Evidently, it was realized (even then) that the practice was common and had certain "natural" advantages so that, while it warranted denouncing, the denunciation was (evidently) intended as a control factor to diminish rather than eliminate (*Parent Education for Parents of Adolescents: Teacher's Manual*, p. 48, quoted by Rabbi Michael Gold, p. 175-176).

c. If teen sexual activity is to be discouraged, what can teenagers do to relieve the very real sexual tension they feel? With the onset of puberty, the hormones are raging and the sexual drive is immense. The only realistic solution is that perhaps it is time for rabbis to rethink the Jewish prohibition against masturbation (Rabbi Michael Gold, *Does God Belong in the Bedroom?* p. 175).

d. Masturbation is a risk-free sexual activity because no body fluids are shared with a partner. Some people are embarrassed to talk about it, but most people enjoy masturbation throughout their lives (*Sexual Health Series:* "A Young Woman's Guide to Sexuality," Planned Parenthood Federation of America, 2001).

What Do You Think?

What are some traditional reasons for the disapproval of masturbation? Why do many modern Jewish thinkers take issue with "tradition" on this topic?

Do you feel the reasons for taking issue are valid? Explain.

Related Middot and Mitzvot

These virtues and commandments can help when making decisions about masturbation:

Lo Levayesh (Not Embarrassing): For example, taunting and teasing others about masturbation is wrong.

Ma'akeh (Preventing Accidents): Masturbation may alleviate sexual tension. This in turn may help young couples resist engaging in intercourse prematurely, and therefore prevent risks of unwanted pregnancy and/or sexually transmitted disease.

Shmirat HaGuf (Taking Care of Your Body): Depending on your perspective, this might mean masturbating or refraining from masturbation.

Tzeniyut (Modesty): Masturbation is a personal matter, engaged in only in private.

Where Do I Go From Here?

When taken at face value the ancient reaction to masturbation may seem arcane. However, we always have something to learn from the rabbis, even when modern technology and medical discoveries prove they sometimes misunderstood the workings of the human body. The texts on masturbation show us how the rabbis first and foremost affirmed life and the perpetuation of our people, something they believed masturbation threatened. Furthermore, engaging the rabbis on every issue helps us to learn more about them and how their minds worked. As Jews, we are obliged to delve into the rabbis' minds in order to understand their perspective on the world. Only then can we shape our own opinions about these hot topics.

An extensive list of resources on masturbation and other issues of sexuality can be found at the end of Chapter 11, "Foundations of Sexual Ethics," on pages 173-176. These will be helpful as you continue your exploration of this sensitive topic.

CHAPTER 13
BIRTH CONTROL

Overview

Jewish Perspectives

One reason to have sex is to make babies. Procreation is an integral component of Jewish sexual ethics. Yet, according to Jewish texts, other worthy elements of a sexual relationship include expressing love, and giving and receiving pleasure. For many reasons having children could present problems to a couple. Jewish ethics on birth control must try to resolve the tensions between competing values. Love and pleasure should not be off-limits when childbearing is not reasonable or practical. The difficulty is this: How are we to decide what grounds are reasonable and practical for refraining from the mitzvah of procreation? This question underlies our discussion of birth control in this section.

We addressed the mitzvah of procreation in some detail in "Foundations of Sexual Ethics" (see that chapter's "Jewish Perspectives," page 161, and Text Study #2, p. 165). There, we discussed the commandment to "be fruitful and multiply" (Genesis 1:28). By having children, we assure the continuity of generations, and experience a special kind of love and joy. Concerns of overpopulation in the world may be legitimate, yet most Jewish authorities argue that the worthiness of having children overcomes these concerns, especially in light of our small numbers and the great losses our people has sustained over the years. Of course, if people cannot physically bear children, the mitzvah does not apply.

Traditional Jewish sources assign the mitzvah of procreation to men, but not women. Most authorities agree that a woman may use birth control if a pregnancy would endanger her life or cause her unbearable suffering.

The dangers of pregnancy are behind a classic Rabbinic text affecting birth control for women. It deals with minors, pregnant women, and nursing mothers. Because of pregnancy concerns, birth control was permitted, some say required, for these women (see Text Study #1B below). This text has had significant influence on the development of Jewish birth control ethics, and today's rabbis and scholars continue to derive insights and guidelines concerning the permissibility of birth control from it.

"Spilling the seed" or "wasting the seed" is an issue that affects birth control (as it does masturbation and homosexuality). Traditional Jewish sources seem to view a man's "seed" (semen) as his very life force and of limited supply. Thus, birth control methods that interfere with the natural flow of semen (such as coitus interruptus and condoms) are especially problematic from a traditional point of view (see Text Study #1a below). Most liberal Jews dismiss concerns of "spilling the seed" as irrelevant to present lifestyles, knowledge, and beliefs.

Because of the same concern for "spilling the seed," Orthodox authorities do not approve of vasectomy (a surgical procedure that causes male sterility). Since vasectomy is a nearly irreversible decision, many liberal Jewish ethicists object to this procedure, too.

When halachic authorities do authorize use of birth control, they give preference to some forms of birth control over others — for example, from an Orthodox perspective the "rhythm method" is not as controversial as other methods. Oral contraceptives ("the Pill") are preferred to the diaphragm, and the diaphragm is preferred to condoms. Liberal Jews feel less concerned, if at all, about using the "right" kind of birth control.

A sensitive birth control issue involves single people. Of course, some traditional Jewish authorities say that single people should not be having sex in the first place, making talk of birth control irrelevant. Yet the reality is that unmarried people do have sex. Many liberal Jews choose to address the issue in two notable ways. First, couples are urged to use of birth control. The consequences of an unwanted pregnancy are inevitably problematic (see Text Study #2e and #2f below). Second is an emphasis on the importance of using condoms since sexually transmitted disease is always a threat. Unprotected (condom-less) sex can lead to irritating, lifetime problems involving the sex organs (and other body parts). Worse, sexually transmitted disease can be deadly.

What if a married couple does not want to have children? Perhaps they want to focus on learning, a career, or other pursuits. Perhaps they don't feel they would be good parents, or simply have no interest in rearing children. Similarly, what if a couple wants to limit the size of their family? Perhaps they feel they can only provide adequately for a specific number of children. Perhaps their work or other interests limits the amount of time and energy they have for a family. In the most traditionally observant communities, these arguments would not be considered worthy. In Modern Orthodox communities, it is difficult to know how couples reconcile their personal needs and values with tradition birth control guidelines — birth control is a personal issue. Modern Orthodox couples may choose to limit their birth control to methods that are deemed acceptable, or may choose to consult a halachic authority regarding their personal decision.

The Rabbis of the Talmud were challenged by Ben Azzai, who preferred to study Torah than marry and have children (see Chapter 11, "Foundations of Sexual Ethics," Text Study #2C and 2a) The rabbis express disapproval about Ben Azzai's preference, though the text does seem to give some credence to his feelings. Discussion of this text brings to light the fact that there were and are competing values when it comes to raising a family.

Besides weighing "personal" needs and values, some Jews feel it is appropriate to limit the size of their family because of competing Jewish values. For instance, justice is a primary value in Judaism; yet justice in the world is compromised by overpopulation and poverty. Some may feel that we promote justice when we limit the size of our families, and when we work for reproductive freedom all around the world, especially through education and making birth control widely available.

Being more observant or more liberal does not determine the ease of your path regarding birth control decisions. Relying on halachic authorities (strictly adhering to Jewish law) is challenging, but so is relying on your own conscience and learning to make informed, ethical decisions.

General Perspectives

Historically, Jews were not the only ones concerned with infant mortality, fertility, and simply having enough people. This concern likely influenced attitudes about birth control the world over.

Religious leaders representing a variety of traditions are finding ways to recognize the value of reproductive freedom. Some openness to birth control exists in many major world religions (including, Judaism, Catholicism, Protestantism, Islam, and several Eastern religions). But, like Judaism, most religions have some followers who are very conservative in interpreting birth control traditions, even if new thinkers suggest innovative ways of reframing familiar teachings to allow for more reproductive freedom.

Especially in democratic societies, belief in individual choice and personal autonomy often trumps traditional religious beliefs. That is, people decide for themselves. In fact, believers in autonomy may find it offensive for any authority (religious or political) to seek to impose rules that limit reproductive freedom. They may argue that such rules are particularly oppressive to women who usually bear the brunt of the consequences of not being able to control their fertility.

Individuals may wrestle with a variety of personal issues, some of which we discussed in the "Jewish Perspectives" section above. Family planning is generally the most significant issue, raising such concerns as balancing family and career, providing adequately for a specific number of children, interest in parenting, feeling too young or too old to parent, health issues, and stability of a couple's relationship.

Overpopulation is a serious world problem. Some people feel they must respond personally to this concern by limiting the number of children they bear.

Other issues may affect attitudes toward birth control. In this culture, the prevailing view is that minors or teens should not be having children, or for that matter even be having sex. However, if they do, they should use birth control. Similarly, any unmarried couples of childbearing age should use contraception. Condoms not only provide contraception, but prevent the spread of sexually transmitted disease. Finally is the issue of sex education, which raises difficult and controversial questions. There are many views on how, when, and who should teach about sex, and which values should be promoted. Whether parents, clergy, and/or schools teach about sex; whatever age the children are; and whatever resources are used, adequate sex education must include teaching about birth control.

Summary of the Overview

- Judaism teaches that procreation is a mitzvah (commandment).

- While halachic authorities may shun certain methods of birth control, there are certain exceptions to the mitzvah of procreation that are acceptable in a traditional Jewish view.

- Personal circumstances, feelings, beliefs, and needs may affect an individual's birth control decisions.

- One's general orientation to Jewish observance will likely influence one's attitude towards birth control.

Scenarios: How Things Have Changed

For centuries, Jews have debated about when to use birth control and which type to use. Below are two imaginary scenarios, one set in ancient days and one set in contemporary times. These scenarios are intended to raise questions and spark discussion. Read each scenario and reflect, either individually or in group discussion, on the questions in the "For Thought and Discussion" section that follows. Then continue on to the "Text Study" section to see what Jewish and other sources have to say on the subject. Finally, you may wish to come back and discuss the scenarios a second time, to see if your views have changed.

Scenario I: In Ancient Days

Yoni and Rivka have known tragedy. Prior to giving birth to their son Uziel, Rivka suffered three miscarriages and a stillbirth. After Uziel was born, Rivka had two more miscarriages before giving birth to Sarah. When Sarah was 18 months old, she became ill with a respiratory ailment and died. Two years later Rivka gave birth to another girl Devorah. Uziel and Devorah both seem to be thriving well.

After a couple of more years, with another pregnancy ending in stillbirth, a friend comes to comfort Rivka. The friend says, "Rivka, why don't you take the potion that Judith, Rabbi Chiyya's wife took to prevent her from ever becoming pregnant again? You wouldn't have to suffer anymore from such terrible pregnancies" (see Text Study #1C below). But Rivka worries. Who knows if Uziel and Devorah will make it past childhood? She and Yoni love children. They would like children to be part of and develop the family trade. They want sons who will be able to become Torah scholars and enrich Jewish learning in the community. They want daughters who will perpetuate family traditions. No, she would not consider intentionally making herself sterile.

Scenario II: Nowadays

Jon and Risa have struggled with fertility issues for two years. After three miscarriages, Risa undergoes medical tests to find out if there is anything clearly wrong. The tests detect a health condition that can be treated with a prescription medicine. The condition had made her susceptible to miscarriages. The doctors assure her that she should be able to have as many children as she would like, now that she is taking the medicine. During the next four years, Risa gives birth to two healthy children. For a variety of reasons, they have decided they don't want more children. Besides, they feel they have fulfilled the Jewish value of procreation by having two children. During the years that follow, Risa and Jon are diligent about using contraception.

For Thought and Discussion:

What factors did Rivka consider in deciding about birth control?

Would she have been wrong if she did decide to

make herself sterile? Explain.

What factors did Jon and Risa consider in deciding about birth control?

Could they support their decision from a Jewish point of view? Explain.

Text Study

The attitude that contemporary Jews hold in regard to birth control can vary depending on a variety of factors: level of observance, community affiliation, sociological factors, and personal values. Jewish texts and other sources express varying viewpoints which highlight the tension between seemingly opposing considerations. The chart at the top of the next page highlights the key Jewish question about birth control. Text sources supporting the two opposing points of view follow.

Note: Beliefs regarding the mitzvah of procreation are also relevant here. See passages in "Foundations of Jewish Sexual Ethics," Text #2, page 165.

1. **What are Jewish views on birth control?**

On the One Hand:

Traditional Jewish sources restrict the use of birth control devices.

A. It is forbidden to destroy [improperly emit] seed. Therefore, a man may not practice coitus interruptus (Maimonides, *Mishneh Torah, Isuray Bi-ah* 21:18).

B. Commentators differ as to whether the following three types of women may use birth control (and others may not), or whether they must do so (and others may).

> Three types of women use an absorbent [contraceptive device, called a *mokh*]: a minor, a pregnant woman, and a nursing mother.
> The minor [from eleven years and one day to twelve years and one day], lest she become pregnant and die; a pregnant woman, lest she cause her

fetus to become a sandal [a flat, fish-shaped fetus]; and a nursing woman [otherwise], she might have to wean her child too soon and the child would die (*Yevamot* 12b. For an extensive discussion of this text, see *Marital Relations, Birth Control, and Abortion in Jewish Law* by David M. Feldman.)

C. Judah and Hezekiah were twins. One was completely developed at the end of nine months, and the other at the beginning of the seventh month [the implication being that they were born three months apart].

> Their mother Judith, wife of Rabbi Chiyya, suffered agonizing pains during childbirth. When she recovered, she disguised herself and appeared before Rabbi Chiyya.
> "Is a woman commanded to propagate the race? she asked.
> "No," he answered.
> As a result of that conversation, she drank a sterilizing potion so that she would have no more children.
> When her action finally became known, he exclaimed, "Would that you bore me only one more issue of the womb" (*Yevamot* 65b).
> Thus, the rabbis ruled: A man is not permitted to drink a cup of roots, but a woman is permitted to drink a cup of roots so that she does not give birth (*Tosefta Yevamot* 8:2).

D. Only the most competent Torah authority, whose piety, erudition and sensitivity to family and social problems are well established, can advise on the complex issue of family planning. In general, only the health requirements of the wife, both physical and psychological, can modify the halakhic disapproval of all contraceptive techniques (Rabbi Moshe Tendler, *Pardes Rimonim*, p. 17).

On the Other Hand:

For many Jews, personal needs and modern science play a central role in influencing birth control choices.

Birth Control: A Question to Consider

The Question	On the One Hand	On the Other Hand
1. What are Jewish views on birth control? (see page 184)	Traditional Jewish sources restrict the use of birth control devices.	For many Jews, personal needs and modern science play a central role in influencing birth control choices.

a. At the time of the birth of Jesus, Jews and most other people believed that it was the man and his semen who provides the actual life, the "seed," and that the woman was merely the soil, so to speak, in which the seed grew to maturity to be born. It was considered almost like murder to allow the "seed" to be "wasted" through masturbation, homosexuality, or sexual intercourse without intent to procreate. It was also erroneously believed . . . that semen, "the precious fluid," was limited in quantity so that if it was "wasted" the energy and strength of the man would thereby be reduced (Mary Calderone and Eric Johnson, *The Family Book about Sexuality,* p. 158, quoted by Rabbi Michael Gold, p. 107).

b. Jewish sources from as early as the second century C.E. describe methods of contraception and prescribe when they may or should be used. Until the later half of the twentieth century, though, Jews never contemplated using contraceptives for purposes of family planning. Judaism, after all, values large families. Moreover, if one wanted even two children to survive to adulthood, one had to try to have children continually, for many such attempts would be frustrated in miscarriages or in stillbirths, and many of the children who survived birth would die of childhood diseases or infections before being ready to propagate themselves. In addition, many Jews would find that they could not beget or bear children, as the stories of the difficulties endured by Abraham and Sarah and by Jacob and Rachel so poignantly describe.

In judging the permissibility of contra-

ceptive, then, we must recognize that we are asking an entirely new question. Not only have the techniques of contraception improved considerably, but the very purpose for which Jewish couples use them has changed. Thus although the use of contraceptives in our time may bear some formal resemblance to their use in times past, these changes in method and purpose must be kept clearly in mind as we examine traditional sources on contraception (Rabbi Elliot N. Dorff, *Matters of Life and Death,* p. 121).

c. As Jews, we take pride in our historic emphasis upon the values of family life. We believe that it is the sacred duty of married couples to "be fruitful and multiply," unless child-bearing is likely to impair the health of the mother or the offspring . . . We believe, moreover, that a righteous God does not require the unlimited birth of children who may, by unfavorable social and economic circumstances, be denied a chance for a decent and wholesome life. Therefore, we declare that parents have the right to determine the number, and to space the births of their children in accordance with what they believe to be the best interests of their families (Commission on Justice and Peace of the Central Conference of American Rabbis, *Yearbook* 1960).

d. Condoms are problematic from the perspective of traditional Jewish law and are not always effective:

Nevertheless, condoms must be used if unprotected sexual intercourse poses a medical risk to either spouse, for condoms do offer some measure of protection against the spread of some diseases, and the duty to maintain health and life supersedes the positive duty of the male to propagate (*This Is My Beloved, This Is My Friend: A Rabbinic Letter on Intimate Relations*, p. 27).

e. Year after year a large number of supposedly intelligent people continue to get involved in extramarital pregnancy . . . Careful, effective contraception is an ethical necessity if there is to be any legimitation of premarital sexual intercourse (Eugene B. Borowitz, *Choosing a Sex Ethic*, p. 21).

f. For single people who are sexually active, it is patently irresponsible not to use birth control . . . For a single woman, an unplanned pregnancy raises numerous difficult issues of Jewish law and morality. Abortion as a form of birth control is a serious violation of Jewish law. Single parenting, although not uncommon, is recognized as less than ideal for imparting Jewish values to children. Rushing into a marriage on account of pregnancy is hardly an auspicious start for a healthy, lifelong relationship. Placing a baby for adoption, an option rarely practiced by Jewish women, is a wrenching emotional decision (Rabbi Michael Gold, *Does God Belong in the Bedroom?*, p. 110).

What Do You Think?

Summarize what you understand to be the traditional Jewish attitude toward contraception according to the first group of texts (#1A-D).

Summarize how a liberal Jewish community might view contraception, referring to the second group of texts (#1-f).

Which text do you find most difficult to understand, or challenging to your current views?

Are you surprised by what any of the texts say? Explain.

What do texts #1d, #1e, and #1f suggest should be the role of contraception for unmarried couples? Do you agree or disagree? Explain.

Related Middot and Mitzvot

These virtues and commandments help infuse decisions about sex with Jewish values:

Emet (Truthfulness): Lovers must be able to trust one another. Being truthful is a necessary element of building trust, particularly around issues of birth control.

Ma'akeh (Preventing Accidents): Unwanted pregnancies and sexually transmitted diseases can occur when people do not take the necessary precautions. Those who engage in sex must be responsible for preventing "accidents."

Ohev Zeh et Zeh (Loving Others): Love for our fellow human beings, especially love for a spouse or partner, requires that we be open, honest, and cautious about birth control.

Shmirat HaGuf (Taking Care of Your Body): This includes being responsible about birth control and avoiding circumstances that might lead to getting or giving a sexually transmitted disease.

Where Do I Go From Here?

You have learned in this chapter that birth control is a more complicated issue than one might think. The decision to use it affects people who are both single and married. The reasons for using it vary greatly. For Jews, it is a particularly interesting topic because of our relatively small population. Hopefully the texts here have helped you better understand how birth control decisions not only affect people on a personal level, but also how they affect the Jewish people as a whole. As Jews, finding the right balance between these two is our task, and, our tradition offers us great insight and help.

An extensive list of resources on issues of sexuality, including birth control, can be found at the end of Chapter 11, "Foundations of Sexual Ethics," on pages 173-176. These will be helpful as you continue your exploration of this complex and sensitive topic.

CHAPTER 14

HOMOSEXUALITY

Overview

Jewish and General Perspectives

Homosexuality is perhaps the most emotional sub-topic of sexuality. The sexual orientation of gays, lesbians, and bisexuals influences their life on many levels: physical attractions and desires, social connections, emotional relationships, and cultural experience. In short, homosexuality is an essential part of their identity.

Some cultures and communities have grown in their acceptance of homosexuality, but discrimination is still widespread, with denial, ambivalence, and even hostility toward gays, lesbians, and bisexuals. Where do these sentiments come from?

From a Jewish perspective, traditional texts undeniably convey negative attitudes toward homosexuality. The Bible, Talmud, Medieval Codes, and Responsa literature all contain statements severely disapproving of homosexual acts. However, modern liberal scholars are taking a hard look at traditional perceptions of homosexuality. They are doing so in light of historical and scientific findings (see Text Study #1a and #5a-c below). That is, they feel we need to have a sense of who wrote these statements, why they wrote them, what the context was, what people didn't understand about homosexuality then that we now do, and so on.

Probably the most significant modern finding is the widely accepted conclusion that most gays and lesbians have no choice about their sexual identity. It is a "fixed," organic, and authentic part of their beings (see Text Study #5a below). Another concern is that male homosexual acts "waste" precious "seed". Modern scholarship addresses this issue by explaining the context of this concern (see Text Study #1a in Chapter 13, "Birth Control," page 184).

We sometimes attach the word "homophobic" to those who feel antagonism toward homosexuals. To be homophobic is to have fears regarding homosexuality. The "fears" expressed in Jewish sources seem to involve expectations of the community's social order. Perhaps condoning homosexuality would lead to the devaluing and disintegration of marriage and family life (see Text Study #3A, #4A, and #6A below).

Advocates for homosexual issues today willingly respond to such concerns. They point out that homosexuals also can and do uphold institutions so dearly cherished by Judaism and others. That is, many homosexuals commit to long-term, monogamous relationships similar to marriage, and many homosexuals raise children in loving homes (see Text Study #4a and #6a-c below).

Certain fears about homosexuality have led some people to hatred, bigotry, harassment, and violence. Ignorance and misinformation are undoubtedly factors. Besides addressing myths about homosexuality, Jewish values would insist that we not tolerate cruel acts committed by homophobic individuals. Judaism teaches that all people are created in the image of God, that you must "love your neighbor as yourself" (Leviticus 19:18); and that we can make the world a better place by living righteously and doing good works (*tikkun olam*).

As we consider issues related to homosexuality, our primary responsibilities are to be humble in the face of things we don't fully understand (and no one fully understands homosexuality), and to be compassionate, loving, and respectful of other human beings. Those who are homosexual will perhaps need to make extra efforts in fulfilling the additional challenges of being true to themselves, and being honest and unashamed about who they are in the world.

Summary of the Overview

- Historically, for Jews and others, predominant attitudes toward homosexuality have been negative.

- Modern Jews are re-envisioning historical attitudes about homosexuality in light of current findings and beliefs.

- The majority of today's Jewish community falls somewhere along a spectrum of belief regarding homosexuality. Those at one end may suggest greater compassion and understanding toward gays and lesbians, but still maintain disapproval of homosexual acts; on the other end are those who emphasize fully equal and non-discriminatory treatment in all realms of life for gays and lesbians. This includes equal treatment as Jews.

Scenarios: How Things Have Changed

Throughout history, human societies have wrestled with how to address issues raised by homosexuality. The options open to homosexuals typically have reflected the times and places in which they lived. Below are two imaginary scenarios, one set in ancient days and one set in contemporary times, intended to raise questions and spark discussion. Read each scenario and reflect, either individually or in group discussion, on the questions that follow in the "For Thought and Discussion" section. Then continue on to the "Text Study" section to see what Jewish and other sources have to say on the subject. Finally, you may wish to come back and discuss the scenarios a second time, to see if your views have changed.

Scenario I: In the Days of the Talmud

Rabbi Noam Mordecai always felt attracted to men. He remembers having homosexual feelings since he was a child. Of course, he never spoke about this with anyone. As he became a teenager, his homosexual feelings became more intense. Despite his "secret," talk of an appropriate wife for him began in his household. Already, he was a

diligent student at the Yeshiva. As talk of a "match" intensified, the young Noam Mordecai spent more and more time studying. When he was seventeen, he told his mother and father that he wanted to delay marriage. He begged his parents to help him in his efforts to study in Pumpedita, 150 miles from his home. His plan was to spend a year or so in a village between his hometown and Pumpedita. There he would earn some money as a day laborer, then continue to Pumpedita. His parents gave their support, and Noam Mordecai was off on his own.

Shortly after arriving in the village, Noam Mordecai and another man befriended each other. Their relationship slowly evolved into a sexual affair. Noam Mordecai was overjoyed to be so in love, to be so physically and emotionally fulfilled. But he was also torn apart. It was impossible that the relationship could continue. He knew that his sexual behavior was considered sinful. After a torrentially emotional year, Noam Mordecai broke off the affair, then continued on, by himself, to Pumpedita. There he became one of the finest scholars of his day.

Rabbi Noam Mordecai never married, insisting that his love of Torah (study) was all-consuming, leaving no time for a family. But he never forgot the happiness he experienced in the village on the way to Pumpedita. It seemed strange to repent for the happiness he felt, however, that is what he did. Throughout his life, though he felt something central was missing, he never loved another man again.

Scenario II: New York City, 2005

Noam always felt attracted to men. He remembers having homosexual feelings since he was a child. Of course, he never spoke about this in his early years, because kids teased boys who showed interest in other boys. Still, he knew that it wasn't so unusual that people of the same sex might get together as couples. There were several kids in his school with two moms or two dads.

As Noam entered his teenage years, his homosexual feelings became more intense. Sex education classes gave him some sense that his feelings were not so unusual. Yet, he felt he needed to understand more about himself, more about his sexual feelings. Over the years, he had noticed a bookstore focused on gay, lesbian, and bisexual interests in Greenwich Village (a neighborhood in New York City). One day, he visited. Besides picking up a book about teens and homosexuality, he spent time looking at the bulletin board. He noticed there was a support group for gay, lesbian, and bisexual teens held at a local synagogue. This particular synagogue had a special interest in outreach to gays, lesbians, and homosexuals. Through attending the support group, Noam was able to work through conflicted feelings regarding his sexuality. He also met other teenagers like him.

At first, Noam was secretive with his family about attending the group. After a few months however, he felt he wanted to be honest with them. While his parents weren't openly critical of Noam, it did take several months for them to accept that Noam wasn't "just going through a phase." Even during this rough period, Noam always knew his parents loved him. Eventually, they became fully accepting of his homosexuality.

By the time he was in college, Noam felt very comfortable with and clear about his sexuality. He enjoyed learning in a wide variety of areas, including Jewish studies. During his senior year of college, Noam was weighing whether he should continue his studies in biology or apply to rabbinical school. Whatever the decision, he felt strongly that he wanted to remain close to Daniel, the man he had been dating for the past two years, the man he loved.

For Thought and Discussion:

How is Noam Mordecai's situation different from Noam's? What are the societal pressures that each faces?

What options for coming to terms with his sexuality are available to Noam Mordecai, living in the time and place that he did? To Noam, the New Yorker, in his time and place?

If either of these young men had confided in you, what would you have advised him?

Text Study

As we have seen, homosexuality is an emotional and complex topic. While some cultures and communities have grown in their acceptance of homosexuality, others maintain strong disapproval. Jewish texts and other sources express varying viewpoints, highlighting the tension between seemingly opposing considerations. The chart on the next page poses the questions and offers two opposing points of view. Text sources supporting each of these points of view follow below.

Note: Text Study #1a in Chapter 13, "Birth Control," (p. 184) concisely explains historical attitudes regarding "wasting the seed" — an issue relevant to homosexuality, as well.

1. **Must we accept traditional Jewish beliefs about homosexuality?**

On the One Hand:

Beliefs that male homosexuality is an abhorrence (*toe-ay-vah*) and lesbianism is licentious (*p'ree-tzoo-ta*) are rooted in the Bible and Talmud.

A. Do not lie with a male as one lies with a woman: it is an abhorrence (*toe-ay-vah*) (Leviticus 18:22).

B. [Concerning] women who practice lewdness with one another . . . the action is regarded as mere obscenity (*Yevamot* 76a).

On the Other Hand:

In light of the context in which our ancestors formed their beliefs, it is legitimate to challenge their views about homosexuality.

a. In the Talmud, a deaf-mute was considered to be retarded, mentally incompetent, an imbecile not able to serve or witness, or to be counted in the *minyan*, or to effect marriage or divorce. But that ruling was based on empirically false data. On a visit to the Vienna Institute for the Deaf and Dumb, Rabbi Simchah Sofer saw that their impaired speech and hearing had nothing to do with their intelligence and accounta-

Homosexuality: Questions to Consider

The Question	On the One Hand	On the Other Hand
1. Must we accept traditional Jewish beliefs about homosexuality? (see page 189)	Beliefs that male homosexuality is an abhorrence (*toe-ay-vah*) and lesbianism is licentious or obscene (*p'ree-tzoo-ta*) are rooted in the Bible and Talmud.	In light of the context in which our ancestors formed their beliefs, it is legitimate to challenge their views about homosexuality.
2. Might it be best simply to ignore homosexuality? (see page 191)	Denial is one way traditional Jewish sources deal with homosexuality.	To believe that Jews are not involved in homosexuality is simply inaccurate. We need to deal with reality.
3. Does being accepting of homosexuality deny "the natural order of things"? (see page 191)	Homosexuality is "unnatural."	God created all kinds of people, both heterosexuals and homosexuals.
4. Does homosexuality threaten "family values"? (see page 192)	Homosexuality violates family values.	There are many ways to contribute to the Jewish community. One is establishing a loving home and raising children — something many homosexuals choose to do.
5. What is the range of responses to homosexuality in the Jewish community? (see page 192)	Mainstream Orthodoxy today generally condemns homosexual acts, though may encourage compassion for individual "sufferers."	Scientific, social, and moral concerns have propelled many Jewish communities to reexamine homosexuality with increasing openness.
6. Does homosexuality threaten the cherished institution of marriage? (see page 194)	Homosexuality can destroy marriages.	A homosexual person's constitution prevents him/her from finding happiness and fulfillment in marriage with someone of the opposite sex. Sanctifying same-sex partnerships promotes the Jewish values of long-term, monogamous relationships.

bility, and urged altering the older rabbinic judgment. The law and its legal interpretation are rooted in history. Every text has its context . . .

The rabbis of the Talmud assumed that homosexual acts were acts of free will, even ideological. They did not know of "constitutional" gay and lesbians who had no control over their sexual orientation. Moreover it is far from clear what the Biblical term ["*toe-ay-vah*"] translated as "abomination" means or to what it refers. Some Biblical scholars maintain that the Biblical word for abomination "[*toe-ay-vah*]" refers not to homosexuality but more likely to cultic prostitution; and that what the Bible inveighed against was the pagan tradition that paid obeisance to pagan gods by all forms of illicit sexual behavior (Rabbi Harold M. Schulweis, "Morality, Legality and Homosexuality," Rosh Hashana sermon, 1992).

What Do You Think?

Why does Rabbi Schulweis make the comparison between deaf-mutes and homosexuals? Is his point a legitimate one? What problems does he find in applying the term "*toe-ay-vah*" to homosexuals today?

Suppose we assume the Bible actually does consider homosexuality a "sin." Do you believe changing historical contexts and beliefs should allow us to discount what is written in the Bible?

⇒◆⇐

2. **Might it be best simply to ignore homosexuality?**

On the One Hand:

Denial is one way traditional Jewish sources deal with homosexuality.

A. Rabbi Judah said an unmarried man must not tend cattle nor may two unmarried men sleep together under the same cover. But the sages permit it . . . They said to Rabbi Judah: Israel is suspected of neither homosexuality nor bestiality (Mishnah,

Kiddushin 4:14 and *Kiddushin* 82a; see also Maimonides, *Issuray Bi-ah* 22:2; Rabbi Joseph Karo, *Even Ha-Ezer* 24; and Rabbi Joel Sirkes, *Bayit Chadash* to *Tur, Even Ha-Ezer* 24).

On the Other Hand:

To believe that Jews are not involved in homosexuality is simply inaccurate. We need to deal with reality.

a. The following passage is included in a longer citation below (see Text Study #4b).

I, for one, cannot believe that the God who created us all produced a certain percentage of us to have sexual drives that cannot be legally expressed under any circumstances. That is simply mind-boggling — and, frankly, un-Jewish . . . (Rabbi Elliot Dorff, *Matters of Life and Death,* p. 145).

What Do You Think?

The Sages maintain that Jews are not (or were not) homosexuals. What reasons might there be for saying such a thing? Should we in our day, claim as the Sages did that Jews are "not suspected of homosexuality"? Explain.

Does Rabbi Dorff make a valid point? Do you agree with his point? Explain.

⇒◆⇐

3. **Does being accepting of homosexuality deny "the natural order of things?"**

On the One Hand:

Homosexuality is "unnatural."

A. You are going astray from the foundations of the creation (Rabbi Aruch Halevi Epstein, *Torah Temimah* to Leviticus 18:22).

On the Other Hand:

God created all kinds of people, both heterosexuals and homosexuals.

a. See Text Study #2a above.

What Do You Think?

What difficulties might someone have in defining the word "natural"? How do you define "natural"?

What do you think Rabbi Epstein means by the phrase, "going astray from the foundations of the creation"?

Is there more that one way to understand what are the foundations of creation? If we say, "yes, but one way is more legitimate than other ways," by what authority do we do so?

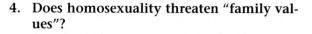

4. **Does homosexuality threaten "family values"?**

On the One Hand:

Homosexuality violates family values.

A. At the root of the precept [against homosexuality] lies the reason that the Eternal Who Is Blessed desires the settlement of the world God created. Therefore God commanded us that human seed should not be destroyed by carnal relations with males: for this is indeed destruction, since there can be no fruitful benefit of offspring from it, nor the fulfillment of the religious duty of conjugal rights [due one's wife] . . . (*Sefer Ha-Chinuch*, no. 209).

On the Other Hand:

There are many ways to contribute to the Jewish community. One is by establishing a loving home and raising children — something many homosexuals choose to do.

a. What grounds could there be, Jewishly speaking, for a more permissive stand [concerning homosexuality]?

As to concern for populating the earth, overpopulation would today be a greater concern — were it not for our equal concern for perpetuating the Jewish people, a concern shared by all loyal Jews, homosexual no less than heterosexual. There are other ways, however, of contributing to the survival of the Jewish people, aside from physically begetting or bearing chil-

dren: many Jewish homosexuals support worthy Jewish causes and institutions . . . some make their contributions as teachers of Judaism . . .

As to the crucial importance of the family for providing a nurturing, loving, and caring relationship, many homosexuals establish a home in which mutual love, genuine sharing, responsiveness and responsibility and lifelong faithfulness are a reality: many are prepared, when society allows, to serve as adoptive or foster parents: and some homosexuals lovingly rear children that they themselves have begotten or borne in a previously heterosexual marriage (Rabbi Herschel Matt, *Conservative Judaism*, Spring 1987).

What Do You Think?

Why might someone suggest that homosexuality violates family values?

What would Rabbi Matt's arguments be for contesting such a suggestion?

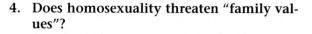

5. **What is the range of responses to homosexuality in the Jewish community?**

On the One Hand:

Mainstream Orthodoxy today generally condemns homosexual acts, though may encourage compassion for individual "sufferers".

A. Clearly, while Judaism needs no defense or apology in regard to its esteem for neighborly love and compassion for the individual sufferer, it cannot possibly abide a wholesale dismissal of its most basic moral principles on the grounds that those subject to its judgments find them repressive . . .

Homosexuality is no different from any other anti-social or anti-halachic act, where it is legitimate to distinguish between the objective act itself, including its social and moral consequences, and the mentality and inner development of the person who perpetuates the act . . . To use halachic terminology, the objective crime remains a *ma'aseh averah* (a forbidden act) whereas the person who transgresses is considered innocent on the grounds of ["*oh-ness*"] (force beyond one's control) (Rabbi Norman Lamm, "Judaism and the Modern Attitude Toward Homosexuality, " *Encyclopaedia Judaica Yearbook*, 1974).

On the Other Hand:

Scientific, social, and moral concerns have propelled many Jewish communities to reexamine homosexuality with increasing openness.

a. The American Psychiatric Association, in its April 1993 Fact Sheet (p. 1) states:

> There is no evidence that any treatment can change a homosexual person's deep-seated sexual feelings for others of the same sex. Clinical experience suggests that any person who seeks conversion therapy may be doing so because of social bias that has resulted in internalized homophobia, and that gay men and lesbians who have accepted their sexual orientation positively are better adjusted than those who have not done so.

b. Rabbi Elliot N. Dorff presents numerous sources, including the previous one, indicating that homosexuals cannot alter their sexual orientation. He continues:

> It seems to me, [there is a necessity for] a rethinking and recasting of the law, for if anything is clear about the tradition, it is that it assumed that gay behavior is a matter of choice. Otherwise, a commandment forbidding it would logically make no sense — any more than would a commandment that prohibited breathing for any but the shortest periods of time.
>
> Now of course it is logically possible to say to gays and lesbians, as some rabbis writing on the subject have said, that if they cannot change their homosexual orientation, they should remain celibate all their lives. That result, however, is downright cruel.
>
> Moreover, I find such a position theologically untenable. I, for one, cannot believe that the God who created us all produced a certain percentage of us to have sexual drives that cannot be legally expressed under any circumstances. That is simply mind-boggling — and, frankly, un-Jewish . . .
>
> Furthermore, it seems to me that to ask gays and lesbians to remain celibate all their lives is not halachically required. If gays and lesbians are right in asserting that they have no choice in being homosexual . . . then they are as forced to be gay as straights are forced to be straight . . .
>
> Putting the matter theologically, as the texts on compulsion do, if human beings can never reasonably require a person to do what is impossible for him or her, one would surely expect that to be even more true of God, who presumably knows the nature of each of us and therefore commands only what is appropriate to the various groups of us . . . (Rabbi Elliot Dorff, *Matters of Life and Death*, pp. 144-147).

c. [The] basic choice [for homosexuals] is not whether "to be homosexual" but whether to live openly and with integrity what they truly are — men and women, who, for reasons not of their own making or choosing, are able to know the blessing of true sexual fulfillment primarily or exclusively through relationship with someone of their own sex . . .

As for the Torah's condemnation of homosexuality, we follow those teachers who have taught us that though the Torah contains God's word, it is not identical with God's word; it is both divine and human. Insofar as the Torah reflects the divine intent, its prohibition of homosexuality could not have had in mind the kind of homosexuality we have been speaking of: insofar as it reflects mere human attempts to grasp the divine intent, it reflects also a human misunderstanding of the kind of homosexuality that is forbidden . . . (Rabbi Herschel Matt, *Conservative Judaism*, Spring 1987).

What Do You Think?

Rabbi Norman Lamm uses these halachic terms: *ma'aseh averah* (a forbidden act) and *oh-ness* (force beyond one's control). How does he apply the terms to homosexuality?

In what ways is Rabbi Lamm's statement consistent with views expressed in traditional Jewish texts? In what ways does his statement reflect modern attitudes regarding homosexuality?

Do you feel Rabbi Lamm succeeds in balancing traditional beliefs with modern concerns? Why or why not?

What are some reasons why many Jewish communities are reexamining homosexuality with increasing openness?

If you were (are) homosexual and felt you wanted to talk to someone about personal issues regarding your sexual identity, who would you go to: Rabbi Lamm, Rabbi Dorff, or Rabbi Matt? Explain your choice.

6. **Does homosexuality threaten the cherished institution of marriage?**

On the One Hand:

Homosexuality can destroy marriages.

A. *Toe-ay atah bah*, "you are going astray" is regarding — those who abandon their wives and indulge in homosexuality (Rabbi Asher ben Jehiel).

On the Other Hand:

A homosexual person's constitution prevents him/her from finding happiness and fulfillment in marriage with someone of the opposite sex. Sanctifying same-sex partnerships promotes the Jewish values of long-term, monogamous relationships.

a. The Jewish values and principles which I regard as eternal, transcendent and divinely ordained do not condemn homosexuality. The Judaism I cherish and affirm teaches love of humanity, respect for the spark of divinity in every person and the human right to live with dignity. The God I worship endorses loving, responsible and committed human relationships, regardless of the sex of the persons involved (Rabbi Janet Marder, "Jewish and Gay," *Keeping Posted* 32, 2; November 1986).

b. The Jewish tradition sanctifies monogamous, loving sex among heterosexuals as marriage, and, the argument goes, we should do the same in our time for homosexuals (Rabbi Elliot Dorff, *Matters of Life and Death*, p. 149).

c. A statement from the Reform Movement's Central Conference of American Rabbis (CCAR):

> WHEREAS justice and human dignity are cherished Jewish values, and . . .
>
> WHEREAS, the institutions of Reform Judaism have a long history of support for civil and equal rights for gays and lesbians, and
>
> WHEREAS, North American organizations of the Reform Movement have passed resolutions in support of civil marriage for gays and lesbians, therefore
>
> WE DO HEREBY RESOLVE, that the relationship of a Jewish, same-gender couple is worthy of affirmation through appropriate Jewish ritual, and
>
> FURTHER RESOLVED, that we recognize the diversity of opinions within our ranks on this issue. We support the decision of those who choose to officiate at rituals of union for same-gender couples, and we support the decision of those who do not, and
>
> FURTHER RESOLVED, that we call upon the CCAR to support all col-

leagues in their choices in this matter, and

FURTHER RESOLVED, that we also call upon the CCAR to develop both educational and liturgical resources in this area (Ad Hoc Committee on Human Sexuality, CCAR, 1998).

What Do You Think?

What might be an objection(s) to Jewish commitment ceremonies or same-sex marriages? What are reasons to endorse them?

Related Middot and Mitzvot

These virtues and commandments can help us approach the issues of homosexuality with a solid understanding of applicable Jewish values:

Emet (Truthfulness): Homosexuals must be true to themselves and honest and unashamed about who they are in the world.

Lo Levayesh (Not Embarrassing): A person's body and sexuality are private. What happens between two people as part of their intimate life is private as well. It is wrong to tease or embarrass others about personal matters.

Ma'akeh (Preventing Accidents): Sexually transmitted diseases are of special concern in the homosexual community. AIDS in particular can be spread when people do not take the necessary precautions. Those who engage in sex must be responsible for practicing "safe sex."

Mechabayd Zeh et Zeh (Honoring Others): Honor and care about others' dignity. Hatred, harassment, and violence against gays, lesbians, and bisexuals is wrong. Judaism encourages us to be compassionate, loving, and respectful of other human beings.

Where Do I Go From Here?

Homosexuality is an issue that permeates the lives of all of us, gay or straight, in some way or another: generally accepted studies show that somewhere between three and ten percent of the population is homosexual.[1] Issues of gay rights and the definition of marriage are constantly in the news, and are certain to continue being "hot topics." In order to make informed choices, you should be aware of traditional and contemporary Jewish thought on this deeply divisive issue.

An extensive list of resources on homosexuality and other issues of sexuality can be found at the end of Chapter 11, "Foundations of Sexual Ethics," on pages 173-176. These will be helpful as you continue your exploration of this sensitive topic.

CHAPTER 15
SEX OUTSIDE OF MARRIAGE

Overview

Introduction

Judaism, like many other religions and cultures, places a high value on marriage. Sex between spouses does involve ethical considerations, but the marital relationship provides well-established boundaries for appropriate sexual intimacy. Sex outside of marriage, however, raises multiple ethical dilemmas.

Defining ethical standards is a challenge for unmarried sex partners whose responsibilities in a relationship are poorly defined. Can we expect love to be a prerequisite, even if we don't require long-term commitment? Can we insist on mutual respect, even if we don't require love? Nonmarital sex becomes an ethical "slippery slope," forcing us to consider if we can we legitimately draw any boundaries for appropriate sex, once we remove the boundary of marriage. The primary reason to make such an effort is that we face new cultural and sociological realities in our day.

Especially relevant is the fact that most sexually mature individuals spend a significant portion of their lives not married. Some may delay marriage in order to realize professional or educational goals, or because they do not feel emotionally ready for the commitment of marriage. For divorced individuals or widows/widowers, remarriage raises complicated issues if its own. Yet, rushing into marriage so as to "legally" have sex is not particularly wise. Our challenge is to find innovative guidelines that will both recognize the realities of our circumstances, yet respect cherished Jewish values.

Jewish Perspectives

"Black and White" and "Gray" Areas of Sexuality

Sex outside of marriage can imply a wide range of sexual interactions, from monogamous "living together" situations to orgies. Some sexual behaviors are never acceptable from a Jewish point of view. These "black and white" cases include forbidden sexual relations such as incest and adultery.

Putting these examples aside, modern Jews recognize the commonplace occurrence of intercourse outside of marriage. If we turn to Judaism to help us apply ethical guidelines to relationships that aren't forbidden, but aren't marriage either, we navigate a "gray area." An example "gray area" relationship might be two twenty-year-old individuals who have dated steadily, love each other, and enjoy sexual intimacy with each other. But for personal and professional reasons, these individuals are not ready to commit to marriage.

The rabbi and theologian Eugene B. Borowitz presents a nuanced understanding of sexual relationships in his book *Choosing a Sex Ethic: A Jewish Inquiry*. The ethics he examines include: (1) healthy orgasm; (2) mutual consent; (3) love; and (4) marriage.

Borowitz first examines the ethics of the healthy orgasm. He finds its criterion for sex to be ethically defective, primarily because it makes "possible the subordination of one person's rights to that of the other."[1]

The mutual-consent criterion for sex is an ethical advance over intercourse that may involve coercion or exploitation, but because mutual-consent is interested only in two aspects of a person — his/her will and his/her sexuality — it is unsatisfactory as well. Mutual consent may not be unethical, but it compromises essential aspects of what it is to be a human being. Meaningful relationships ask individuals to embrace the fullness of who the other is.[2]

What about love? A sexual relationship that is born of love and is an expression of love is not unethical. Love and friendship are highly esteemed values in a relationship, and a sexual relationship that grows out of love and friendship can be a source of great pleasure and an expression of deeply felt emotion.

Still, Borowitz would view an "ordinary" love relationship on a continuum of values. Love may be wonderful in the present moment, and perhaps carry past meaning as well. However, the future, too is integral to the wholeness of a person's identity. Thus, lifelong love allows for the most meaningful human relationship.

Rabbi Arthur Green suggests another innovative way to frame sexuality. He proposes a "sliding scale of sexual values" (see Text Study #1a below). Suppose we place Borowitz's four ethics on this sliding scale. A fully loving, committed relationship — that is, marriage — would stand at the top of the scale. Love (without commitment) would be a little lower. Mutual-consent would be lower still. And below that would be healthy orgasm.

Holiness

Judaism advocates marriage as the ideal vehicle for attaining holiness in a relationship. Likewise, marriage would be at the top of a Jewish "sliding scale of sexual values." However, if we become involved in a sexual relationship outside of marriage, we are not to lose sight of Jewish aspirations. We can incorporate holiness into our intimate lives through such values as honesty, integrity, respect, humility, love, and modesty. All of these elevate our relationships.

Modesty (Tzeniyut)

For a discussion of modesty (*tzeniyut*), refer to Chapter 11, "Foundations of Sexual Ethics," page 162.

Revealing Ourselves

In meaningful sexual encounters, two people who reveal themselves sexually to each other, reveal vulnerability, as well. That is, sexual sharing involves more than a physical revelation of self. True, some individuals so detach their emotional selves from their physical selves that sex becomes hardly different from an animal act (as in the healthy orgasm "ethic"). But for those who seek a holier way of relating, a higher level on the "sliding scale," sexual intimacy will expose our most sensitive spots. In making love, we reveal body, heart, and soul.

A healthy sexual relationship requires the emotional maturity and self-confidence to endure the impact of full self-revelation. Suppose a person exposes too much of him/herself too soon in a relationship. Possible reasons might be because of peer pressure, pressure from a partner, low self-worth, or a desire for the partner to feel more committed to a shaky relationship. When the relationship inevitably falls apart, the result can be extraordinarily painful. Feelings of humiliation and perhaps violation can be intense. Carelessly revealing our emotional and spiritual vulnerability can cause suffering lasting longer than we might ever imagine.

Ready for Sex, but Not Ready for Marriage: Some Practical Guidelines

To review so far: We won't find a Jewish ethic urging unmarried individuals to "go out and have sex." Judaism considers marriage to be the ideal relationship for sexual intercourse. Yet, given our modern reality, we understand people will engage in intercourse outside of marriage. We can and should bring Jewish values into our relationships even if they are not marriages. Still, non-marital sexual relationships are not all equal. We mentioned the "defects" of the ethics of "healthy orgasm" and "mutual consent," and also the benefits and limits of "ordinary love." We suggested the goal of aiming to place ourselves on the higher end of the "sliding scale of Jewish sexual values."

Certainly it can be helpful to have an awareness of some philosophical underpinnings involved in making decisions regarding non-marital sex. But such awareness doesn't mean making a decision of "should I?" or "shouldn't I?" will be easy. When emotions and ethics are involved, feeling absolutely confident about a decision is rare. Even so, we can add a few more practical insights regarding non-marital sex to the general guidelines presented thus far.

Making Decisions

The most important guideline is that we must take responsibility for making decisions. We are not passive players in a life that unfolds around us. Specifically, we should never fall into bed with someone because passion overtakes us. Simply allowing sexual intercourse to happen is equivalent to accepting no guidelines. At its very foundation, Judaism teaches that we have choices, and that we make choices. Therefore, a desire for intercourse should only become an act of intercourse after conscious and conscientious consideration. In other words, we choose and plan to make love because we have thought about it, because we have discussed it with our partner, and because we have come to a reasoned and ethical decision regarding this significant step.

Choosing Influences

This is related to the idea above. We not only decide, but we decide how to decide. What ideas and values do we want to influence our sexual decisions?

There is no shortage of frivolous and even harmful attitudes toward sex in our society. We must ask ourselves two questions regarding what should influence our sexual behavior: Do we believe that (1) sex should be a sacred encounter between two individuals who love and trust each other; or (2) sex is a response to passions, urges, and social pressures? Given these two choices, Judaism clearly would embrace the former.

Questions to Ask, Values to Consider

As stated before, it is important for individuals not to engage in sex prematurely. But what does "prematurely" mean? Outside of marriage, what criteria might we use to figure out when taking the step to engage in sexual intercourse is appropriate in a given relationship? For some specific ideas, see the "General Perspectives" section of Chapter 11, "Foundations of Sexual Ethics," page 162. Also see the following paragraphs and Text Study #1B below.

Fleeting versus Enduring Values

When faced with decisions regarding non-marital sex, we weigh competing considerations. Some values may conflict with others. Judaism guides us to embrace enduring values. While pleasure, fun, excitement, and heeding social pressures may be values, they are fleeting ones. Enduring values include trust, respect, honesty, love, modesty, and responsibility. Abiding by fleeting values in isolation from enduring ones is an insufficient standard for sex.

Teen Sex

Our discussion of ethics pertaining to non-marital sex assumes it happens between adults (eighteen or older). As Rabbi Michael Gold writes, "Teens are physically ready to have sex long before they are emotionally ready . . . " See Text Study #1c for a fuller exploration of teen sex issues.

Masturbation

This subject relates to teens and others. If, as Rabbi Gold puts it, "teens are physically ready to have sex long before they are emotionally ready . . . ," they need safe and appropriate ways to relieve the sexual tension they feel. Perhaps a relaxation of Judaism's traditional disapproval of masturbation is in order (see Text Study #1c and #1d in Chapter 12, "Masturbation," p. 179, and also "Scenarios: How Things Have Changed" in that chapter, page 178).

Birth Control

In Chapter 13, "Birth Control," we discussed the responsibility of those who engage in sex outside of marriage to use contraception. As Eugene B. Borowitz puts it, "Careful, effective contraception is an ethical necessity if there is to be any legitimation of premarital sexual intercourse" (see Text Study #1e and #1f in Chapter 13, "Birth Control," page 186).

General Perspectives

Refer to the information in the "General Perspectives" section of Chapter 11, "Foundations of Sexual Ethics," page 162. The notions of ethical sexual behavior outlined there apply to our topic here, as well.

Summary of the Overview

- Marriage is Judaism's ideal relationship for sexual intercourse.
- Yet, current trends suggest that some people will engage in intercourse outside of marriage.
- To remain relevant, Judaism must respond meaningfully to these trends rather than ignore or deny them.
- A meaningful response begins by teaching the importance of bringing enduring Jewish values into intimate nonmarital relationships.

Scenarios: How Things Have Changed

More and more, communities find themselves wrestling with the issue of sex outside of marriage. The "Scenarios: How Things Have Changed" section in Chapter 11, "Foundations of Sexual Ethics" (page 163) addressed the tensions between physical readiness for sex and emotional and practical unpreparedness for marriage. In "Scenario II," we met the high school sweethearts Marc and Liana. Marc is 18 years old, and Liana is 16. Here, the continuation of their story raises additional questions and invites further discussion. Read the "next episode" of Marc and Liana's scenario and reflect on the questions in the "For Thought and Discussion" section that follows, either individually or in group discussion. Then continue on to the "Text Study" section to see what Jewish and other sources have to say about sex outside of marriage. Finally, you may wish to come back and discuss the scenario a second time, to see if your views have changed.

Marc and Liana: A Scenario Update

Marc and Liana continue to date exclusively and continue to feel they want to be together the rest of their lives. But they also are clear they won't be ready for marriage at least until both are in their mid-twenties. Their physical relationship progresses from kissing to intimate touching over the course of two years. When Liana is eighteen, they begin to bring each other to orgasm manually. During those months of more intense sexual intimacy, they also start to talk about having sexual intercourse with each other. After discussing birth control, they agree that Liana will take oral contraceptives. Marc and Liana now are enjoying sexual intercourse with each other. They have been making love for a few months now. When Liana goes to study abroad next year, they wonder what will happen to their relationship. Meanwhile, they feel that for now, they are relating to each other in a meaningful and worthy way.

Marc and Liana's decision process is similar to that which many young people will go through. While they have few concrete signposts to guide them in their choices, we sense that they have tried to anchor their decision in important standards and values, including many Jewish ethical

values. Their choice reflects their effort to live and relate ethically to each other as lovers.

Clearly, some communities will accept only marriage as the appropriate place for sexual expression. But for those who venture outside traditional standards, Jewish wisdom can provide relevant, meaningful, and supportive guidance.

For Thought and Discussion:

What values guide Marc and Liana in making their decision to engage in sexual intercourse? How have they balanced short-term, fleeting pleasures with more enduring values?

How are these values compatible with Judaism and how do they conflict with Judaism?

If Marc and Liana had sought your advice before making their decision, what would you have told them?

Text Study

We face difficult questions regarding sex outside of marriage. Jewish textual sources provide many answers, but these answers often highlight the tension between seemingly opposing considerations. The chart below poses the key question on this topic and offers two opposing points of view. Text sources supporting each of these points of view follow.

Note: For other relevant texts, see Text Study #2E, #3B, #5A, #5a, and #5b in Chapter 11, "Foundations of Sexual Ethics," pages 161-176, and Text Study #1c and #1d in Chapter 12, "Masturbation," pages 177-180.

1. **Should sex always and only take place between married adults?**

    On the One Hand:

    Sexual relations belong in the confines of marriage.

    A. The following passage summarizes the traditional attitude regarding sex outside of marriage:

Sex Outside of Marriage: A Question to Consider

The Question	On the One Hand	On the Other Hand
1. Is sex outside of marriage permissible? (see p. 199)	Sexual relations belong only within the confines of marriage.	Recognizing the realities of modern life, rabbis and others are rethinking guidelines for sexual relations between unmarried, consenting adults.

Chastity before marriage has been considered an obvious requirement for all and was taken for granted by the tradition . . . There are many statements that support this point of view and demand that an unmarried person refrain from sexual intercourse. The references deal particularly with males (*Pesachim* 113a, b; *Shabbat* 152a). A statement of Rabbi Yochanan makes this very clear: "There is a small organ in man; he who satisfies it goes hungry and he who allows it to go hungry is satisfied" (*Sanhedrin* 107a) . . . All females were expected to be virgins at the time of their first marriage. The dowry of a nonvirgin was less than that of a virgin, and anyone falsely claiming virginity was subject to severe punishment (*American Reform Responsa*, p. 477).

B. Elliot N. Dorff, a Conservative rabbi and theologian, writes:

Marriage (*Kiddushin*) is holy precisely because a man and woman set each other apart from all others to live their lives together, taking responsibility for the children they bear. The willingness to assume these responsibilities is critical both for their own pleasure and growth and for the perpetuation of the Jewish community and the Jewish tradition. Marriage is also important in Judaism because it provides a structure for achieving core Jewish values in our intimate lives — values like honesty, modesty, love, health and safety, and holiness. Marriage is no guarantee that

we will succeed in this, but it does help us attain those values. Thus Judaism is not being irrational, prudish, old-fashioned, unrealistic, or mean in demanding that we limit our sexual intercourse to the context of marriage; it is rather responding to concerns that are at least as real and important in the fragmented society of today as they were in the more stable society of times past (*Matters of Life and Death*, p. 136).

C. Eugene B. Borowitz, a Reform rabbi and theologian, writes:

The most ethical form of human relationship I know is love-for-life. Its appropriate social and religious structure is the monogamous marriage. This being so, marriage is, if I may use the strange formulation of ethical pluralism, the most right context, that is, the best criterion for the validity of sexual intercourse. And I think every human being should try to reach the highest possible level of ethical behavior (*Choosing a Sex Ethic*, p. 113-114).

On the Other Hand:

Recognizing the realities of modern life, rabbis and others are rethinking guidelines for sexual relations between unmarried, consenting adults.

a. Living in a world where we cannot advocate either ideal sex or no sex as the alternatives, what we must begin to evolve is a sliding scale of sexual values . . . At the top of this scale would stand the fully knowing and loving relationship . . . , while rape — fully unconsenting and anonymous sexuality — would stand at the bottom. Somewhere near the middle of the scale, neither glorified nor condemned, would be the relationship of two consenting persons, treating one another with decency, fulfilling the biological aspects of one another's love-needs, while making no pretense at deeper intimacy. Given such a scale, a Jew might begin to judge his/her own sexual behavior in terms of a series of challenges which s/he might want to address (Rabbi Arthur Green, "A Contemporary Approach to Jewish Sexuality," in *The Second Jewish Catalog*, p. 99).

(Please note: This passage makes important points for Jews to ponder today. However, most current thinking would object to including "rape" on any scale of sexual values, even if we call rape a "sexual sin." Although rape involves a sex act, it more fittingly belongs in the category of violent crime.)

b. Those values that lead Judaism to advocate marriage — honesty, modesty, health and safety, love, and holiness — still apply to sexual relations outside marriage; they are just harder to achieve in that context. Indeed, precisely because unmarried couples cannot rely on the support of a marital bond to foster those values, it is all the more critical that if they engage in sexual intercourse, they must consciously strive to live by them. Even though their behavior will not be ideal by Jewish standards, to the extent that they can make those values real in their lives, they will be preserving their own humanity, their Jewishness, and their own mental and physical health, as well as that of their partner (Rabbi Elliot N. Dorff, *Matters of Life and Death*, p. 137. For a fuller treatment of these issues, see Dorff, *This Is My Beloved, This Is My Friend*, p. 30-36.).

c. Regarding sexual relations between unmarried, consenting adults, Michael Gold, a Conservative rabbi, writes:

Each of these three words is important. If one of the adults is married, the relationship becomes adulterous. If one of the adults is nonconsenting, it is a case of rape. If one of the partners is not an adult (eighteen or older), the relationship involves another dimension — teenage sex . . . (p. 58)

d. About teenage sex, Rabbi Gold writes:

Teens are physically ready to have sex long before they are emotionally ready . . . Teens, however, lack the emotional maturity necessary for a sexual relationship. They usually have neither the self-esteem nor the self-confidence to be truly consenting when confronted with sexual choices . . . Teens are especially susceptible to powerful peer pressure as well as to pressure from the media. They all too easily confuse lust or physical infatuation with love . . . Often teens are involved in reckless behavior [which can lead to pregnancy or the contraction of venereal diseases, including AIDS] . . . Too late, teens discover that they are vulnerable, for people who engage in sex open themselves to another in a very intimate way. An irresponsible sex partner can leave a young person emotionally if not physically scarred. Because of this risk and its serious repercussions, I believe teens are too young to be sexually active . . .

Of course, youngsters do not leap from no sex to full genital intercourse in one step; they move through various levels of sexual experimentation, from rather tentative kissing, to heavy petting with clothes, to genital contact and mutual masturbation. Traditional Judaism forbids all such physical activity between unmarried partners because of fear of the "slippery slope" — that any of these activities will lead to improper sexual intercourse.

However, most young people in our society do not and will not abide by a prohibition against all physical contact between members of the opposite sex. Flirting and physical experimentation are part of growing up in today's society.

Recognizing this reality, parents can tell their children that they may draw boundaries within this continuum of physical activity. As we learn in the fourth blessing of the *Amidah*, *chochmah* (wisdom) is the ability to distinguish boundaries and to abide by them. Thus we can teach our children that kissing is acceptable at a certain age, whereas genital manipulation is not. Parents can help their children set reasonable boundaries for themselves and their partners (pp. 173, 178-179).

d. About sex education:

Nobody should make assumptions about what kids know about sex. Research shows that while they're highly aware of sex generally, they're often pretty ignorant about the details. Good sex education is safe sex education too. Helping kids to be aware of their bodies — of health and contraception, masturbation, sensual touching, and fantasy as well as intercourse — and of their feelings about sexuality can only make them better able to practice safe and egalitarian sex in what could be history's most honest chapter of sexual relations (Judith Levine, "Thinking About Sex" in *Tikkun, an Anthology*, edited by Michael Lerner, Oakland, CA and Jerusalem: Tikkun Books, 1992, p. 211).

What Do You Think?

Why does Judaism view sex in the context of marriage as the ideal?

In Text #1a Rabbi Green describes a "sliding scale of sexual values." What does he mean by this? What are the advantages of such a scale? What are the disadvantages? Does the "sliding scale of sexual values" make sense to you?

What is Rabbi Dorff's main point in Text Study #1b? What advice would he have for a couple that chooses to engage in sexual relations outside of marriage?

In Text Study #1c, why does Rabbi Gold say these three words — "unmarried," "consenting," and "adults" — are so important in discussing sex outside of marriage? Why should a committed Jew agree with him? What are Rabbi Gold's concerns about teen sex? Are his concerns valid?

Do you believe Rabbi Gold's advice for teens (and their parents) is worthwhile? Explain.

Related Middot and Mitzvot

These virtues and commandmen ts can help when wrestling with issues of sex outside of marriage:

Emet (Truthfulness): Lovers must be able to trust one another. Being truthful is a necessary element of building trust.

Emunah (Trustworthiness): In sexual relationships, partners make themselves vulnerable as they reveal themselves to each other. This requires the individuals to deeply trust each other.

Lo Levayesh (Not Embarrassing): A person's body and sexuality are private. What happens between two people as part of their intimate life is private as well. It is wrong to tease or embarrass others about personal matters.

Ma'akeh (Preventing Accidents): Unwanted pregnancies and sexually transmitted diseases can occur when people do not take the necessary precautions. Those who engage in sex must be responsible for preventing "accidents."

Mechabayd Zeh et Zeh (Honoring Others): Honor and care about others' dignity. Do not treat people as objects (i.e., physical machines), but respect them as full, complex human beings.

Ohev Zeh et Zeh (Loving Others): At some time in our lives, we may have a special love for one person. Along the way, as we encounter potential partners, love for our fellow human beings requires us not cause hurt.

Shmirat HaGuf (Taking Care of Your Body): In terms of sexuality, this includes getting regular physical check-ups, being responsible about birth control, keeping clean, avoiding circumstances that might lead to getting or giving a sexually transmitted disease, and getting help when a relationship feels dangerous or has become violent.

Simchah (Joy and Happiness): We celebrate the pleasures of sexual relationship.

Tzeniyut (Modesty): This includes being respectful and humble, not showing off. Casually revealing your body and allowing easy access to it by others, makes you more like an object than a "vehicle for holiness."

Where Do I Go From Here?

The texts in this chapter demonstrate, among other things, that sex is a highly complex topic. It is all too easy to get swept into sexual activity quickly and carelessly. The bond of marriage is meant to be stronger than any other between two people. Does sex belong exclusively to that bond, or can Judaism sanction sexual intercourse outside of marriage? This is a decision that nearly every person faces at some point. An understanding of both traditional and modern Jewish texts regarding sex, love, and marriage can help you make informed, ethically sound choices.

An extensive list of resources on issues of sexuality can be found at the end of Chapter 11, "Foundations of Sexual Ethics," on pages 173-176. These will be helpful to you as you continue your exploration of this complex topic.

NOTES

Chapter 1: Abortion

1. Mei Ling Rein, *Abortion: An Eternal Social and Moral Issue*, 8.

Chapter 2: Cloning and Other Genetic Technologies

1. Adapted from "Human Cloning—Scientific, Moral, and Jewish Perspectives" by Avraham Steinberg, 2.

2. Ibid., 2-3.

3. Ibid., 10.

4. Regenerative medicine: repairing the body by harnessing its own repair mechanisms — stem cells and signaling proteins — to renew damaged tissues and organs. ("Glossary," The New York Times, Science Times, D10)

Chapter 3: Euthanasia and Assisted Suicide

1. The Supreme Court (in the Cruzan v. Missouri case) considered the insertion of feeding tubes to be a medical treatment that a competent patient could refuse by living will or proxy decision maker. It is difficult to impose a definitive Jewish position on whether the insertion of feeding tubes should be considered "routine" or not.

2. These categories are described in "Euthanasia, Physician Assisted Suicide and the Dying Patient: Medical Status" by Philippa Newfield, M.D., a paper given at the Institute for Jewish Medical Ethics, 1997, 3 - 4.

3. Ibid., 4.

4. Adapted from "Making Sacred Choices at the End of Life" by Rabbi Richard F. Address, in *Lifelights*, 4.

5. English definitions adapted from "Euthanasia, Physician Assisted Suicide and the Dying Patient: Medical Status" by Philippa Newfield, M.D., 1.

Chapter 4: Harmful Behaviors: Smoking, Alcohol Abuse, and Over/Undereating

1. As reported in "Death in the Ashes" by Bob Herbert in his column, "In America," New York Times, July 26, 2001, A23.

2. "Drug Use in the General Population," *Drug and Crime Facts*, Bureau of Justice Statistics, December 1999.

3. "Youth Risk Behavior Surveillance — United States, 1999," *Morbidity and Mortality Weekly Report*, vol. 49, no. ss-5, June 9, 2002.

4. Chris Varley, *Life Issues: Alcoholism*, p. 31.

5. Marlene Boskind-White and William C. White, *Bulimia/Anorexia: The Binge/Purge Cycle and Self-Starvation*, p. 219.

6. Robert J. Kuczmarski et al., "Increasing Prevalence of Overweight Among U.S. Adults," *Journal of the American Medical Association* 272 (3[20 July 1994]): 205-211.

7. Center for Disease Control, The Third National Health and Nutrition Examination Survey (NHANES III: 1988-1994).

8. According to a group of adults responding to a survey, approximately a third did not participate in any leisure time activity as part of their weight loss program. Only about a fifth of these adults exercised the recommended 30 minutes or more, five or more times a week. These findings are reported in "Prevalence of Leisure-Time Activity Among Overweight Adults — United States, 1998," *Morbidity and Mortality Weekly Report*, vol. 49, no. 15, April 21, 2000.

9. "Youth Risk Behavior Surveillance — United States, 1999," *Morbidity and Mortality Weekly Report*, vol. 49, no. ss-5, June 9, 2000.

10. *Youth Risk Behavior Surveillance — United States, 1997*; Centers for Disease Control and Prevention, Atlanta, Georgia, 1997.

11. Moshe Zemer, *Evolving Halachah: A Progressive Approach to Traditional Jewish Law,* 349-350.

12. Much of the material for this section is drawn from "Intervening in the Life of an Alcoholic" (1989) by Judith Brazen and Susan Freeman, in *Reform Jewish Ethics and the Halakhah*, edited by Eugene B. Borowitz. NJ: Behrman House, Inc., 1994, pp. 79-95.

13. *Sanhedrin* 42a with *Tosafot, Sh'elot U'teshuvot* of *Bayit Chadash* #41, Leviticus 10:9, *Mishneh Torah — Hilchot Biat Hamikdash* 1:3, *Shulchan Aruch — Yoreh De'ah* 1:8.

14. These questions are adapted from *The New Our Bodies Ourselves*, Boston Women's Health Collective, 59.

15. Ibid, questions about drug and alcohol use adapted here for eating disorders.

Chapter 5: Ethics of Business

1. These categories of *g'nayvah* are detailed in Meir Tamari's book, *In the Marketplace*, 46.

2. Ibid, 48-49.

3. These categories are discussed in detail in "Employee Rights in a Situation of Dismissal" by Gayle Pomerantz and David Stern in *Reform Jewish Ethics and the Halakhah* by Borowitz, 278ff.

Chapter 6: The Death Penalty

1. Elie Spitz, "The Jewish Tradition and Capital Punishment" in *Contemporary Jewish Ethics and Morality*, 344.

2. Basil F. Herring, *Jewish Ethics and Halakhah for Our Time*, 155. For details of court procedure in capital cases, see Maimonides, *Mishneh Torah, Hilchot Sanhedrin* 11-15.

3. Herring, 169.

4. Mei Ling Rein, *Capital Punishment*, 44.

5. Robert J. Lifton and Greg Mitchell, *Who Owns Death? Capital Punishment, The American Conscience, and the End of Executions*, 200-201.

6. Hugo Adam Beadau, "The Case Against the Death Penalty," www.aclu.org.

7. This information is discussed in a position paper published by the Religious Action Center of Reform Judaism ("Issues: Death Penalty," www.rac.org, June 11, 2001, 2) and publicized in a statement made by the American Civil Liberties Union, www.aclu.org.

Chapter 7: School Violence

1. "A Brain Too Young for Good Judgement" by Daniel R. Weinberger, *The New York Times*, Op-Ed, March 10, 2001.

2. Raymond B. Flannery, Jr., *Preventing Youth Violence: A Guide for Parents, Techers, and Counselors*, 32-33.

3. Ibid, 37.

4. Elliot Aronson, *Nobody Left to Hate*, 59.

5. Richard L. Curwin and Allen N. Mendler, *As Tough as Necessary: Countering Violence, Aggression, and Hostility in Our Schools*, 24ff.

6. *Nobody Left to Hate*, 46.

Chapter 8: Ethics of War

1. Some *halachic* sources further distinguish types of obligatory war, naming a third category called *milchemet chovah*, or "a compulsory war."

2. These reasons are gleaned from the chapter, "War, Terrorism, and the Balance of Power" in

Social Problems by James M. Henslin, pp. 578-611.

3. From "The Four Freedoms," a booklet published by the Office of War Information, Washington, DC, 1942, which includes prior remarks made by Roosevelt on January 6, 1941.

4. From "Ends and Means: Defining a Just War," by Richard Falk, professor emeritus of internatinal law at Princeton University. In *The Nation*, October 29, 2001.

5. For a thorough study on this topic, see *A Responsum of Surrender* by Elijah J. Schochet.

6. The three texts here are cited in "War in the Jewish Tradition by Everett Gendler, in *Contemporary Jewish Ethics*, 205.

Chapter 9: Animal Experimentation

1. As quoted in *Who Renews Creation* by Earl Schwartz and Barry D. Cytron, 78.

2. Chimpanzees share 99.5% of the same base sequences along every double strand of DNA as human beings. This finding is described by Nicholas Wade in "Human or Chimp? 50 Genes are the Key," *New York Times*, D1, October 20, 1998.

3. For a thorough treatment of these categories in the context of animal rights, see *Rattling the Cage: Toward Legal Rights for Animals* by Steven M. Wise.

4. Hugh LaFollette and Niall Shanks, *Brute Science: Dilemmas of Animal Experimentation*, 266-269.

Chapter 10: Consumerism: How Much is Too Much?

1. From the Web site "Enough: Anticonsumerism Campaign," www.enough.org.uk. See also Text Study #2f.

2. Ibid, definitions adapted.

3. Jeremy Brecher and Tim Costello, *Global Village or Global Pillage: Economic Reconstruction from the Bottom Up*, 72.

4. Ibid.

5. Robert H. Frank, *Luxury Fever: Why Money Fails to Satisfy in an Era of Excess*, "The Price of Luxury," 45-63.

6. Ibid.

7. Some of these policy ideas are adapted from *Global Village or Global Pillage*, 170.

Chapter 11: The Foundations of Sexual Ethics

1. Linda and Richard Eyre, *Teaching Your Children Values*.

2. Planned Parenthood Federation of America, "Responsible Choices" series, "Is This Love: How to Tell If Your Relationship Is Good for You," 2000.

3. Ibid.

4. Leviticus 19:18.

5. Michael Gold, *Does God Belong in the Bedroom?*, 40.

Chapter 14: Homosexuality

1. Kinsey, Pomeroy, & Martin, 1948; Kinsey, Pomeroy, Martin, & Gebhard, 1953; Fay, Turner, Klassen, & Gagnon, 1989; Hatfield, 1989; Laumann, Gagnon, Michael, and Michaels, 1994; Lever & Kanouse, 1996; Rogers & Turner, 1991.

Chapter 15: Sex Outside of Marriage

1. Eugene B. Borowitz, *Choosing a Sex Ethic: A Jewish Inquiry*, 104.

2. Ibid., 105.

MY HOT TOPICS JOURNAL

MY HOT TOPICS JOURNAL

MY HOT TOPICS JOURNAL

MY HOT TOPICS JOURNAL

MY HOT TOPICS JOURNAL

MY HOT TOPICS JOURNAL

MY HOT TOPICS JOURNAL

MY HOT TOPICS JOURNAL